GUERRILLA

GUERRILLA

Insurgents, Patriots and Terrorists
from Sun Tzu to Bin Laden

DAVID ROONEY

BRASSEY'S

First published in 2004 by Brassey's

An imprint of **Chrysalis** Books Group plc

Brassey's
The Chrysalis Building, Bramley Road, London W10 6SP

David Rooney has asserted his moral right to be identified
as the author of this work.

ISBN 1 85753 352 6

Illustrations courtesy Chrysalis Images, *Illustrated London News*,
US Department of Defense, PageantPix and the author's collection

Edited and designed by DAG Publications Ltd
Designed by David Gibbons
Edited by Jonathan North. Layout by Meredith MacArdle
Cartography by Anthony A. Evans

Printed in the USA

CONTENTS

 # PREFACE

This is not a history of guerrilla warfare, but rather a study of some outstanding and brilliant military leaders who became successful guerrilla warriors, and added their own slant to this fascinating story. Many of them wrote their memoirs or wrote manuals outlining their philosophy and their views on strategy and tactics.

My purpose in picking on these leaders – all of them charismatic characters – is to illustrate how they adapted their guerrilla theories to their particular terrain and situation, or developed new ideas as the struggle continued. Some are not well known, and it is my hope that these brief chapters will help the reader to grasp the main issues involved, and, perhaps, to inquire and study further.

There is no reason why the average reader should be familiar with Afghanistan, Bolivia, China or Yugoslavia and, therefore, to assist in understanding the text, I have tried to ensure – as I did in my previous books on the Burma campaign – that place names which occur in the text also appear in a map in the same chapter. The brief bibliography lists books which should be fairly easily available for those who wish to read further.

I should like to thank the following for their help, advice and support: the staff of the Cambridge University Library, who, as ever, have been most helpful; Diane and Jim Gracey, formerly of Blackstaff Press; Professor David Harkness; and our daughter Kathy Rooney. Sadly, while this book was being written my wife suffered a severe stroke. I dedicate it to her, with my affectionate thanks for fifty-five wonderful years.

David Rooney
Cambridge, 2004

INTRODUCTION

An assessment of two of the guerrilla theorists of the twentieth century – Mao Zedong and Che Guevara – might suggest that nothing fundamentally significant had been added to the ideas expressed by Sun Tzu in 400 BC. Yet there have been guerrilla leaders from that time onwards, fighting against oppression, injustice or alien occupation, who have learnt and absorbed some or all of Sun Tzu's ideas, and have been driven by their own passions and have added their own contribution. So, guerrilla warriors through the ages have demonstrated leadership and bravery to achieve their ultimate aim of removing unjust rule and establishing a new society. Where there has been widespread alien occupation, as under the Romans, under Napoleon or under the Nazis, guerrilla activity has usually flourished, but within those parameters are guerrilla leaders who have had a purely military aim, rather than the wider social and political targets of the true guerrilla warrior. Thus the World War II threw up some remarkable guerrilla leaders, such as David Stirling in the SAS, Wingate in the Chindits, Blair Mayne, Calvert and others, but they are in a different category from Mao Zedong, Tito or Che Guevara, who operated within the wider social and political sphere.

King David fought for the poor and dispossessed, Judas Maccabee fought to secure Jerusalem, but the Roman occupation of Europe gave rise to the earliest widespread recognisable guerrilla activity. Plutarch described the Romans in Spain suffering from 'the fleet mountaineers never brought to battle', and, east of the Rhine, Arminius, trained by the Romans, emerged as an outstanding guerrilla leader, now revered by present day Germans. In medieval Britain, Robert the Bruce and Owen Glendower illustrated considerable guerrilla skills in opposing English domination.

Napoleon's domination of Europe gave rise to widespread guerrilla activity. Spain coined the word guerrilla, and in the uprisings in Aragon and Catalonia proved – as the Cossacks did in Russia – that guerrilla activity can influence the outcome of a major campaign. The overthrow of Napoleon, and the rejection of the ideas of liberty and democracy by the reactionary regimes set up by the Congress of Vienna, ultimately gave scope to one of the great guerrilla warriors – Garibaldi – who initially developed his skills in the wars of South America.

Most guerrilla activity relied on secure bases in mountains, forests or swamps. At the end of the nineteenth century, two new developments emerged, with the Boer Commandos – driven by both patriotism and religion – flourishing across the open spaces of the Veldt, whilst Lawrence, both a theorist and a practitioner, adapted his ideas to the desert. At the same time, and not unconnected, Michael Collins developed a new and original approach to guerrilla war, and successfully challenged Britain at the height of its power.

In the twentieth century the outstanding guerrilla warriors were those – notably Mao Zedong and Tito – who initially led their guerrilla bands, but were driven by their wider political aims, and achieved final victory as head of state. Che Guevara, who took part as a close colleague of Castro in the Cuban revolution, wrote a brilliant thesis on guerrilla warfare, but learnt entirely the wrong lessons from his experience, and after several abortive campaigns, paid with his life in Bolivia.

The basic guerrilla precepts – defeating alien occupation, having a cause to die for, having the support of the people, attacking when least expected and never risking defeat in set battle – have not changed in 2,500 years, but over the centuries they have been adapted by brave and inspiring leaders. In the twenty-first century, blurring the distinction between guerrilla and terrorist, they have been most effectively adapted by the new type of modern guerrilla warrior – Osama Bin Laden and Al-Qaeda.

GUERRILLA WAR ORIGINS

Several guerrilla campaigns are described in the early books of the Bible, and from the detail of these stories, many of the critical factors in effective guerrilla war emerge. The Bible records in remarkable and colourful detail the activities of Joshua, who led a guerrilla band to attack Jericho. He sent spies in to Jericho, and they went to a prostitute, Rahab, who hid them when the Philistines arrived to search the house. Later she let them down by rope over the city wall. Soon, Joshua returned, captured Jericho, and sacked it, but Rahab and her family were saved.

Soon afterwards, in turbulent times, David was anointed king. He escaped from his enemies, and made his base in the caves of Adullam, where all the people who were suffering or in distress came to join him. From such small beginnings, based on the caves, David built up a powerful force, which, in a series of guerrilla campaigns, attacked and defeated the Philistines. From Hebron and Jerusalem, he established an empire, which stretched as far as the Euphrates river. He defeated the Philistines again, captured Damascus, and 'took gold and brass to Jerusalem' (1 Samuel, chapter 22). He continued to fight against the Philistines or Syrians, who were followers of Ammon or Zeus. Although David is held up as a role model, some of his actions are deplorable. He slept with Bathsheba, the wife of Uriah the Hittite, and made her pregnant. David then made certain that Uriah was put in the front line of the next battle, and he was duly killed. Bathsheba lost the child, but later David married her and they had a son, Solomon. Some modern scholars dispute the actual existence of King David, despite much well-established evidence, but there is no doubt at all about the existence of Judah, the great leader of the Maccabees, whose military skills and whose campaigns illustrate nearly all the key facets of guerrilla war.

In 160 BC Judea lay uncomfortably on the fringe of two empires – the Ptolemaic empire based in Egypt under the descendants of Ptolemy, the general of Alexander the Great, and the Seleucid empire, based on Syria. Both these empires were threatened by the expanding power of Rome. Judea was prosperous and was virtually self-governing, and the Syrian king, Antiochus, decided that to strengthen and expand his empire, he must first subdue Judea and establish the Hellenistic customs, which his people followed. The Greek culture with its worship of Zeus, its tradition of wrestling and athletics, and its admiration of the naked human body, offended the Jews, who held to their monotheistic beliefs and practised circumcision. They also refused to eat pork.

In order to subdue the Jews, Antiochus destroyed the temple in Jerusalem, re-dedicated it to Zeus, sacrificed pigs on the altar, and organised sexual orgies in the temple precincts. The Jews were outraged and, after their elderly leader, Mattathias, killed a man who was profaning the altar with a pig, they rose in revolt, under the leadership of Judah, one of the sons of Mattathias.

The people fled from the towns, leaving at night, and took with them their sheep and goats, together with implements and food loaded on to donkeys and carts. Following Judah's lead they assembled in the Gophna hills to the north of Jerusalem. Fortunately for Judah, the Seleucid authorities did not attack at once, and so he had time to organise and train his forces, and to prepare the defence of his base in the hills. He reconnoitred the whole area, established sentries, and prepared defensive ambush positions on every approach to the hills.

As soon as he had trained enough men, he led small groups by night to other villages to spread the news of the revolt, to gain recruits, and to establish an intelligence network. Very rapidly, an intelligence and supply system was set up with a commander in each village. Supplies, weapons and equipment were taken to the Gophna base at night, usually accompanied by eager young volunteers going for further training. Before the revolt had started, a Jewish force had been massacred because they refused to fight on the Sabbath, so now it was decided to fight on every day of the week. Judah based his guerrilla training on secret movement at night, when most of the Seleucid mercenaries stayed in their barracks; on detailed defence tactics to cover every approach to the base; and on strengthening the faith to ensure success in the long term.

Judah's chance of success seemed remote, and the Seleucid forces appeared impregnable. They had large battle-hardened armies, with infantry, cavalry, artillery, engineers, and chariots, as well as elephants and camels. The Jews cherished the tradition of Joshua and of David, and Judah quickly enunciated a sound guerrilla doctrine. Descriptions of Judah's leadership and achievements, by modern writers, raise interesting questions. One description giving details of Judah's guerrilla policy suggests that it followed the standard principles of guerrilla war. The question has to be asked whether these principles were not super-imposed by the writer on the description of Judah's doctrine, just because he had been a successful guerrilla leader. One description reads 'Desist from open battle. Choose the time and place of your encounters, don't leave it to the enemy. When he attacks, melt. When he shies from fighting, assault. When he halts, harass him. When he flees, pursue.' This is quite remarkably close to the very well-known outline of the principles enunciated by Sun Tzu in his work on guerrilla war.

Despite this slight caveat, there is no doubt that Judah and his brothers did build up a most successful guerrilla force, which trained by day but operated by night. Led initially by the brothers, the groups would visit a village by night, destroy any pagan altars, kill any collaborators, take on volunteers and arrange circumcisions when needed. These actions appear to have kept the solid support of the people in the villages. Circumcision, which was crucial to Jewish belief, remained a major issue in religious development at the time, and later was retained by Muhammad as well as by several Christian groups.

After Judah had established a reliable system his groups, in order to extend their area of influence, were trained to lie up in safe areas overnight, and to be alert to the opportunity of attacking small enemy units, An enemy patrol would be ambushed, and the men killed with daggers or swords. After the attack, any bodies would be carefully hidden in order to avoid reprisals on local communities, and all captured weapons taken away. This became the main source of armament for the Maccabees. Despite these precautions, the Seleucids did carry out savage reprisals, especially if they found that children in a village had recently been circumcised.

Initially, the Seleucid forces were not seriously concerned at what they saw as sporadic and isolated attacks on their troops, so Judah had a year or more to build up his system. Above all, he gained the support of hardy and tough countrymen, who knew the land and treasured it. The wild hill country of Gophna proved an ideal base, and hundreds of young men were trained there, and then returned to their own villages, where a cell would be established under a commander. Every volunteer became a trained observer and passed details of all enemy troop movements to the head-quarters in Gophna. On the farms every effort was made to increase production so that, if the men were called away to fight, the community would not suffer.

As his strength grew, Judah organised and led fighting patrols of fifty or more highly-trained men to ambush Seleucid units. After some months these attacks had virtually confined Seleucid troops to Jerusalem, and had forced

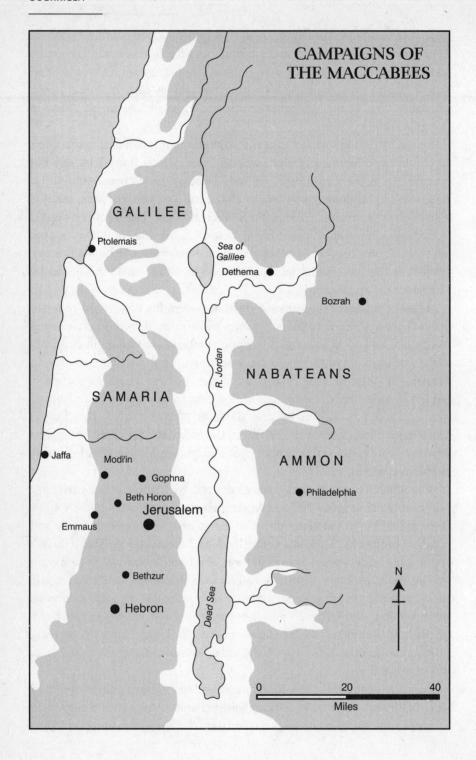

CAMPAIGNS OF THE MACCABEES

GALILEE

Ptolemais

Sea of Galilee

Dethema

Bozrah

R. Jordan

NABATEANS

SAMARIA

Jaffa

Modi'in

Gophna

AMMON

Beth Horon

Philadelphia

Emmaus

Jerusalem

Bethzur

Dead Sea

Hebron

N

0   20   40
Miles

the Jerusalem commander to send for help to the garrisons in Samaria, some 100 kilometres to the north. When help was eventually sent from Samaria, Judah's intelligence gave him advanced information about the Seleucid troop movements, and he was able to plan an ambush in a steep and narrow defile some distance north of the base at Gophna.

The Seleucid forces advanced with two major units under the commander Apollonius. They were not expecting an attack, they were marching four deep, and then they had to close up because of the narrow defile. Judah had organised his defenders into four groups, each under an experienced commander. One group lay at the top of the pass, one on either side, and one at the bottom. They were all very carefully concealed, and well disciplined to hold their fire. Judah waited until the leading enemy units had reached the top of the pass. Then he gave the signal, and all four groups attacked with slings, swords and daggers. The Seleucids had not been vigilant and were ill-prepared for an attack. The sudden violence of the assault by Judah's men caused chaos as the rear columns continued to blunder forward. Apollonius was killed in the first assault, and this added to the confusion. His troops suffered very heavy casualties, then retreated down through the defile and hurried back north to Samaria. Judah's men had also suffered casualties, but his victory at Gophna gave heart to all the people of Judea, gave him virtual control over the whole province, and, equally important, brought him a very large supply of weapons with which to arm his guerrillas. At the same time, he realised that the Seleucids would return with more powerful forces, and he had to prepare for that situation. Relying on his advanced intelligence of troop movements, he planned to harass the enemy and wear them down, so that they would abandon their attempt to hold down Judea and to crush the Jewish religion.

Expecting another attack down the road from Samaria, Judah reconnoitred the whole Judean countryside and prepared ambushes on all the approach roads, where they came up from the plain into the hills. He used his advantages, with the support of nearly all the people of Judea, to expand his intelligence network up into Samaria, so that he would have ample warning when any large body of troops moved against him.

Antiochus, the King, sent an experienced general, Seron, the overall commander in Samaria, to march over 150 kilometres from Acre, down the coast to Jaffa, and from there to move eastwards into the centre of Judea, to approach Judah's stronghold through the pass of Beth Horon. Contemporary estimates suggest that there was a force of over 4,000 men in four units organised as a grand phalanx. Seron planned to eliminate Judah and his forces, to occupy Jerusalem and from there to crush all opposition in the country.

Judah received advanced warning of the approach of Seron's army and prepared a main attack at the pass of Beth Horon. After a relatively easy march down the coast road, the advancing Seleucid troops became more alert as they approached the hills. Flank units were posted, but the daunting hills at the approach to Beth Horon forced them back close to the main body, and, weighed down by heavy equipment, they began to labour up towards the pass. Judah had about 1,000 men organised in three units – one at the head of the pass, and one on each side of the ascent. A well-disciplined and silent body, they waited while the heavily-laden enemy troops trudged up the road towards the summit of the pass. At a given signal, Judah's unit at the head of the pass attacked the enemy with slings, and with archers shooting rapidly. Then the whole unit closed in with swords and daggers. Like Apollonius before him, Seron was killed at the start of the action. The leading Seleucid troops halted under the weight of the attack, and some men ran back down the hill causing confusion among those behind. At that moment, Judah's two other units stormed into the attack and completely routed the whole of Seron's force. Contemporary descriptions give detail of how over 800 men were killed, and the rest – demoralised and without their commander – were pursued towards the sea.

This resounding defeat of a large and experienced army came at a time when Antiochus was about to embark on a major campaign to re-establish his rule across his whole territory as far as the Euphrates and Tigris. Conscious of the threat to his base, he decided to divert a substantial force under the experienced general Lysias to crush Judah as rapidly as possible. The defeat of Seron had clearly made a serious impact, because Lysias was instructed to destroy Judea and Jerusalem, to slaughter the people and to repopulate the country with other settlers. There is some dispute over the number of the forces under Lysias, but the lowest estimate is 20,000 troops.

Lysias, determined not to repeat the mistakes of Seron, sent two experienced commanders, Nicanor and Gorgias, to set up a strong base at Emmaus, 15 miles north-west of Jerusalem. Nicanor was so confident of victory that he invited slave dealers to his camp so that he could profit from selling his expected captives instead of killing them.

After his previous victories, Judah had recognised the danger, and realised that the Seleucids would send a much more powerful army against him, but he had the full backing of the people, and he had had time to train his men into larger formations. When the enemy advance was confirmed, he assembled his fighting units, sending home the weak or faint-hearted. He had 6,000 men available, and he assembled them where he could deploy them swiftly to meet any threatened danger. He sent out constant reconnaissance patrols and soon learnt that the enemy were fortifying Emmaus.

The Seleucid commander, Gorgias, having strengthened Emmaus, took a strong force out of the town in order to attack Judah's base camp. When he learnt of this, Judah moved rapidly to attack Emmaus while the main force was away. He also lit fires at his own camp to deceive the enemy. This ruse succeeded. Gorgias attacked Judah's camp, found it deserted, and assumed its defenders had run away. At about that moment, Judah was addressing his troops ready to attack Emmaus. As he led them forward, they discovered that the enemy were not asleep but armed and ready. Judah, like Alexander the Great in his battles, was in the forefront of the fighting, and able to make an immediate decision. He wheeled his troops to a flank in order to wipe out the enemy cavalry, and then attacked the cumbersome phalanxes from the side. Then his training with sword and dagger for hand-to-hand fighting proved decisive. Although outnumbered, his men routed the Seleucid troops who broke away and fled towards the coast. Then Judah – like Cromwell rather than Prince Rupert – reined in his men, and prepared to attack Gorgias and his units returning from their fruitless advance. When the leading Seleucid troops saw the destruction of Emmaus, and the fields littered with corpses, they fled in a panic and did not fight again.

After this serious setback to Gorgias and Nicanor, Lysias himself set out from Jaffa and marched towards Hebron, some 25 kilometres south of Jerusalem. He had an army of 20,000 including a strong force of cavalry. Having now to face an attack from the south towards Jerusalem, Judah had to change his plan. He had reconnoitred all the ground along the road from Hebron to Jerusalem, and had discovered a good spot for an ambush at Beth Zur. There, because of the narrow valley, the enemy would have to move in close column, and would therefore be more vulnerable. Once again, a swift and determined attack on the forward units as they reached the head of the pass caused chaos. These troops turned back just as the rest of the column was attacked by the main bulk of Judah's army. Lysias then withdrew and, surprisingly, did not counterattack – perhaps because of the fear and low morale of his men, who were all mercenaries.

Judah, having started with a handful of men, had proved himself an outstanding guerrilla commander, and had now inflicted a major defeat on the army of the Seleucid empire. He now had a final challenge – to recover Jerusalem and the Temple Mount. The Temple Mount lay several hundred metres from the powerful fortress of Acra. Judah, with a strong and well-armed force, decided to capture the Temple Mount and leave the Acra fort until later. The Temple and all the surrounding buildings had been desecrated and destroyed. Judah therefore despatched a strong force to neutralise the enemy garrison in the Acra, while the main body were used to clean and purify the sacred places on the Temple Mount and to rebuild the Temple. The book of Maccabees records the details of the great religious celebration when the Temple was re-consecrated in 164 BC. The celebration lasted for eight days – an occasion still observed by the Jewish people.

After the re-establishment of the Temple, Judah decided not to attack the Acra fortress because he was likely to incur heavy casualties. He did, however, feel strong enough to send fighting patrols to rescue Jewish settlements lying further north up the River Jordan, and others to the east of the Sea of Galilee. These Jewish communities were being persecuted partly because of Judah's success, and, after a decision by an Assembly of the people, Judah planned the attack. Once again he used sound guerrilla tactics.

He decided that speed of movement would be the key factor. He therefore prepared and trained his men to march swiftly and for long hours, carrying their weapons and only the most basic rations. This campaign was supported by the Nabatean people, who opposed the Seleucid power. They gave valuable information about the strength and movement of Seleucid military units. Their information enabled Judah to move rapidly and to capture the important town of Bozra, lying nearly 100 kilometres to the east of the Sea of Galilee. Records show that after the capture of Bozra, Judah again moved swiftly north and was able to rescue another Jewish settlement close to the Sea of Galilee just as it was being attacked by the Seleucids. After these successes, most Jewish communities were brought back to Judea for protection.

In the following year, 162 BC, the Seleucid commander, Lysias, determined to avenge his earlier defeat, assembled a powerful army to overrun Judea. He even included a force of elephants as part of his army. Elephants had been used in battle at the time of Alexander the Great, around 333 BC, but, in recent times, it had been agreed – like the curbs on gas warfare after 1918 – that elephants would not be used in battle.

This campaign has been well documented. Lysias marched south along the coast road, as the Crusaders were to do centuries later, and wheeled east towards Jerusalem. He clearly had a very strong force, though numbers have probably been exaggerated – indeed over the centuries an occasional nought has often been added to army numbers. Judah faced a difficult decision. He needed to protect Jerusalem and, to do this, he had to abandon the guerrilla precepts which had brought him such remarkable success. This crucial issue of guerrilla mobility, as against static sieges, again came to the fore in the campaigns of Robert the Bruce, Owen Glendower and the Boer Commandos. For Judah this proved disastrous. The forces of Lysias had learnt the lessons of ambush in hilly country, and as they moved forward they were ready for battle. The elephants led the advance, surrounded by specialist groups of both infantry and cavalry to protect them. Each elephant carried a howdah full of heavily armed soldiers. Judah had little chance of countering this overwhelming force, and he moved his army back to the hills of Judea, but left a fairly strong defensive group on the Temple Mount, which had been very carefully fortified. This held out bravely for months against the attack of Lysias. Then, when the defenders were starving, short of water and almost ready to capitulate, Lysias suddenly offered them a truce.

This final campaign raises two interesting issues. Judah was renowned for his effective intelligence gathering, and he must have known that Lysias was advancing with elephants. Two centuries before this, Alexander the Great, when he faced the Indian king, Porus, who also had a large force of elephants, had trained his special group of commandos to go forward and slash the trunks and legs of the elephants. This brilliant attention to detail won Alexander his last great victory. Perhaps his brilliant ideas had been lost over the centuries, but this does illustrate his pre-eminence as a supreme tactician. The siege of the Temple Mount illustrates a military truism, that however bad things are for you, they are probably worse for the enemy. This sage thought was frequently enunciated by that outstanding Chindit leader, Brigadier Mike Calvert, in Burma in 1944 when he led his brigade behind the Japanese lines for five months. In the case of Lysias at the Temple Mount, his decision to offer a truce saved the Jewish cause. He made the decision for mainly political reasons, but it meant that Jerusalem was saved, and the campaign of the Seleucids to destroy the Jewish religion and customs was finished. Thus the guerrilla campaign of Judah, which began with a small group of fighters at Gophna, had defeated the most powerful empire of the time, and had achieved independence for its people – the ultimate test for the success of guerrilla war.

The Jewish guerrilla struggle continued, first against the declining power of the Seleucids, and then against the growing and aggressive force of Rome. During this phase of the struggle, the Zealots fought fiercely against the Roman occupation, and in 67 AD were strong enough to capture Jerusalem, but this carried a heavy military legacy of static siege war as opposed to the success of mobile guerrilla attacks. The struggle against Rome continued at least to the reign of Hadrian, who, in 133 AD launched a major campaign to crush the Jewish guerrillas. Hadrian showed great skill in what would now be called counter-insurgency tactics. By a deliberate policy of road development, he isolated the guerrillas and cut them off from their support and from their supplies of food and weapons. In addition, he organised his forces into small groups, which could move swiftly and beat the guerrillas at their own game.

When the Romans attacked Britain – an episode documented in Caesar's *Gallic Wars* – soon after they landed, a legion foraging for corn was ambushed by a group of the native people under Cassivellaunus. The Britons had enticed the legion forward, and then attacked them with cavalry and chariots. This was a new type of warfare for the Romans. The Britons charged in among the legions, then jumped from their horses and from their chariots and fought on foot. The chariot driver parked the chariot as close as possible so that if the fight went against them the fighters could disengage, rush to the chariots and escape. In spite of this initial setback, Caesar's legions advanced successfully against the opposition of Cassivellaunus, but he did employ sound guerrilla tactics to harass the Roman advance. He removed corn and cattle from areas threatened by the Romans, and attacked them from thickly wooded places. Gradually, as the Romans established control, warfare became more static, and Cassivellaunus lost his advantage and was defeated.

Alien domination has always given rise to guerrilla opposition – witness the Napoleonic and Nazi eras – and the Roman empire, stretching from Hadrian's Wall across Europe to the Middle East and deep into North Africa, produced countless examples of effective guerrilla risings. Few were more successful than those in Spain.

For centuries southern Spain had been subject to the influence of the Phoenicians and of Carthage, but by 200 BC, after a series of victories by the outstanding military leader, Scipio Africanus, Rome had established control. The Romans held towns, ports and strips of the coast from Andalucia to Valencia, but faced fierce resistance from the people of the interior.

The Romans considered the local people barbarians, and imposed a savage and oppressive regime, designed primarily to plunder and exploit the wealth of the country, which was rich in corn, olives, wine, gold and silver. Thousands were forced to work as slaves in the silver mines. This calculated oppression caused frequent protests against the brutality of Roman rule. For decades – indeed centuries – the clashes between Roman troops and their guerrilla opponents were marked by appalling atrocities. Prisoners frequently had their hands or their heads chopped off. Although Roman power appeared impregnable, the constant drain on its resources from the continuing guerrilla war in Spain caused serious repercussions across the Empire. Increasingly, mutinous grumbles arose from the soldiers, who did not share in the booty and whose lives varied from tedious garrison duty to harsh and dangerous campaigning into the interior.

There are remarkably detailed contemporary accounts of these prolonged and brutal wars – by Appian, Plutarch, Polybius and others – but most accounts are viewed from the Roman angle. In spite of this slant, one Spanish leader, Viriathus, does emerge as an outstanding guerrilla commander, and he features in one of the best known descriptions of a battle in the campaign, taken from Appian.

Viriathus drew up his forces to face the Roman legions, as if deploying for a set battle. He kept 1,000 picked troops to stay with him – rather like Alexander and his Companions – and as the battle started he warned the rest that as soon as he mounted his horse they were to scatter in all directions. As soon as action had been joined, he mounted his horse and in the ensuing chaos he used his specialist unit first to attack, then to feign retreat and then to attack again. He kept up this tactic all day, and finally galloped off to his mountain base, with the cumbersome and heavily armed Romans unable to pursue him. Viriathus kept up his harassment of the Romans for more than a decade, with sudden swift attacks and ambushes, but, in the end, while terms were being discussed, the Romans, perfidious to the end, had Viriathus stabbed to death while he was sleeping. For all his skill, Viriathus was never likely to drive the Romans out of his country – the vital yardstick of guerrilla success.

All over Europe, wherever they faced opposition, the Romans referred to their opponents as brigands. Often they were just that, for those men on the fringes of society with nothing to lose, were more likely to volunteer and to gain from military action. This factor reappears in the many conflicts in Africa today, where youths swagger about carrying Kalashnikov rifles rather than endure the boredom and hardship of farming the land in an unkind and hostile environment.

When the Romans crossed the Rhine, they encountered stronger resistance from the German tribes. Although at first the Germans did not seriously impede the advance of the legions, they gradually learnt from their mistakes, and their tactics improved. Tacitus records that they developed the art of making more disciplined attacks followed by a controlled withdrawal, and learnt to use the marshes and forests of the north German plain for their own advantage. Their greatest leader, Arminius – known in Germany today as Herman – was a brave warrior and used effective guerrilla tactics against the Romans. He is honoured by a statue – Herman's Denkmal – at the peak of the Teutoburger Wald, a spur of rounded hills running northward into the German plain near the small town of Gutersloh. Herman proved himself a sound military leader and tactician. He established discipline, and he care- fully controlled his units in battle, often enticing the legions forward and then attacking their flanks with other units emerging from the forests.

The principles of successful guerrilla war were already established by the time of the Roman empire. The best-known and most highly respected treatise comes not from the Jews or the Romans, but from a Chinese scholar of the fourth century BC – Sun Tzu, author of *The Art of War*. He lived during the period of the Warring States – the fifth to the third century BC – a time of prolonged civil war when 'violent military opera- tions filled the fields with bloodshed'. Unlike Clausewitz, many centuries later, Sun Tzu argued that understanding should be used if at all possible to prevent or overcome conflict, and that to win without fighting is best. War should only be the last resort. He believed that war was always destructive and counter-productive even for the victors, an argument taken up in 1910, when Norman Angell wrote *The Great Illusion*, arguing, vainly, that no country can benefit from war. Sun Tzu, having argued the case for avoiding war at all cost, then gives the most detailed and compre- hensive advice on how to wage war successfully. His theory is general but it applies particularly to guerrilla war.

After stressing that war must only be a last resort, he continues:

'Be subtle, be mysterious in order to confuse your opponent. Planning must be secret, attack must be swift, like a hawk striking its prey; when strong appear weak; when competent appear incompetent and inept; when orderly appear chaotic; when many appear as few; before any action consider the weather, the ground, the quality of your troops and the enemy, and the level of discipline.'

Other Chinese military leaders have frequently referred to Sun Tzu, and he is usually known as Master Sun. He constantly stressed that the most important military factors are intelligence, trustworthiness, courage, sternness, humaneness, deception and surprise. Master Sun advised:

'Avoid set battles; wear down the enemy by feigned flight; when the enemy attacks disperse; treat captives well and use them; avoid a long campaign which can ruin a country; feed your army in enemy territory if possible ... If you are equal fight if you are able. If you are few, keep away if you are able. If you are not as good, flee if you are able.'

He compares a military formation to water, which has no consistent shape – victory is gained by changing shape and adapting, like flowing water.

Master Sun always emphasised the significance of terrain, and the importance of a commander knowing and seeing the land before giving orders, saying 'Unless a commander knows the mountains, the forests, the defiles and the impasses he cannot manoeuvre an armed group.' In the centuries since Sun Tzu, how many men have lost their lives because a commander was behind the lines and had not seen the ground before he gave an order? He continued:

'If there are narrow defiles, that route should not be taken; stay by the valleys, close to water, food and fodder; fight going down hill not climbing up; where there are hills keep on the sunny side; when advancing through hills or forests, these must be searched carefully; watch and listen for birds, for dust and for smoke, for evidence of the enemy; if you have to fight, choose ground where you will surely win.'

Master Sun deals at length with the importance, whether for armies or small guerrilla groups, of using spies to gain all possible detail about the enemy – command, numbers, disposition, movement and plans. It is equally important to be alert for enemy spies and, if they are caught, they should be well treated so that they might be turned and become double agents in order to spread misinformation. His sound psychology is illustrated in his advice that if you have surrounded an enemy you should leave an escape route because men surrounded will always fight desperately. Conversely, if your force is surrounded, your men will always fight desperately.

A summary of his wisdom is especially applicable to guerrilla war: use every form of deception to confuse and mislead the enemy; always avoid a set battle; when opponents are at ease tire them; choose the time when you attack; when he halts harass him; when he attacks disperse; move at night for better cover; let the enemy come to you. Ten victories is not the best – the best is to win victory without fighting.

Today, there is great interest in the ideas and philosophy of Sun Tzu, not only in military circles, but also in business schools and the development of corporate management. It is disconcerting to think that modern management is, perhaps, being trained with the emphasis above all on deception and spying.

With the break-up of the Roman empire there were centuries of violence and war as successive aggressors attempted to take control. The Vandals, the Huns and the Vikings extended their depredations across most of Europe, while to the south, Islam spread rapidly across North Africa and into southern Spain. Finally, the Normans established their empire in northern France and gradually extended their influence more widely. The Norman conquest of Britain after 1066 led to more decades of fighting but these are well documented and illustrate the efforts of a native people to resist an alien conqueror.

There had been sporadic warfare between the people of the border counties of England and the Welsh for a long time before the Norman conquest. In 1062 King Harold had advanced with a strong army against Welsh forces in the Snowdon area and, after the conquest, there was growing Welsh opposition to the increasing power of the Normans. In 1095 King William II led a campaign into Wales and imposed a brutal system, with vicious reprisals against the Welsh people. He ruthlessly destroyed villages, crops and woods, whilst the Welsh, in traditional guerrilla style, set up ambushes in the valleys and woods. Increasingly, Snowdonia became the secure base for the Welsh fighters and for their families and cattle. Their life-style of cattle grazing and cattle raiding made it relatively easy to adapt to mobile guerrilla tactics against the advancing power of the Normans. In reply, the Normans, as they had done in England, started to build castles in order to dominate an area, and, especially in north Wales, to curb the rebels from Snowdonia.

The Welsh continued their guerrilla opposition to the aggressive intrusion of the Normans for nearly 200 years, and then Edward I, the most powerful English medieval king, having established effective control in England, turned his attention to Wales and Scotland. When the Welsh leaders refused to pay homage, Edward planned a large-scale invasion. Considerable detail is known about the Welsh wars because a medieval chronicler, Giraldus

Cambrensis, who served in a previous Welsh campaign, left a vivid description of the dangers of advancing into a barren land of thick woods, high mountains, few roads and atrocious weather, where the people were accustomed to rally at the first alarm. Then, using spears and bows, they would either harass or ambush the enemy or try to defeat him with a wild charge. Giraldus even suggested a possible strategy to overcome Welsh resistance.

It is not known if Edward ever saw this document but, in 1277, after careful preparation, and roughly following the guidelines of Giraldus, he invaded Wales with a strong force of infantry and cavalry. He advanced westward from Chester along the north Wales coast, cutting wide swathes through the forests, and also supplying his armies from the sea. This progress led past Conway, to Anglesey, Caernarvon and Harlech. By the end of the summer Edward's occupation of Anglesey had deprived the Welsh leader, Llewellyn, of his main supply of corn and this forced him to sue for peace at Conway. Edward then imposed heavy-handed rule over the whole of north Wales, and started an immense programme of castle building in order to curb the guerrilla tactics of the Welsh. Five years later, Llewellyn, outraged by the unjust and oppressive demands of the Normans, drove into the English Marches in a ferocious attack. Then in this no-holds-barred war, under cover of discussion about a truce, Llewellyn was lured into a trap, killed, and his head taken for display in the Tower of London.

The powerful Norman forces based on the newly built castles had proved too strong for the Welsh guerrillas but their bitter resentment simmered on. Their determination never to be beaten, added to their talent for knowing and using the ground for ambush, and for sudden night-time sallies, was never abandoned. Twenty years later, Owen Glendower, himself a Marcher Lord, led another revolt. He had leadership skills and organising ability, and, using guerrilla tactics based on his people's natural fighting talents, he managed to remove English control from most of Wales. His real power base lay slightly to the south of the mountain mass of Snowdonia, centred on the great castles of Harlech and Aberystwyth. After considerable success, he too made the mistake of abandoning the mobile guerrilla warfare favoured by the ground, the weather and by the natural talents and skills of his followers. Tying himself to static war based on castles and sieges he was eventually defeated and his revolt overcome.

This crucial issue arose again during the years when Edward I and Edward II attempted to gain control of Scotland, and, as alien aggressors were fiercely resisted. The resistance centred on two great Scottish heroes and leaders, William Wallace and Robert the Bruce.

After the death of the Scottish king Alexander VI in 1286, there was a disputed succession and Edward I, who had already subdued Wales, came forward in 1292 to adjudicate between the claims of Bruce and Balliol – a situation described by the Scots as putting a fox in the hen house. Edward chose the more compliant Balliol – nicknamed the Toom Tabbard, or Empty Coat – and then imposed heavy taxes and demanded that the Scots support his war against France. This quickly aroused opposition and Edward returned, sacked Berwick, beat the Scottish army and took away the Stone of Destiny, which remained in Westminster Abbey until the 1950s, when it was recovered by Scottish patriots. By 1297 most of Scotland had risen in rebellion. Three effective young leaders emerged: William Wallace, Bruce and Moray, their main power lying in the Selkirk forest, on the Borders, some 30 miles south of Edinburgh. The career of Wallace has always been controversial – the controversy increased by the film *Braveheart*. His reputation is attributed partly to the Scottish poet Blind Harry, who lived 100 years later, but the facts appear to be that Wallace was a man of great physical strength and powerful character. By using guerrilla tactics to harry the English, Wallace and Moray seized control of much of Scotland and, by 1297, had besieged Dundee and had reached Stirling. Here, in September of that year, Wallace showed that in addition to being a successful guerrilla leader he had the disciplined control and tactical ability to lead an army in battle. At Stirling Bridge, the English advanced into boggy ground, while Wallace had drawn up his schiltrons – powerful groups of over a thousand pikemen – on higher ground overlooking the bog. Seizing the moment, Wallace charged wildly downhill with his schiltrons and overran the English who were slaughtered. This battle was an early and rare example of foot soldiers beating an army of cavalry and archers.

Wallace became the sole Guardian of Scotland. He realised that Edward would exact revenge for the English defeat at Stirling Bridge, and he therefore continued to avoid battle, and to conduct a scorched earth policy in those areas where Edward was likely to advance. In the summer of 1298, Edward did lead his army north and, at Falkirk, Wallace foolishly relying on his schiltrons as he had done at Stirling Bridge, engaged in a set battle. He was no match for Edward who used his longbowmen with deadly effect on the closely packed schiltrons, and then launched his cavalry. The Scots were slaughtered, just as the English had been at Stirling Bridge. Wallace paid a heavy price for giving up his guerrilla tactics and engaging in battle against one of the ablest commanders of the Middle Ages.

Wallace kept up his opposition for some years, but eventually was betrayed and caught by the English. In 1305 he suffered the gruesome penalty for treason. He was hanged, drawn and quartered, and his head displayed on London Bridge.

Edward died in 1307 but his harsh and brutal policy, accompanied by threats of disembowelling and castration, had already ensured ready support for Robert Bruce, who had supported Wallace, and now came forward as a positive and successful leader. Bruce had learnt valuable lessons from Wallace and for years he continued the campaigns of guerrilla war against the English. He ambushed their columns, struck at isolated posts, and was even strong enough to attack and overcome castles in the Borders. At the same time, he led powerful raids into the northern counties of England and exacted heavy fines or retribution.

Bruce established a treaty with France, but failed to gain the support of the Papacy, which had excommunicated him because he had murdered Comyn, a rival claimant to the throne, in the church at Dumfries. Although he had setbacks and periods of exile, Bruce was crowned king of Scotland in 1306. Edward I died while actually leading a new expedition against Bruce, and his death marked a turning point in Scottish history.

The foppish and openly gay Edward II lacked all his father's military skills, and withdrew the expedition. By 1311, Bruce, with the support of most of the turbulent Scottish nobles, had won control of the north of Scotland by consistent guerrilla attacks on the English lines of communication and garrisons and had driven the English from Edinburgh, Perth and Dundee.

There are detailed descriptions, both Scottish and English, of Bruce's campaigns and his tactical methods. He trained his troops not to rely on fortresses but to make their base in the forests, to hide their stores in remote places and, where possible, to attack at night. Castles were usually attacked at night by scaling parties using subterfuge, sometimes helped by a disloyal servant opening a door to admit a guerrilla group. Bruce's successes finally forced Edward II to organise an expedition to rescue Stirling Castle and he reached Stirling by June 1314.

The English force had 3,000 mounted knights – the medieval panzers – whose terrifying charge often decided the outcome of the battle. The Scots had only a small cavalry unit, but their strength again lay in the schiltron, a mass of some 3,000 pikemen armed with twelve-foot pikes. It looked like a hedgehog and was strong enough to withstand a cavalry charge. Bruce had been fighting for years, and was an outstanding commander, able to adapt the lessons of guerrilla war to the set piece battle. Using all his experience, he chose his ground carefully, to cover the old Roman road as it approached Stirling, along which he expected Edward to advance. Edward did carry out a reconnaissance and, on the night of 23 June 1314, he decided to move his forces under cover of darkness to turn the Scottish flank. Clearly, he did not realise that the flood plain of the Bannockburn was boggy and marshy. When dawn broke, Bruce saw the whole English host milling about in muddy chaos in the valley below him, and he ordered his schiltrons to advance.

The historian Sir Charles Oman described Edward's generalship as 'nearly insane'. He had bogged down his whole force in face of the enemy. He had already had difficulty with his over-mighty subjects who commanded the cavalry groups, and he had no control over the battle. As Bruce's schiltrons charged down the hill, the English cavalry could not charge, the archers could not shoot and the infantry were ready to flee. While the Scottish losses were negligible, the slaughter of the English was almost complete. No prisoners were taken, and the English infantry and cavalry alike were driven back into the bog. Many were drowned in the Bannockburn, and Edward himself barely escaped.

This decisive battle was won by Bruce because he used all his experience of years of guerrilla war. He had chosen his ground carefully and kept control of the battle from the start. Bannockburn showed that a cavalry charge could not always overcome determined pikemen, and archers were not decisive unless they were protected. Bruce as a guerrilla leader had passed one ultimate test – that the purpose of guerrilla war is to rid your country of the oppressor.

In the fourteenth and early-fifteenth centuries, the English longbow became the decisive weapon in feudal warfare and helped substantially in the victories of Edward III at Crecy, 1346; the Black Prince at Poitiers, 1356; and Henry V at Agincourt, 1415. These successes were made easier by the arrogant, ill-disciplined and irresponsible attitude of the French cavalry leaders, who, as Oman said 'Tended to despise all types of infantry as useless peasants'. This was a view which may even have been heard in some officers' messes in the Household Cavalry up to World War II.

The prolonged English successes under the Black Prince and Henry V did lead to one significant development of guerrilla warfare. Because of their constant defeats, the French retreated to their chateaux and refused to engage in battle. A man then emerged who illustrated all the qualities of a brilliant guerrilla commander. He was Bertrand du Guesclin, an uncouth, semi-literate Breton, who had the same qualities of cheerful audacity which made Mike Calvert such an outstanding Chindit leader in Burma in 1944. At the age of eighteen, Guesclin led a Breton group to ambush the occupying English forces. He next won fame at Fougeray by pretending his group were woodcutters, tricking his way in and capturing the chateau. He was taken on by the king and, using rapid movement, detailed preparation and sudden attacks, gradually rescued northern France from English control. King Charles V made him Constable of France (commander in chief). Then, using the same guerrilla tactics of harassment, surprise, ambush and sudden assault, he continued his campaign. Liddell Hart recorded that, in five years, Guesclin had reduced the vast English possessions in France to a narrow strip of land between Bordeaux and Bayonne.

In Europe in the fifteenth century an unlikely religious leader hastened the end of the feudal army. The Czech Hussite leader, Ziska, whose followers fought with religious fervour, developed the use of firearms. He also encouraged the use of horse-drawn wagons, which moved rapidly, carrying arms and supplies, but could then be chained together as an effective defence against a cavalry charge. Finally, they could be used again to carry off the booty after a successful fight.

Thus the feudal host, which was ridiculed by Oman as 'An assemblage of unsoldierlike qualities such as have seldom been known to co-exist', was gradually superseded by the development of gunpowder and firearms. The dramatic changes which this brought about during the sixteenth and seventeenth centuries featured in a series of prolonged wars, most of which were decided, not by major battles but by marauding forces waging a type of guerrilla war.

THE AGE OF NAPOLEON

Gunpowder presaged the end of medieval warfare, and, as its use was developed and refined, warfare changed dramatically. Whilst the great dynastic rivalries between Hapsburg and Bourbon, or the national rivalries between England and France, would continue and later spread to India and across America, a new and dangerous element of war was introduced by Martin Luther – religion. Luther has been considered the bravest man in history, because he took on the terrifying power of the medieval Roman Catholic Church, and, by his actions, risked the condemnation to hell and damnation in the afterlife. These threats – illustrated so vividly by the Renaissance painters – were very real to Luther, yet he defied the Church's power. His public protest at Wittenberg in 1517 led to his excommunication and his arraignment before Charles V at the Diet of Worms – that source of so much puerile humour. His brave stand led eventually to the division of Europe into the Protestant north and the Roman Catholic south. Thus the great religious struggle between the Protestant Elizabeth I and the Roman Catholic champion, Philip II of Spain, continued into the seventeenth century, when Protestant northern Europe, exemplified by the Swedish king Gustavus Adolphus, fought the Thirty Years' War (1618–48) against Austria and the Roman Catholic south and devastated much of central Europe.

Gustavus Adolphus, an able military commander and an outstanding king, who briefly made Sweden a significant European power, played a decisive role in the Thirty Years' War. Having his lines of communication stretching from Sweden across the Baltic Sea and through Germany as far south as Nuremberg and Vienna, he was always conscious of the danger of guerrilla attacks. Although, as the saviour of the Protestant cause, he had few problems in north Germany. He proved himself an all-round leader, fearless in battle, and with both strategic and tactical acumen. In his many engagements he developed the use of light mobile artillery, the tactical use of muskets, and the controlled cavalry charge.

Gustavus shares his fame with other rival commanders like Wallenstein, Condé, and Tilly, but although there were major battles like Lützen in 1632, when Gustavus was killed leading a cavalry charge, many of the campaigns of the Thirty Years' War were conducted as guerrilla warfare. Many of the local German counts – like Brandenberg and Brunswick – were renowned as guerrilla commanders.

At the same time as the skirmishes and ambushes of the Thirty Years' War a similar conflict, largely based on guerrilla techniques, was being fought in the Balkans. Here, for racial, political and religious reasons, the Turkish advance northwards from Constantinople was fiercely opposed by the Bulgarians, the Serbs and the Hungarians.

In the eighteenth century, warfare was dominated by Frederick the Great of Prussia (1713–86). Considered as the brutal Prussian drill sergeant, Frederick waged war throughout most of his reign. In 1740, he made an unprovoked attack on the province of Silesia, hoping to defeat Maria Theresa of Austria. History has recorded his great battles like Rossbach and Leuthen, in 1757, where he established himself as an outstanding commander by his use of the ground, by his control of the battle, by the effective use of mobile artillery, and by the close co-operation of infantry and cavalry.

In contrast to these great battles, much of the war consisted of guerrilla attacks on the lengthy Prussian lines of communication, as Frederick's men campaigned through Silesia and Bohemia. The Prussians suffered severely from the attacks of Maria Theresa's Croat skirmishers – virtually guerrilla fighters. Frederick himself described the dangerous effects of what he called the enemy light troops. In his Silesian campaign his food supplies were often cut off and, as the Prussian armies advanced, the Austrians ordered all people to flee the area and either to hide or take away all their corn and cattle. Because of the guerrilla activity in Silesia, Frederick's army was unable to obtain food or fodder, it suffered heavy casualties, its communications were destroyed, and he was forced to retreat the way he had come. In another early campaign, Frederick recorded that when patrols went out to find food for men and horses, they had to be protected by thousands of both cavalry and infantry. He even used the phrase 'kleine krieg' or ' little war'.

Later, during the Seven Years' War (1756–63), having learnt the lessons of his earlier campaigns, Frederick established 'Frei Regementen' or free battalions, whose role initially was to counter guerrilla attacks.

Frederick is given credit for this development in military thinking, but in fact it was forced on him by the guerrilla attacks of the Austrian and Croat skirmishers on his lengthy lines of communication. These stretched across central Europe from Berlin to Vienna and, in the east, as far as Torgau on the Elbe, where he fought one of his last bloody battles against the Russians. This took place on the very site where, in April 1945, Patton's tank force met up with the Russians. The Prussian free battalions – which Frederick described as detestable scum – were recruited from the gamekeepers on the

Junker estates. They were poorly armed and ill-disciplined and normally used to defend lines of communication and to do outpost duty. In battle they were deployed to cover the flank of the main army, by searching surrounding woodland, or, occasionally, to rush wildly at the enemy and, without opening fire, to engage in hand-to-hand fighting.

Frederick preferred not to campaign during the winter months, and he used this time for his voluminous writings about every aspect of war. These included his *Instructions to the Free Regiments*, his *Instructions to the Generals* and *The General Principles of War*.

In the course of his many campaigns he acquired the nickname 'The Grave Digger' and, by 1786, when he died, he was a cowed and tragic figure, described as 'a demented scarecrow'. He destroyed his country and caused half a million deaths by his constant wars but, despite his military failure and the widespread destruction he caused, he was an outstanding military leader and one of the first to recognise and study the significance of guerrilla war. He established the Prussian military tradition, which led to Scharnhorst, Moltke and Bismarck.

The Peninsular War

The Peninsular campaigns of Wellington, waged in Spain and Portugal between 1807 and 1813, provided the name Guerrilla War, although, as we have seen, decades before this, Frederick the Great had used the phrase 'kleine krieg' or little war to describe the Austrian and Croat skirmishers. The Peninsular War was to give the word a totally new meaning.

By 1807, when the French emperor Napoleon had won victories across most of Europe, including Jena and Austerlitz, Britain remained his most dangerous rival. Therefore, in order to isolate Britain and damage her trade, he sent General Junot across Spain in 1807 in order to seize Lisbon and eliminate one of the most valuable ports in southern Europe for the British Navy and her commerce. To follow up this success, Napoleon sent the swashbuckling Murat – married to his younger sister – to take control in Spain. As Murat approached Madrid in 1808, serious riots broke out. The weak and vacillating Spanish king, Charles IV, abdicated in favour of his effete son Ferdinand, but then Napoleon, with overweening arrogance, called the Spanish royal family to Bayonne in southern France. He dismissed both Charles and Ferdinand and appointed his brother, Joseph – who had been king of Naples – as king of Spain.

The Spanish royal family had not been popular and were regarded with indifference by the majority of Spanish people but Napoleon's high-handed arrogance in brusquely dismissing them created a country–wide uproar. This widespread outrage made the Spanish guerrilla movement significantly different from most other guerrilla operations. The Spanish Army was badly led by appalling officers and – except for the unexpected victory at Bailen in Andalucia in July 1808 – was more likely to run away than to stand and fight. Wellington treated it with derision. In contrast to the regular Spanish Army the whole Spanish people were prepared to support the activities of the guerrillas after Napoleon's monumental blunder. Not only did the guerrillas have the almost total support of the people, wherever they operated, but a very wide cross-section of able people came forward to lead guerrilla bands. Unlike the situation in the Civil War in the 1930s, when the church lined up with the landowners against the peasants and the working class, now aristocrats, landowners, priests and monks came forward to lead guerrilla bands. As the guerrilla uprising continued, and as the Spanish armies suffered a succession of defeats, more and more officers and soldiers went over to the guerrillas.

Murat was taken ill, but Napoleon promoted him to be king of Naples. Before he left for his new kingdom his forces had been defeated largely by guerrilla activity and driven north across the Ebro river. This significant guerrilla achievement prompted the British government to seize the opportunity of damaging Napoleon by sending an expeditionary force to Portugal in order to re-establish their links with the crucial port and harbour of Lisbon. The British operations were not, initially, a great success. Arthur Wellesley – later to become Duke of Wellington – defeated the French commander Junot at Vimiero, just north of Lisbon, in August 1808. But this success was marred when two British commanders, senior to Wellesley, agreed to the Convention of Cintra. This allowed Junot and 25,000 French troops, with masses of loot, to be taken back to France in British ships. The uproar which this caused in England did not, fortunately, damage Wellesley's career.

Napoleon himself then came to Spain with over 140,000 troops and swiftly drove out the expedition of Sir John Moore. Moore was killed in January 1809 during the final battle as his forces were being evacuated from the safe anchorage of Corunna. The British general, who had developed light infantry training and revolutionised military training generally, had already anticipated and encouraged the role of guerrillas before he was killed. After defeating the British at Corunna, Napoleon used the substantial French forces in the peninsula to eliminate the remaining Spanish armies. This was swiftly achieved in spite of guerrilla activity, but it soon

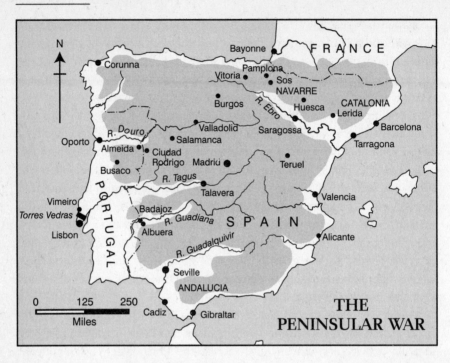

THE
PENINSULAR WAR

established the vicious system of reprisals that was to characterise the remaining five years of the French occupation of Spain.

As guerrilla activity increased, French reprisals became more and more brutal. Frequently, when a village had helped the guerrillas, it was surrounded, torched and all the inhabitants were burnt to death or shot as they tried to escape. Everywhere there were examples of torture, destruction, burning, and even the rape of nuns on the altars of convents. While the French could hold the towns, they increasingly found that they had to employ large numbers of troops – usually dragoons or hussars – to escort every convoy, because the guerrillas controlled the countryside. During the early actions in Portugal, one notorious event took place in Oporto. During an action, a bridge collapsed and hundreds of Portuguese civilians fell into the river. The French continued firing at the struggling survivors, and then built a plank bridge over the corpses. The Portuguese estimated that 10,000 people were deliberately killed. Ghastly retribution against the French started at once. Reprisals – part and parcel of occupying powers from the Romans to the Nazis and beyond – usually favour the occupying power, but in Spain, especially in Aragon and Catalonia, the guerrillas were so strong that they curbed the French punitive policies, by killing ten French prisoners for every Spaniard killed.

Several significant factors swiftly emerged in the increasingly bloody struggle between the French armies and the Spanish people. The French always considered it their right to loot the area they occupied, and now guerrilla bands developed the technique of attacking French convoys to recapture the loot – especially religious paintings and artefacts. It was always French policy to raise taxes from occupied territory and to collect food for the troops and fodder for the numerous horses. Here again the spreading guerrilla bands were able to attack the French marauders and take back the money, food, fodder and other supplies. Their attentions soon began to affect the morale of the occupying forces. Quite early in the campaign one French commander commented 'We fear to walk alone'. As the guerrilla movement grew stronger, the Spanish partisans attacked collaborators, especially some aristocrats and higher clergy who had initially welcomed the more liberal attitudes of the French invaders.

In July 1809 Wellesley had advanced from Portugal towards Madrid and then won a significant victory at Talavera on the Tagus river, about 100 miles south-west of the Spanish capital. He considered this the bitterest battle he ever fought and he lost a quarter of his strength, but the French, under Joseph and Jourdan, lost even more. Wellesley won the victory by his outstanding control of his army during the battle, and he then added to his stature as a commander, by retreating to the safety of his Portuguese bases. The rest of his campaigns can be more easily understood if attention is focused on Lisbon and his carefully constructed defensive lines at Torres Vedras. In this secure and well-supplied base, he could retire with relative impunity, and then at his chosen time, he could advance to action in and around the fortress towns along the Portuguese–Spanish border. Hence the great battles at Albuera, Badajoz, Ciudad Rodrigo and Almeida.

Wellington – a viscount after Talavera – despised the regular Spanish troops, and more particularly their officers, but when he withdrew to the security of the lines at Torres Vedras he was already using both Spanish and Portuguese guerrillas to bring him up-to-date intelligence about French movements. He gave British support to the guerrillas to harass the advancing French units. During the winter of 1809 Wellington had the ground in front of the Torres Vedras lines systematically flattened so that there was no cover at all for any French attack.

In an attempt to eradicate Wellington's base, Napoleon had sent Marshal Massena – considered one of his ablest commanders – to Portugal. Massena, consumed by greed and with a voracious appetite for women – he even had his mistress disguised as a dragoon officer – had pillaged his way across Italy,

Poland and Germany. With inadequate information, no detailed reconnaissance, and almost condescending in his approach, Massena was bloodily repulsed at Bussaco in September 1810. Wellington once again retired to Torres Vedras, and as Massena faced the daunting defences, his forces were constantly harried by Portuguese guerrilla attacks, their supply columns were annihilated and they were forced to withdraw.

Wellington continued to frustrate Massena's plans and, in May 1811, he again showed his superiority as a military commander in the hard-fought and prolonged battle against Massena's superior numbers at Fuentes d'Onoro. Wellington was able to use his favourite divisions – Picton and the Third Division, and Crauford and the Light Division – and inflicted a serious defeat on the French. The battle is significant, because, for the first time, a guerrilla cavalry unit was positioned on one wing of Wellington's force. It was commanded by Julian Sanchez, one of the really successful guerrilla commanders.

Wellington's defeat of the French gave a huge impetus to the guerrillas across the country and they eagerly seized the initiative. As the French retreated, watched constantly and harassed by guerrilla bands, they committed even more brutal atrocities. The French were incensed that priests were sometimes leaders of guerrilla groups, and they impaled priests by the throat and conducted unspeakable atrocities on church altars. The guerrillas' control of information was so complete that, as soon as a garrison was weakened by troops being moved elsewhere, an attack could be mounted instantly. Although many were supported by patriotic fervour, the lasting image of the guerrillas' activities is of horror and brutality. One gang, which was not in any way unique, was led by a sergeant who had deserted from the French forces and was known as Marshal Stockpot. He and his followers gained a widespread reputation for savagery and butchery. Wellington said 'When inflamed, the Spaniard is an undisciplined savage', although this remark must be balanced against his other comment that his own troops were the scum of the earth. Among guerrilla leaders whose names are recalled with pride is the Maid of Saragossa, who manned a cannon after her fiancé was killed, and who was portrayed by Goya, among his many paintings of the Peninsular campaign, in an image known as 'Que Valor'.

It is remarkable that, apart from the voluminous official detail about these campaigns, there is a wealth of contemporary comment by NCOs and privates, now recently republished, which present a vivid picture of their adventures and their suffering. Notable among these are: *The Recollections of Sergeant Morris, The Letters of Private Wheeler* (Windrush Press), and *The Tale of the Peninsula and Waterloo* by J. Douglas (Leo Cooper). Describing the French retreat, Douglas wrote 'The French committed the most wanton barbarities on the defenceless inhabitants', and he added that when passing the revolting remains of mortality the stench was intolerable.

As early as 1810, Wellington, who the previous year had lost a golden opportunity because he had refused to speak to a Portuguese officer, had started to encourage both Spanish and Portuguese guerrillas, by judicious bribes in silver, to bring in despatches captured from the French. In that year, the capture of despatches from Marshal Soult warned Wellington that the combined forces of Soult and Ney together heavily outnumbered him, and he was thus able to avoid an almost certain defeat.

After the success of Sanchez at the battle of Fuentes d'Onoro, he became an increasingly important colleague for the British forces. He had served in the Spanish army, but had left and raised his own marauding band, and started his lethal feud with the French. He had been brought up in the area of Salamanca, where he enjoyed his favourite hobby of hunting wild pig, and he led his guerrilla band with panache and ferocity. The emergence of Sanchez as a reliable and outstanding guerrilla leader, coincided with another development at Wellington's HQ. The French needed to send secure despatches, particularly from Joseph in Madrid to the commanders of the French armies all over Spain, and to his brother Napoleon. He therefore developed a system of codes. Fortunately for Wellington he had a lowly and relatively junior officer, George Scovell, whose passion was codes and how to break them. Scovell had left a smart cavalry regiment because he could not keep up with all the toffs financially, but now he was given an opportunity. Wellington appointed him to command a small unit of mounted Guides, to liaise with Sanchez, and to collect and decipher all the despatches, which were now being brought in on a regular and well-organised basis.

At this critical juncture, as more and more despatches arrived from Sanchez's guerrillas, Scovell worked long hours and at last began to unravel the French codes. The combination of Scovell's skill in deciphering the codes, and the ruthless operations of Sanchez against French couriers and spies, provided Wellington with invaluable intelligence. In the summer of 1811, he received intelligence about a very large concentration of French troops under Marshal Marmont in the area of Ciudad Rodrigo. Wellington therefore judiciously withdrew towards his secure bases in Portugal, while leaving effective spies in both Ciudad Rodrigo and Salamanca. There they were able to communicate quite easily with the ever-active guerrillas just outside the cities.

By the end of 1811 Napoleon's plans to withdraw troops from most of Spain to support his Russian campaign, to support a major attack on Valencia and to eliminate the powerful guerrillas in Navarre, had been picked up from the captured despatches and by observation of troop movements. Early in January 1812, acting on this information, Wellington sprang a surprise attack, and within a few days Ciudad Rodrigo was surrounded. It was captured in twelve days, and this setback proved a major disaster for the French. Among a huge supply of stores and equipment, Wellington captured over 150 cannon – enough to weaken any French counter-attack.

After the capture of Ciudad Rodrigo, Wellington advanced further south towards Badajoz. Here, after a bitterly fought struggle, the city was captured in April 1812. As was customary at the time, after a fiercely contested siege, the victorious troops were given a free hand. Badajoz has gone down in history as the occasion when British troops, completely out of control, in an orgy of drunkenness, burnt, pillaged and raped until they collapsed in a drunken stupor. While Wellington was occupied at Badajoz, Marmont, under orders from Napoleon, advanced into northern Portugal, but, as Wellington already knew – thanks to the guerrillas who harassed Marmont and intercepted his despatches – Marmont's supply crisis would prevent him taking any really effective action.

The French commanders, Joseph, Marmont in northern Portugal, and Soult in Andalucia, all wanted to accompany Napoleon on the Russian campaign. They resented having to stay in Spain to face Wellington and, as well, the humiliation and frustration of the widespread attacks by the guerrillas who captured their supplies and virtually bottled them up inside their fortresses. Much better, they reasoned, to win glory and prestige with Napoleon in a successful attack on Moscow.

In the spring of 1812, as Wellington pondered on whether to attack Marmont in the Salamanca area, or Soult further south, he received valuable new intelligence, which persuaded him to move against Marmont. At the same time the guerrillas all over the country were encouraged to step up their activities in order to pin down the French forces in their own area. This was not difficult because all the French commanders were always loath to help each other. Thus, after his victories of Ciudad Rodrigo and Badajoz, Wellington, in July 1812, moved against Salamanca. As he and Marmont fenced and manoeuvred around the city, it looked at one stage as if Marmont had outwitted his enemy. Then, at a critical moment, the Spanish guerrillas brought in intelligence about likely reinforcements for Marmont. Using this information, Wellington, by the brilliant handling of his divisions at the heart of the battle, and after desperately hard fighting, won a resounding victory. This defeat shattered the French control over central Spain. After Salamanca, a French general compared Wellington to both Marlborough and Frederick the Great.

Scovell, the man who did more than anyone to break the French codes, was present at the battle. His skill, linked to the operations of the guerrillas against French couriers, had given Wellington decisive and timely information, and he was promoted to lieutenant colonel. Scovell's full story is told in the admirable book *The Man who broke Napoleon's Codes* by Mark Urban (Faber, 2001).

As a result of his victory at Salamanca, Wellington was able to advance and occupy Madrid. There were still threats from powerful French armies, but he reckoned that Soult in Andalucia would not come to help his fellow commanders. Wellington therefore took this risk and advanced rapidly to the ancient and formidable fortress of Burgos, more than 100 miles north of Madrid and half way to the French border. As this advance continued, the guerrillas of Sanchez and others across northern Spain continued to play an effective role both in providing Wellington with intelligence from captured despatches, and in destroying isolated French units.

Burgos was stoutly defended by the French garrison, and despite several attacks – during which Wellington's tactics were criticised by his staff – he failed to capture it. Although Wellington received a serious check at Burgos, elsewhere in Spain, because of the victory at Salamanca, the Spanish guerrillas were everywhere in the ascendant. Wellington was also helped at this time by the hostility between the French marshals, and especially that of Soult, who from Seville sent a despatch to Napoleon accusing his brother Joseph of treason. The despatch was intercepted and taken to Joseph, who wrote to Napoleon and demanded Soult's dismissal.

In spite of the squabbling among the French commanders, Wellington's failure at Burgos forced him to retreat again from both Burgos and Madrid to the safety of winter quarters on the Portuguese frontier. This withdrawal during the autumn of 1812, after resounding successes earlier in the year, caused untold suffering to the weary troops of Wellington's armies. Thousands of men deserted, even from the most hardened and loyal units. Fortunately this reverse did not curb the activities of the guerrillas and over many parts of Spain guerrilla commanders, such as Sanchez and Julian

Longa, ruled vast areas, collected taxes and acted as the warlords, which, indeed, they were.

At the end of 1812, in grim winter quarters on the northern Portuguese border, the British HQ received the first news of Napoleon's retreat from Moscow. At the same time, there was encouragement from the increasing number of despatches brought in by the guerrillas. A notorious local brigand, Saornil, handed over new despatches from King Joseph to Soult and Marshal Suchet. From the north of Spain, from the hands of Juan Longa, who dominated Navarre and the vital French route past the Pyrenees to France, came copies of Joseph's despatch to Napoleon in which he demanded Soult's dismissal. Another despatch gave details of the concentration of French forces to counter-attack the powerful guerrillas of Aragon and Catalonia.

The campaigns of Wellington from the secure bases in Portugal through the border towns of Ciudad Rodrigo, Badajoz, and Salamanca, and past Madrid to Burgos, are well known in the story of the Peninsular War. Less well known is the French occupation of Navarre, Aragon and Catalonia. Here guerrilla activity was more widespread and effective than elsewhere in Spain and, in the end, forced Napoleon himself to intervene, and it substantially affected the outcome of the war.

Soon after the initial French incursion into Spain, Suchet, who was to win his marshal's baton for his work in Aragon, was given command of all French troops in Aragon. His first role involved him in the attack on the city of Saragossa. The city was stormed in February 1809 after which 'not a house was left standing' and 40,000 Spanish corpses were found. Suchet was the only French commander in Spain who gave his full attention to the problems of guerrilla activity. After the capture of Saragossa, he took stock of his situation. He understood 'The force of a fanatical insurgent population that detested the godless French invaders, and preferred death to rule by these foreigners' (Napoleon's Marshals, p.491). He saw for himself that when the French devastated the country, the people were not cowed, but reacted with fury. Brutal repression brought brutal retaliation. So Suchet, who became Governor of Aragon, as well as commander of the French III Corps, worked out a positive hearts and minds policy to counteract the guerrillas. He announced that the Aragonese would be ruled according to their own customs. He said 'We will not impede your harvests nor overcrowd your cities'. Religion and clergy would be respected, but priests leading guerrilla bands would be shot. He established councils and encouraged the gentry to take part in local government.

Suchet was highly critical of the other French commanders and appalled at their petty wrangling and their failures in battle. He reorganised the army of Aragon, which had often been an ill-disciplined rabble. The army had not been fed and had not been paid and he saw that this inevitably had a damaging effect on relations with the local people; he therefore disciplined his troops, and ensured that they were paid and properly supplied. Until his reforms were carried out it was said that 'the French only controlled the ground in the shadow of their bayonets'.

In Aragon Suchet faced a new development in guerrilla war. In the Saragossa area, Spanish army units were commanded by General Blake, one of several successful Spanish commanders of Scottish and Irish extraction. Blake made several serious military blunders, but he was the first Spanish commander to see the value of working with the guerrillas and of supplying them with arms. In addition to supporting the guerrillas, Blake implemented an order, in reaction to the French occupation, that all able-bodied men should join a *partida*, i.e., guerrilla band. It was estimated that by 1809 there were over 8,000 guerrillas in north-east Spain and French units several hundred strong were being attacked and butchered. Early in 1809, one of Blake's ablest subordinates, Xavier Mina, left the army and went to his home country Navarre, to organise guerrilla activity and to threaten the French communication and supply route from Pamplona to Bayonne. Even as early as 1809, before the guerrillas had completed their stranglehold, many French units across north-east Spain were close to starvation because the guerrillas intercepted their supplies and prevented them from collecting local produce.

Blake made the mistake of challenging the French to battle instead of relying on guerrilla pressure, but, initially the guerrillas also made the mistake of trying to defend specific areas instead of refusing contact and they too suffered some serious reverses. At the same time, Suchet was introducing his counter-insurgency policy, and he did establish an effective measure of control over parts of Aragon. He also gained some support from the local people. While encouraging support, he was ruthless in dealing with opposition. He issued proclamations warning people to choose peace or war, and threatening that war would bring fire and devastation. Typical of the operations at that time, was a sweep by a French unit of 1,500 men from a garrison in the Pyrenees, which seized 5,000 sheep and 200 cattle, and wiped out every village in the area. Soon the guerrillas learnt the lesson that they should not defend fixed points but slip away before the French attacked. In places where they were strong enough, the French would seal off an area, collect grain and taxes and seize hostages. This policy backfired, because the guerrilla leaders were even more ruthless and executed ten French for every Spaniard killed.

By 1810, Suchet had established some measure of control in Upper Aragon north of the Ebro river and was able to collect taxes. South of the Ebro, where Blake co-operated with the guerrillas, the French faced much greater difficulties, and the guerrillas were joined by many former officers and soldiers as well as French deserters. French garrisons were often attacked by guerrilla groups several thousand strong and were unable to collect taxes or food.

While Suchet established some control in Aragon, elsewhere, notably in Navarre, the French were too weak to suppress the guerrillas. There, Xavier Mina could often attack with units of 2,000 infantry and 300 cavalry, and was easily able to seize towns or roads. The French need to have strong garrisons to resist guerrilla attacks, kept thousands of troops idle, a point picked up by Napoleon. Whether in Paris, or even Moscow, he issued orders to his armies in Spain. Suchet was totally frustrated when, having pacified much of Aragon, Napoleon ordered him to take troops away and launch an attack on Valencia. This order was to have widespread reper-cussions. In Navarre, as soon as the French garrisons were run down, the guerrillas stepped up their attacks. In Aragon, Suchet, before moving against Valencia, made a powerful sweep across Aragon to subdue the *partidas*, but he still had to leave large garrisons. By March, 1810, he was besieging Valencia, and had three divisions under command, but the city was strongly defended. Villacampa, an able guerrilla leader, was then strong enough to attack Teruel, some eighty miles north of Valencia, and to cut Suchet's links with Aragon. At the same time, in Navarre, Mina started operations aimed at disrupting supplies to Suchet in Valencia. Mina was captured in that campaign, and Suchet wanted him to be executed, but he was imprisoned in France. Ironically, his uncle, called Francisco Mina, took over his nephew's *partida*, and became one of the most formidable guerrilla leaders.

Napoleon was angry and frustrated at the lack of success in northern Spain, and ordered Suchet to capture Lerida, a key communications town about fifty miles north of Tarragona. This operation clearly illustrates the role of the guerrillas in the struggle against France. Out of his III Corps, Suchet had to leave one division to garrison Aragon, and took two for the attack on Lerida. In addition, for this attack he needed the siege train brought down from Pamplona in Navarre, which in itself was a huge logistic operation. This gave endless opportunities to the guerrillas for ambush and disruption, with an effective threat to the whole supply position of Suchet's command. In spite of further interference by Napoleon, Suchet was such an outstanding commander that he quickly captured Lerida, in May 1810, and destroyed several important guerrilla units. This was a blow to the guerrillas, but Villacampa in the Valencia region was still strong enough to win significant victories by ambushing major French convoys, and capturing small towns. In one of these, the mayor who had co-operated with the French was burnt alive. After the capture of Lerida, the people in Aragon began to tire of the constant demands of the guerrillas, and there was at last some response to Suchet's measured policy.

Napoleon still wanted Suchet to capture Valencia, and, at the same time demanded the aggressive collection of taxes – for example a fine of three million francs on Lerida. This, of course, heightened Suchet's dilemma between exploitation and pacification. During the summer of 1810, the guerrillas became even more powerful. Villacampa was able to destroy French tax-collecting units 200 strong, Catalan guerrillas raided into France and shot hostages, and in Navarre Francisco Mina was strong enough to defeat whole battalions of French troops.

Suchet was outstandingly the best of the French commanders in obtaining food and supplies for his troops and, by the spring of 1811, he had fairly effective control over most of Aragon and the Ebro valley. He then collected three months' food supply before he besieged Tarragona. The city fell in June 1811, and the main regular Spanish forces in that area were eliminated, but the *partidas* were still strong enough to recruit French deserters, and to be a constant threat to French food supplies. After the fall of Tarragona, Suchet moved in force against Valencia, which was still holding out under Blake. The Spanish general made a number of serious mistakes. He called Villacampa, the most successful local guerrilla leader, to help defend Valencia – showing that he had not grasped the real lessons of guerrilla fighting. Towards the end of 1811, Suchet stepped up the pressure on Valencia, but even without the *partidas* of Villacampa, who were inside the city's defences, the guerrillas in the area were able to muster over 6,000 men and, in October, using mining techniques under the ramparts, were able to capture a fortress town which cut the French supply line. Fortunately for Suchet, Blake surrendered Valencia in January 1812, and nearly 20,000 prisoners were taken off to France.

In spite of the loss of the main towns, the *partidas* had increased in numbers and efficiency – an ominous sign for the French. At this juncture,

Mina, having evaded a French build-up in Navarre, was strong enough to invade Aragon with a force of infantry and cavalry nearly 2,000 strong and he took yet another town which threatened Suchet's links with France.

The guerrillas now turned their attention to Catalonia and, by the beginning of 1812, were able to challenge major French units. Using artillery and mining equipment against French held fortresses, the guerrillas were even strong enough to attack and overwhelm the relief columns coming to the help of the besieged towns. In the first two months of 1812, Suchet lost nearly a quarter of his forces.

The terrific upsurge of guerrilla activity across north-east Spain forced the French to re-group a large number of their forces, and this had serious repercussions across the peninsula. It led to the fall of Ciudad Rodrigo to Wellington, and, in Navarre, Mina routed a strong French force which fled to Pamplona. All over Spain, French patrols trying to collect food, supplies or taxes were overwhelmed and butchered. All the French commanders in Spain now called on Napoleon to give the highest priority to the defeat of the guerrillas. He therefore set up the Army of the Ebro, strengthening the existing troops with four additional divisions, intending to crush all the guerrillas and to stop their devastating raids into southern France. Napoleon appointed General Reille to command this operation but, once again, the bad blood and bickering between the different French commanders weakened the effort. There was particularly bad feeling between Reille and Suchet, and the whole campaign was threatened by the failure of all the French units to obtain food and other supplies – the result of guerrilla activity.

French troops were now being transferred for the Russian campaign, and both Reille and Suchet protested that this would be disastrous. Reille's command of the so-called Army of the Ebro had been reduced from 35,000 to about 9,000 not because of a major battle but because of transfers to the eastern front and by the growing power of the guerrillas. The French were everywhere on the defensive, and merely trying to hold on to their fortresses, while the great guerrilla leader, Mina, directing his own division as well as other independent groups, was harrying the French supply routes. Across Navarre, Aragon and Catalonia the *partidas* were strong enough to infiltrate towns, to blow up French ammunition dumps and to prevent the collection of food, supplies or taxes. Everywhere they held the initiative. Their achievements received further recognition when, in August 1812, Wellington, after his victory at Salamanca, planned amphibious landings from Alicante to Valencia. The French had to withdraw more troops to face Wellington's own advance in the north, and this gave the opportunity for Mina, Villacampa and other guerrilla leaders to step up their activities, and, almost at will, to capture supplies, ammunition, cannon, horses and money. Increasingly, they took hostages and demanded ransom.

The French estimated that the guerrillas had 25,000 men in north-east Spain. In desperation they seized hostages, and even shot parents whose sons were guerrillas. But this proved counter-productive. During the summer of 1812, helped by the advance of Wellington, the guerrillas were able to take control of large areas, collect taxes and harvest the corn. Under intense pressure, the French commanders squabbled even more, and rarely co-operated together, and by the end of the year Mina was almost unchallenged north of the Ebro, while south of the river Villacampa held sway.

Early in 1813 an incident took place which illustrates the difficult situation faced by the French. Mina, with two battalions, attacked the small town of Sos, south-west of Pamplona. It was strongly defended by about 150 men under a determined leader. It had sound defensive walls and, as in many other towns the centre of the defence lay in the fortified convent – presumably the sturdiest building complex in the town. Mina attacked with six cannon and had engineers who mined under the defences, but still the defenders held out until a strong rescue force arrived. Mina had to withdraw, but the town was so badly damaged by fire and by explosions that the French withdrew, and he was able to attack the main French column and destroy it as it moved off. All the French garrisons felt threatened, and they faced the daunting fact that they often lost more men in attempting to rescue a garrison than the number in the garrison (a detailed description of these campaigns is given in *Rod of Iron*, by Don W. Alexander, USA, 1985).

In 1813, Napoleon was still considering the annexation to France of all territory north of the Ebro, and he decided, again, to take drastic action against the guerrillas. He put another commander in charge – General Clausel – and sent four additional divisions, but once again the other commanders did little to help. From this time onwards the operations of the guerrillas were directly linked to Wellington's operations. As he advanced, the French had to withdraw troops to face him. At the same time, the British from their base in Alicante, mounted an attack on Tarragona, but in spite of support from both the Spanish army and the guerrillas, this failed.

In May 1813, Wellington, who had used the winter wisely, was ready to move forward with a force of over 80,000. It was an army which was well-disciplined, re-clothed, re-supplied and backed up by a reorganised supply system. He employed a brilliant strategic plan which deceived the French. Advancing from Salamanca, he sent powerful forces – 40,000 under General Graham – to move north of his expected route. Using this tactic, he was able to by-pass the French defences covering Valladolid, Burgos and the defences on the upper Ebro, and reached Vitoria – the very gateway to France. On 21 June 1813, Wellington attacked Vitoria, which was defended by Joseph and Jourdan with nearly 50,000 men. After a fierce fight, Wellington won an astounding victory, assisted at a critical moment by artillery under the guerrilla leader Longa – a fitting testimony to the role of the Spanish guer- rillas. King Joseph and Marshal Jourdan had assembled mountains of loot to take away to France – priceless pictures as well as a silver chamber pot – and all of this now fell into the hands of the jubilant and victorious Allied troops.

As the French started to withdraw ignominiously over the border, pursued by Wellington's triumphant troops, Suchet, in Valencia, heard the news of Vitoria, and immediately started a controlled withdrawal at the eastern end of the Pyrenees. All over Aragon, Catalonia and Aragon, guerrilla bands stepped up their attacks on the retreating enemy.

Although the defeat of the French in Spain was overshadowed by the more spectacular retreat from Moscow, it substantially weakened and undermined the French power and position in Europe. Napoleon himself must take the blame for the Spanish débâcle. His arrogant decision to remove the Spanish royal family had the unexpected result of creating a national uprising, and created a totally new guerrilla situation, where leading figures from all levels of society joined the *partidas* or guerrilla bands. Once the campaigns had started, Napoleon did little to curb the destructive rivalry between his ambitious marshals. Then he added to their difficulties by intervening – sometimes disastrously – in tactical decisions and in occupation policy. He demanded the collection of heavy taxes, and even in Aragon under Suchet this played into the hands of the guerrillas.

The most effective guerrilla activity took place in Navarre, Catalonia and Aragon, and it was this which wore down the French occupation forces. In south-west Spain and Portugal the guerrillas played a slightly different role. Although they kept up constant pressure on the French armies of Soult, Massena, Marmont and others, they performed the additional role of capturing French despatches and bringing them to Wellington where they were well rewarded. The guerrilla role in this aspect of Wellington's intelli- gence system was crucial, and contributed substantially to his success.

Guerrilla activity, especially in north-east Spain, where it was based on almost total support from the local community, developed something new and established a new name in the annals of military history – guerrilla war.

Russia, Prussia and other Revolts

Spain is rightly credited with the most significant development of guerrilla war but Russia had an even older guerrilla tradition. In the eighteenth century, Pugachev, an officer in an elite light cavalry force in the Russian army, deserted during the Seven Years' War (1756–63). He began a daring uprising with a following of peasants and mineworkers from the Urals. Under his leadership, a Cossack rebellion swept the country and he demanded a separate Cossack state. While the Russians were preoccupied with fighting the Turks, Pugachev was strong enough to seize towns and to threaten Catherine the Great's policy towards the peasants, but, when the Turks were defeated, the Russian army turned on him. He retreated to the Volga region, but was captured and executed in 1775. He remained a hero to the peasants and mineworkers, and his rebellion featured in Pushkin's novel *The Captain's Daughter*.

The repercussions of the French Revolution, and of Napoleon's aggression, spread rapidly across Europe but the first effective guerrilla uprising took place in backward rural France, where the peasants of the Vendée objected to the new ideas. They were deeply attached to their priests and to the old order, and they rose up in rebellion when they were ordered to be ready to serve their country outside their home territory. In 1792, the Vendée revolt erupted in the remote and wild country south of the Loire. The *bocage* was ideal for guerrilla attacks and ambushes – as was rediscovered in 1944 – and the peasants used the marshes and hills effectively. The rebels lacked co-ordination, but their sudden fierce attacks with remarkably accurate firepower, and their swift dispersal so that they could not be pinned down, presented the new French government with a major problem. The rebels enjoyed the additional advantage that the best French troops were away fighting on different fronts, and initially only inexperienced conscripts were deployed against them. As the government brought in more experienced troops to overcome the revolt, the rebels were worn down by the weight of numbers of the Republican forces and, by the end of 1793, the revolt was over.

Almost simultaneously with the Spanish revolt, Napoleon's arrogance sparked another brief but violent guerrilla uprising. The Bavarians had made an alliance with France, and as a reward had gained control over the Tyrol. In 1809, the Tyroleans rose in angry revolt, and used their mountain hideouts to wreak havoc on the enemy. Fiery leaders soon emerged, often supported by the priests, and late in 1809 a force of several thousand was able to capture Innsbruck, the strategic town controlling the Brenner Pass. This success was short-lived, and by the end of that year the leaders were betrayed and the revolt savagely suppressed.

In June 1812, when the Spaniards had already taught him some bitter lessons, Napoleon, driven by almost insane ambition, and ignoring many ominous signs, invaded Russia with the Grande Armée, nearly 600,000 strong. Only half of this vast array were French, and few of those were veterans. As the huge host left Königsberg on the Baltic, poor organis-ation created problems almost from the start. Supplies of weapons, ammunition, food and fodder proved hopelessly inadequate. Even in the summer weeks of July and August there was massive desertion and even starvation. This resulted in French troops plundering the local areas for food, and this, in itself, influenced the attitudes of the Lithuanian people and the Russian peasants towards the invaders. Napoleon could easily have gained the support of both these groups, and their hostility was to cost him dear.

By the beginning of September 1812, the Grande Armée was approaching Moscow, after fighting many minor delaying actions carried out by the ageing General Kutuzov. He and most of the Russian comman-ders agreed on the strategy of allowing Napoleon to advance slowly and to extend his lines of supply and communication. The Tsar finally overruled Kutuzov and demanded a fight. This took place on 7 September at Borodino, less than a hundred miles from Moscow. Napoleon with his experienced marshals Ney, Davout, Junot and Murat launched the attack, but the Russian defences held firm. During a day of awful carnage, with 70,000 casualties, the French attacked in vain, and at the end of the battle, although Kutuzov withdrew, his army was still intact. Napoleon slowly advanced and Kutuzov decided not to fight to save Moscow. Finally, Napoleon entered an almost deserted city, but the people started fires to burn down their city rather than hand it over to the French.

By this time the French supply system had almost completely broken down, and French troops rampaged through Moscow, desperate for food and water. Those still outside the city searched the countryside, but began to encounter a grave and ominous threat. In their advance to Moscow the French had antagonised all the people along the way, and now small groups sprang up, ready to take their revenge. Isolated French soldiers or small groups were attacked, killed and their uniforms and weapons taken. The weapons were eagerly used in the next attack. These guerrilla groups spread rapidly and soon were able to challenge major French units.

A young lieutenant colonel on Kutuzov's staff – Denis Davidov – had witnessed the start of this uprising even before Borodino, and had gained reluctant permission from Kutuzov to use a couple of hundred light cavalry Cossacks to widen the impact of the peasant attackers. This was the nucleus of the Cossack partisans who ruthlessly terrorised and destroyed so much of Napoleon's army as it retreated from the burnt-out ruins of Moscow. Davidov was not only one of the most successful guerrilla leaders in the field, but he is remembered for his *Essay on Partisan Warfare* which vividly illustrated his views on guerrilla tactics. He envisaged guerrilla war as undertaken by regular troops, with the optimum number about 1,500 men supported by light mobile artillery. Although he had set out with his very small force to co-ordinate the attacks on the French by the largely peasant bands, which had sprung up spontaneously, his writing ignores them. He mentions the people or the peasants only in a negative way, by forbidding his troops to plunder, in order not to lose the goodwill of the peasants. In his writing, Davidov stressed the importance of partisan attacks on enemy supply lines in order to destroy convoys, destroy depots of food, ammunition and weapons, and to capture couriers in order to send back information about enemy units and movements. As leader of a strong Cossack unit, he was able to attack and destroy small French units, to free Russian prisoners, to destroy enemy medical services and field hospitals, to destroy bridges, and generally slow down the enemy retreat. He repeated the dictum that partisans should never take part in a set battle, and should always depend on surprise. They should never have a fixed base, which could be vulnerable to enemy attack, and should only set up temporary bases to care for their own wounded. His whole philosophy reflects the Russian fear of arming the peasants in case they used their power to revolt against their serfdom.

In spite of Davidov's reservations, the spontaneous peasant bands wrought most havoc on the retreating French forces. Wherever the starving French soldiers went to forage for food or to find shelter from the fearsome Russian winter, they were immediately at risk. Partisan bands became increasingly well organised. They attacked isolated men, stripped them of weapons and clothes, and, to save a round of ammunition, left them naked to freeze to death. Even French units over 1,000 strong were not immune from attack.

As the French continued to retreat, Kutuzov, who had been forced by the Tsar to do battle at Borodino, now refused to attack in force, but followed the French on a parallel route, constantly harassing them. He was able to observe the vicious and ruthless attacks of the peasant bands, and this convinced him more than ever, of the danger of arming the peasants. When the tattered remnants of the Grande Armée crossed the Russian border, they were again harried across the whole of Poland and into Prussia.

Between 1809 and 1812, three of Prussia's great military figures – Scharnhorst, Gneisenau and Clausewitz – having been well briefed about the situation in Spain, had given much thought to the issue of partisan war, and how it could be used against Napoleon. Clausewitz, who had served in the Prussian Army, had witnessed the effect in Prussia of the defeat at Jena and the humiliation of the treaty of Tilsit. After this, along with some other Prussian officers, he briefly transferred to the Russian Army. When he returned to Prussia, he came under the powerful influence of Scharnhorst, with whom he worked to rebuild the Prussian Army, and to learn the lessons of defeat. Clausewitz gave lectures at the Berlin War Academy on partisan warfare. The initial ideas put forward by these leaders included the establishment of the Landwehr or Prussian militia. All males from 16 to 60 were to be enlisted in the Landwehr, and encouraged to use basic arms – like muskets – but also farming tools, which could be used as weapons. Their role was to ambush enemy forces, to capture enemy couriers carrying despatches, and to pass on information to the regular forces. Partisans were always seen as adjuncts to the regulars – ideas clearly based on the Spanish experience.

At this time, Clausewitz formulated his ideas about guerrilla war, even though his seminal work *On War* was published posthumously many years later. His specific ideas are contained in a chapter entitled 'Arming the Nation'. This is a detailed and impressive treatise, which repeats his strongly held views that guerrilla war must be seen as an adjunct to regular forces, and that partisans can never be decisive by themselves. Within these parameters, Clausewitz gives sound advice on guerrilla tactics: guerrillas must operate in small bands so that one reverse cannot be decisive; they must not be used to attack major enemy units, but must undermine the enemy by ambushes, by attacks on small units or patrols, and by capturing couriers and despatches; after every attack they must rapidly disperse; such tactics will force the enemy to deploy large numbers of troops either to defend garrisons or to escort convoys. Clausewitz coined an apt phrase, which is usually translated as 'A nebulous vapoury essence'.

On War, the main work of Clausewitz, although immensely significant and influential, is generally considered to be dense and academic. It did not gain its pre-eminent position until the age of Bismarck and von Moltke. This general assessment of Clausewitz makes it all the more remarkable that he put forward such sound practical and down to earth advice on partisan warfare. Before peace was achieved in 1815 Scharnhorst and his able colleagues had established another organisation to rouse the people against an invader. The Landsturm, set up in 1813, aimed to be a partisan force of all the people. Its instructions and advice were clear cut and imperative, but were defensive rather than offensive. As an enemy advanced, all people were advised to flee to the woods, to carry away their corn, to destroy all stores and wine, to fill in all wells, and to destroy all bridges and mills. This radical sounding advice for a people in arms was at the same time heavily circumscribed, with a clear warning that any action by the people must take place only under the orders of the army, and must be carefully controlled.

Thus Davidov in Russia, and Clausewitz in Prussia, both of whom did so much to focus attention on partisan war, were always conscious of the danger of a peasant uprising. They remained convinced that all partisan activity should be tightly controlled by the government and the army.

The ideas of the French Revolution – Liberty, Equality, Fraternity – coupled with the aggressive military adventures of Napoleon, obviously impacted most strongly on Europe, but the ramifications were felt across the world. In India, Anglo-French rivalry caused wars between Hindu Mysore and Muslim Hyderabad and Britain fought the USA from the Great Lakes to New Orleans in the often forgotten War of 1812. But the most significant offshoot of the revolutionary ideas and Napoleonic expansion came in the Caribbean.

Before the end of the eighteenth century, the ferment of ideas of the Age of Enlightenment, the spread of scientific knowledge, the radical ideas of the philosophers like Locke, Burke and Rousseau, and the success of American independence, had stirred up strong feelings in the slave colonies of the Caribbean. Slave revolts, with bloodthirsty attacks on the largely white-owned sugar plantations, spread widely. Colonial rivalry between Britain, France and Spain only exacerbated these problems, and nowhere was this more dramatically illustrated than in Santo Domingo (Haiti).

In this island, which still suffers the wretched legacy of colonial division, a massive slave revolt destroyed over a thousand plantations. The revolt spread across the island, and, during the 1790s, an effective leader gradu-ally emerged. Toussaint L'Ouverture, who had served with both the French and Spanish forces in this deeply divided island, proved himself to be an outstanding military leader. In the early days of the revolt the slaves tended to make a wild mass charge against any enemy force, but Toussaint, by establishing a cadre of well disciplined troops, with carefully controlled fire-power, set up a most effective guerrilla organisation. This became strong enough to tackle British, French or Spanish armies. His troops, former slaves who had fled from their plantations, used the mountains as their secure base from which to launch their attacks. They moved swiftly, rarely encumbered by any baggage. Toussaint rapidly gained a reputation for striking suddenly and unexpectedly, and then dispersing to the mountains, where the colonialist forces rarely followed. He appeared to have well-organised supplies and weapons, and, from sound intelligence gathering, seemed always able to anticipate and ambush the ponderous advances of the French or British forces.

Sovereignty and control of the island was continually disputed between the French, British and Spanish but by 1798 Toussaint was powerful enough to force the British to leave. Another phase of the struggle began in 1802, when Napoleon, again forgetting the lofty humanitarian aims of the Revo-lution, decided to recapture the island and re-establish slavery. This started a wretched chapter in its history. Napoleon sent General Leclerc to lead the expedition, but he died of yellow fever. Soon after this, although the French were not in a strong position, Toussaint decided to negotiate – illustrating the old maxim that however bad things are for you, they may be even worse for the enemy. Toussaint's fine leadership ended in betrayal and tragedy, and the French took brutal revenge.

Across Europe after 1815 and in the aftermath of Napoleon, the kings and priests returned, and all the partisan activity of the preceding years appeared to have achieved little. In Italy, where Napoleon had established brief unity under a puppet ruler, the old powers divided up the country, and, except for Piedmont, restored control to reactionary aristocrats and the numbing influence of the Papacy. Yet, it was from this unpromising base that one of the greatest guerrilla leaders was to emerge.

GARIBALDI IN SOUTH AMERICA, PRELUDE TO ITALY

Garibaldi, the greatest guerrilla leader of the nineteenth century, became a world figure during the 1860s and was lionised across Europe, Britain and America. His exploits in support of Italian unity are well known. Less well known are his achievements in South America, where he fought for the cause of freedom and liberty, and developed his remarkable leadership potential.

Born in Nice in 1807, when Napoleon was at the height of his power, Garibaldi had a happy and secure childhood. His parents wanted him to become a doctor, but he had a passion for the sea. Aged 17, he went to sea and his life of adventure began. Pirates captured him and left him destitute in Constantinople. At this early age, after a visit to Rome, he recorded his hopes for a united Italy, free of the Papacy. He returned home in 1831 as an experienced sailor, with his Master's Certificate. He was excited by the current wave of radical ideas sweeping across Italy, which aimed to over-throw despotic kings and reactionary clerical governments. In 1833 he joined the Young Italy movement founded by Mazzini and was soon being hunted by the police for stirring up revolt in the local naval unit. He fled to Marseilles and joined the crew of a ship sailing to Rio de Janeiro.

In the decades after the fall of Napoleon and the end of the Spanish and Portuguese empires in South America, a number of unstable and warring states emerged. Brazil, a country of four million people, half of whom were former negro slaves, stretched across a vast area with few roads, poor communications and with little to hold it together after the removal of the control of the Portuguese royal family. Civil war erupted, and the rebels in the southern province of Rio Grande do Sul struggled for their indepen-dence. Large numbers of Italian immigrants had settled in Rio de Janeiro, in southern Brazil, in neighbouring Uruguay, and in Buenos Aires, the capital of Argentina. Most of the immigrants were active in the Young Italy move-ment, which flourished in all three countries, and there was widespread Italian support for the uprising in the Rio Grande do Sul.

By 1837, Garibaldi, with the support of the local Italian people, had procured a small ship with a few guns, and he set out to help the rebels. He was soon introduced to the brutality of war and civil war in the area, when he put into the estuary of the River Plate and was captured by the Argen-tinians because he had attacked one of their ships. Pirates normally killed

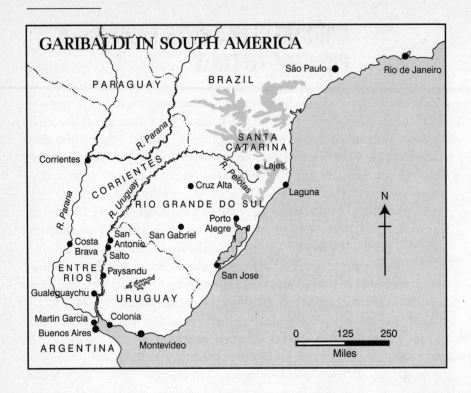

GARIBALDI IN SOUTH AMERICA

their captives, and if they were caught they were executed, but Garibaldi, who suffered a serious neck wound in the exchange of fire before he was captured, was kept in prison and severely tortured. After some months his prison conditions became more relaxed and he learnt Spanish and also learnt to ride a horse – skills which were valuable to him in the following years. In 1838, to his surprise, he was released and he got away to join the rebel forces in Rio Grande do Sul – the start of many years' campaigning in the wars and civil wars in and around the province.

In most of these South American wars a relatively small number of troops were involved in the vast open territory, and, as in medieval times, they often had difficulty in locating the enemy forces. Troops were armed with fairly basic weapons, the cavalry using a lance or sword, and the infantry a carbine and bayonet. When Garibaldi joined the rebels, their competent commander, Goncalves, faced a serious threat from a Brazilian army several thousand strong, which was based on Porto Alegre, on a vast inland lagoon. Despite their large army, the Brazilians held a few seaports, but little else.

Goncalves established a good rapport with Garibaldi, whom he put in command of two ships, with a crew of about 60 men, to attack Brazilian shipping. Garibaldi faced a serious task. His base and his two ships were on the same lagoon – 200 miles long and 30 miles wide – on which the imperial forces also had their headquarters at Porto Alegre. They also controlled the narrow outlet from the lagoon to the sea. Garibaldi, from his base on the western shore of the lagoon, decided to attack Brazilian supply ships going northwards up the lagoon to Porto Alegre. In September 1838 he captured a large vessel with a valuable cargo, but this angered the imperial authorities who, with a naval force of 50 ships, ordered all merchant ships on the lagoon to sail with a naval escort.

A military stalemate then ensued during which the rebels, who now controlled most of Rio Grande do Sul, set up a new administration based on the precepts of the French Revolution. They drew up a constitution, being careful in this backward Roman Catholic country not to attack the church, and they arranged democratic elections and published a newspaper headed by quotations from Mazzini and Young Italy. Goncalves had many aristo-cratic land-owning supporters, with estates on the lagoon, and here they were able to establish a dignified social life. One of the estates became Garibaldi's headquarters.

During April 1839, when security had become very lax, an imperialist patrol attacked Garibaldi. He had about a dozen men to face 150. He led the defence of the main storehouse. The attackers realised they were deep in enemy territory and when their leader was wounded, and Garibaldi continued to hold out, they withdrew. After Garibaldi's success, Goncalves felt strong enough to attack the neighbouring province, Santa Catarina, where there was considerable sympathy for the republican cause.

In July 1839, Garibaldi faced a serious problem. He could not get his ship out of the lagoon, and he therefore consulted an engineer, who constructed a vehicle to lift the ships out of the water and, with 200 oxen, pulled the ships 50 miles across an uninhabited strip of land. After three days they were launched into the Atlantic.

After this amazing achievement the two ships set out for Laguna on the coast of Santa Catarina, but they were hit by a very violent storm and Garibaldi had to abandon ship. He lost all his stores and half his crew. The attack on Laguna went ahead and, in July 1839, after a serious fire-fight in which the enemy lost fifteen killed and over seventy taken prisoner, the town was taken. The booty included several ships, weapons, ammunition and food. Laguna was a prosperous town, and it became the capital of the republic of Santa Catarina, with a provisional government. After initial success the people of Laguna turned against their so-called deliverers. A second base at Laguna enabled Garibaldi to raid shipping all along the Brazilian coast.

Probably the best known romantic incident in Garibaldi's life took place at Laguna soon after its capture. He looked through his telescope from his ship and saw Anita. He went ashore, found her, and said, 'You must be mine'. She, not a great beauty, was a fierce and passionate woman and Garibaldi's proposal was the start of a love affair which continued until her death in his arms in 1849.

In October 1839, Garibaldi resumed his attacks on Brazilian shipping and had three ships under his command. He sailed north to São Paulo and captured several valuable prizes. On his way back he was apprehended by Brazilian warships and after a severe encounter, in which he lost two of his prize ships, he fled for the shore and mounted the gun from his ship on the beach. The Brazilian ships attacked the next day, and were driven off after another bloody engagement. Anita stayed with Garibaldi throughout these battles. Very soon the people of Santa Catarina turned against the invading forces. Garibaldi then had to take a punitive expedition to deal with a town which had opted for the imperial side. He landed his small contingent and, by attacking from the land side, captured the town with ease. He had been ordered to sack the town and this was done, but he wrote that he hoped anyone 'who retains any feelings of humanity will never have to sack another town.' While the enemy forces remained nearby, Garibaldi's men went first to the wine shops and rapidly got drunk. Garibaldi, fearing the enemy could counterattack and wipe out his now incapable troops, used his sword and his fierce discipline to force them back to the boats.

These actions prompted serious retaliation by the Brazilian forces and, in November 1839, a fleet of small ships carrying heavily armed troops attacked Laguna. Anita, once again by Garibaldi's side, fought more bravely than most of the other sailors, and after sustaining heavy casualties, and abandoning their ships, Garibaldi and Anita joined the retreating Rio Grande army. The retreat to the borders of Rio Grande do Sul took several months and during this time Garibaldi commanded many actions in guerrilla-type war, in stopping or delaying the pursuing Brazilian forces. He commented that Anita looked on battles as a pleasure and enjoyed the hardships of camp life. In December 1839, the Republicans won a victory on the River Pelotas and in January 1840 recaptured a sizeable town, Lages. The Republicans had been welcomed in Lages, but after they established a tax-collecting system in which Garibaldi was involved, the people of Lages turned against them and, shortly afterwards, welcomed back the imperialists. The Republicans, including Garibaldi and Anita, were driven over the border back into Rio Grande do Sul.

The Brazilian forces advanced rapidly and, in May 1860, a major battle took place just west of the Republican stronghold of Porto Alegre on the northern shore of the great lagoon. The Republicans had about 6,000 men, most of them gauchos with their horses, facing about 7,000 Imperialists, who also had a few artillery pieces. The Republicans won a clear victory in which a unit of mounted lancers, made up entirely of freed negro slaves, played a decisive role.

Despite this victory the Brazilian forces were able to mount further attacks at the southern end of the lagoon at San Jose del Norte. The Republicans counter-attacked, but were defeated and had to withdraw. During this campaign Anita bore Garibaldi a son, Menotti.

In 1845 a revolution took place in Rio de Janeiro and a more liberal government took power. It attempted to end the clash with Rio Grande do Sul by negotiation, but the rebels rejected the approach. Garibaldi felt that the rebels would have been wiser to consider the offers sent from Rio. The Brazilian forces then drove Goncalves and all his followers including Garibaldi, Anita and their baby, far into the western highlands. As they retreated with Garibaldi often commanding the rearguard, the group sustained casualties and Garibaldi lost more of his close friends. They suffered severely from a particularly cold and wet winter and from serious food shortages. Then, when the weather improved and they found plenty of cattle, their morale improved and they reached Cruz Alta, roughly in the centre of Rio Grande do Sul. Their retreat continued southwards until they reached San Gabriel. The fighting continued in a desultory fashion for some time, but Garibaldi left Rio Grande do Sul, and decided to take Anita and Menotti to Montevideo in Uruguay. In April 1841 he set off with a herd of 900 cattle. Inexperience and bad advice led to near disaster. They lost all the cattle, and the Garibaldi family arrived in Montevideo in June almost destitute and owning a few worthless hides. Facing dire poverty, Garibaldi earned a little money by teaching and, in this quiet period of his life, he married Anita.

At this time there was virtual civil war in Uruguay between two rival political parties. In 1838 one had been defeated and its leader, Oribe, took refuge in Argentina under its dictator, Rosas. This saw the start of a long period of war between Argentina and Uruguay. France became involved in the fracas because it decided to blockade Buenos Aires in order to recover French investments in Argentina. Rosas then used the Argentine navy to blockade Montevideo. The purpose of this was also to hit at the Argentine province of Corrientes, on the upper reaches of the River Parana, which was in revolt and wanted to join neighbouring Rio Grande do Sul. This was the background to a wild, madcap, ill thought-out scheme, which had no prospect of success. The expedition was launched by Uruguay in order to hit at Argentina, and also to bring help to the people of Corrientes. It had to sail through 400 miles of mostly hostile Argentine territory, with no friendly bases, and up rivers which, when the water was low, were hardly navigable. Who better to head this expedition than the intrepid leader who had proved his leadership qualities on both land and sea – Garibaldi.

Two rivers, the Parana and the Uruguay, unite to form the River Plate. This point was controlled by the Argentine fortress of Martin Garcia. In June 1842 Garibaldi set out from Montevideo with three ships, the largest of which, the *Constitucion*, had eighteen guns. The ships managed to pass Martin Garcia without too much damage but, shortly afterwards, the *Constitucion* ran aground. Before it could be refloated Argentine warships arrived but their flagship, the *Belgrano*, also ran aground and blocked any movement for the other ships. Garibaldi refloated the *Constitucion* and then thick fog came down and Garibaldi was able to slip away. The Argentinians assumed Garibaldi would sail up the River Uruguay, which went through friendly territory, along the border of Uruguay, but in fact he and his little fleet went up the River Parana, a fact not discovered for many days by the Argentinians. Their comment: 'Only Garibaldi could be capable of such lunacy.'

As he sailed up the Parana, Garibaldi had to attack local towns and villages in order to obtain food, water and pilots to navigate the treacherous river. He had running battles with shore batteries and occasionally Argentine army units but, eventually, after 48 days, he reached Costa Brava, an important provincial town. During his hectic voyage he had captured several merchant ships, but he realised that the Argentine navy was now pursuing him and, sooner or later, he would have to face them. His original intention had been to take arms and supplies to the rebel forces at Corrientes, about 200 miles further up the river, but the low level of the river meant that he could not proceed beyond Costa Brava.

On 14 August 1842, Admiral Brown, the commander of the Argentine naval force, reached Costa Brava. He commanded about 10 small ships with 50 cannon and 700 men. Garibaldi, with half the number of cannon and far fewer men, had time to draw up his ships, including those he had captured, in a sound battle formation of three lines with the *Constitucion* in front. He had carefully disposed of his stores, sending major loads up the river to Corrientes. He also deployed as many men as possible on the river bank to oppose any land attack.

The battle started when Brown's forces, out of range of Garibaldi's guns, used their artillery at will to inflict serious damage on Garibaldi's ships and men. He lost some of his best and most experienced fighters and faced a daunting situation. As the situation deteriorated, a local unit which had supported Garibaldi, deserted and ran away. The substantial superiority of Brown's forces, and the greater range of his guns, made his victory almost inevitable. Garibaldi fought on until all the ammunition had run out, and then he blew up the remaining ships and led away his remaining forces through swamp and jungle.

Highly controversial accounts of this brief campaign have survived. Argentine sources accuse the barbaric pirate Garibaldi of appalling brutality on his way up the River Parana, and they allege that in Costa Brava at the end of the fight he blew up his ship with men still inside. This tendentious view does not accord with the record of his humane attitude during his subsequent years of fighting for the unification of Italy.

By the end of 1842, the Argentinians and their ally Oribe had driven back their opponents – usually called Unitarians – and were ready to besiege Montevideo. In spite of the strength of Oribe and his Argentinian backers, the people of Montevideo were not prepared to give in. In contrast to their determined stand, the people in the Corrientes province, whom Garibaldi's expedition had intended to help, surrendered to the Argentinians without a fight.

In Montevideo, the people as well as the expatriate communities prepared to defend the city against Oribe who had the significant support of Admiral Brown, who had defeated Garibaldi at Costa Brava. By February 1843 Garibaldi had reached Montevideo, and took part in an early skirmish with his old adversary, Admiral Brown. Within the town, large numbers of French, Italian and Spanish immigrants rallied to its defence, in spite of the threat from Oribe to cut the throats of every expatriate who opposed him. Although Garibaldi made urgent appeals to the Italians, the French volunteered in far greater numbers. When Oribe's troops reached the town he, foolishly, expected it to surrender without a fight, and while he dallied all the communities worked frantically to construct defences.

In March 1843 Garibaldi was given command of the Montevideo naval forces, with a request to build up their strength in order to challenge Admiral Brown's ships which were blockading the town. Garibaldi's task was urgent because Montevideo imported most of its food from the surrounding country and depended for its survival on the import-export trade. In spite of the blockade, Garibaldi found many local villages which were happy to provide food and other supplies, and enough small boats which were prepared to slip though the blockade at night. Fairly soon he had succeeded in building up a fleet of 17 small boats with over 300 men.

The Montevideo siege attracted the interests of the European powers as well as Brazil. France tended to support the Unitarians defending Montevideo, while Britain – generally reflecting Palmerston's stance of arrogant condescension – was primarily interested in expanding its trade in the whole area, and merely wanted the blockade of the River Plate to be finished as soon as possible. Typical of the time, the commander of the British naval squadron strongly supported Garibaldi, against the views of his government, but messages to the British government took six months each way and this gave him considerable latitude. Garibaldi supervised the so-called fleet, but was also active in inland operations, and he commanded the Italian legion in several actions. He sustained serious criticisms because of the lax discipline among the crews on his boats and among the troops in the Italian legion. Perhaps he learnt a valuable lesson of war from this experience, since, in the Italian campaign he was famed for the high level of discipline among his guerrillas. In June 1843 in the middle of an action, Garibaldi appealed to the Italian legion to uphold the honour of Italy, and then led them successfully in a bayonet charge, which won the day, and restored the rather battered reputation of the legion. Thereafter he became famous for his tactic of leading a charge with fixed bayonets and dispersing the enemy.

Both Brazil and Argentina were attempting to extend their influence in the area of Uruguay – sometimes by dubious methods – and there was a diplomatic crisis when Garibaldi, who thought he had been insulted, charged into the Brazilian embassy and challenged the ambassador to a duel. Both Argentina and Brazil blew the incident out of all proportion, but it was settled when Garibaldi apologized and Brazil promised to remain neutral in the situation in Montevideo.

In contrast to this incident, there were brutal reprisals between the two sides in Montevideo, and prisoners frequently had their throats cut. Oribe, who encouraged the throat cutting, hesitated to make a direct assault on Montevideo because he lacked sufficient troops and he continued to hope that it would surrender without a fight. The siege even featured in a book by Dumas, who compared it to the siege of Troy. As the war dragged on,

Garibaldi continued to take part in both naval and military actions. He led the Italian legion in several serious clashes on land and, through his actions with the navy, he managed to capture several merchant ships and bring their cargoes of food and other supplies to help the hard-pressed people besieged in Montevideo.

During this increasingly stressful time, Garibaldi clashed with the English commander of the international fleet, which was monitoring the situation in the River Plate, and notched up the tension still further. Within Montevideo there were growing and bitter divisions between the different factions, made worse by the defection to the enemy of two senior members of the Italian legion, who then proceeded to vilify Garibaldi as a barbaric pirate. Oribe and the attacking forces made the most of the divisions within Montevideo, and they deliberately fomented the dislike of the local people towards the foreign legions, and to the increasingly powerful position held by Garibaldi. They also resented the drunken ill-discipline and offensive behaviour of many of the Italian legion. To instil more discipline and control over his fighters, Garibaldi bought the slaughterhouse shirts – loose red robes with a belt around the waist – which were to become famous as the red shirts of Garibaldi's guerrillas in Italy. They were bought because they were cheap – a failed export order – but they came to symbolise Red Republicans across Europe.

Unexpected help came to Montevideo when Britain, France and Brazil organised an international naval force to bring an end to the hostilities in the River Plate. It came at a time when the defenders of the town were rent by bitter divisions and were very close to surrender. The great powers aimed to curb the Argentinian involvement, and to arrange an election in Uruguay to decide between the two warring factions in the civil war – i.e., the Unitarians, who were inside Montevideo, and Oribe who was besieging them with the help of Argentina.

In August 1845, Garibaldi joined the international naval force in the capture of Colonia from Oribe's forces, who then issued wild propaganda stories about the looting and depredations of Garibaldi's savage Unitarians. Then the allied force advanced and in early September took the strategic town of Martin Garcia. Next Garibaldi was given command of a joint naval and military force moving up the River Uruguay. Settlements on the Uruguayan shore were well treated, but his men gained a bad reputation for looting and destruction in the villages on the shore of the Argentine province of Entre Rios. He captured the town of Gualeguaychu, and while his men looted the town, he ensured the humane treatment of prisoners and civilians. He was severely criticised for this, because, in this war, it was customary on both sides to cut the throats of prisoners. Soon after the victory at Gualeguaychu he captured Paysandu and continued up river with 19 boats including one British and one French pinnace. His largest ship had a crew of 36 and mustered 39 guns.

Garibaldi's expedition was making for the substantial town of Salto, population 10,000, which played an important role in the volatile and confusing civil war between the Unitarians under Rivera and Garibaldi on the one hand and the forces of Oribe, backed by Argentina on the other. Garibaldi was approaching Salto in October 1845, and diplomatically sought the surrender of the town in order to save lives, but his appeal was ignored. As he sailed closer to Salto, the garrison launched a counterattack against the other part of the Italian legion commanded by Garibaldi's able colleague and friend Anzani. With good discipline, he held his fire and then slaughtered the attackers. After this defeat, the garrison fled and Garibaldi with Anzani entered Salto. Garibaldi insisted on the humane treatment of prisoners and civilians, but, as was customary, he was vilified by the enemy propaganda for unspeakable and barbarous crimes.

After capturing Salto, Garibaldi hurriedly fortified it, because two armies of the Oribe faction were swiftly approaching. They had over 3,000 men against Garibaldi's 1,000 and they had threatened to cut the throats of all the Italian legion and all Unitarians. The siege lasted three weeks, but the defenders were never seriously threatened, and the attackers then moved off into Corrientes province.

In February 1846, Garibaldi heard that friendly forces were coming to his assistance, and he marched out from Salto to San Antonio, a few miles away, to link up with them. He had about 200 men and 100 Uruguayan cavalry, when he was taken by surprise and attacked by an enemy force of over 1,000. He rapidly formed his small group into a defensive position around a ruined farm building and they prepared to fight for their lives. Then the Uruguayan cavalry – one third of his total force – after a brief skirmish, and to the disgust of Garibaldi, fled back to the safety of Salto. He, with his fierce control of troops in action, carefully held his fire while the enemy advanced in a rather disorganised straight line, and then opened fire causing heavy casualties. The attackers regrouped and continued their assault, often with hand-to-hand fighting, but never with a single concerted attack. The battle lasted nine hours, and then, with casualties mounting alarmingly and as darkness fell, Garibaldi decided to retreat from the farm building towards the River Uruguay, less than a mile away. This dangerous manoeuvre, in darkness and in the face of continuing enemy attacks, was eventually achieved, and the survivors were able to slake their desperate thirst in the river. The river gave them some cover, and slowly over a period of several hours, they continued their retreat towards Salto.

In this battle, which became a significant part of the Garibaldi legend, he lost 30 killed and 50 wounded out of a force of 200. When, the next day, the enemy withdrew, he went back to the battlefield, and rescued his own and the enemy wounded, and arranged a decent burial for the fallen of both sides. Medical help for the wounded came from the crew of a small French naval ship moored on the river.

This victory, though smaller than a battalion action, was hailed resoundingly in Montevideo, and Garibaldi was promoted to general. His fame spread from South America to Italy. At the same time, the Argentine press, keeping up its hostile propaganda, referred sneeringly to the drubbing he had received. His promotion – although at first he refused it – caused outrage among many Uruguayan leaders, who resented his prominence. Leaving aside the legend, from a purely military point of view, Garibaldi's handling of the fight at San Antonio showed great military skill. He defended his base when taken by surprise by overwhelming odds, he held the defence together when the cavalry deserted, and then he conducted a controlled withdrawal at night over a period of four or five hours. By any standards this was an outstanding military achievement.

After San Antonio and the siege of Salto, during which there was a coup in Montevideo, the political situation rapidly deteriorated, and Garibaldi became increasingly disillusioned. He was nominally commander in chief, but he and the Italian legion refused all pay. Anita and Garibaldi's growing family lived in abject poverty, often without enough money to buy candles. The great powers made another investigation in order to stop the war and to open up the area for trade, and they decided that the war was kept going largely by the French and Italian legions. In a welter of corruption and unprincipled scheming and division, Garibaldi's reputation for complete integrity – including his refusal of 30,000 dollars to change sides – remained unsullied. In the months after San Antonio although the Uruguayan government made him an Honourable (sic) member of the Republic, his disgust and disillusionment continued.

In this situation, news of political stirrings in Italy caused great excitement in the Italian legion and among their supporters, who generously contributed to a fund to help the uprisings in Italy. In April 1848, Garibaldi and his family together with over 70 seasoned guerrilla veterans from the

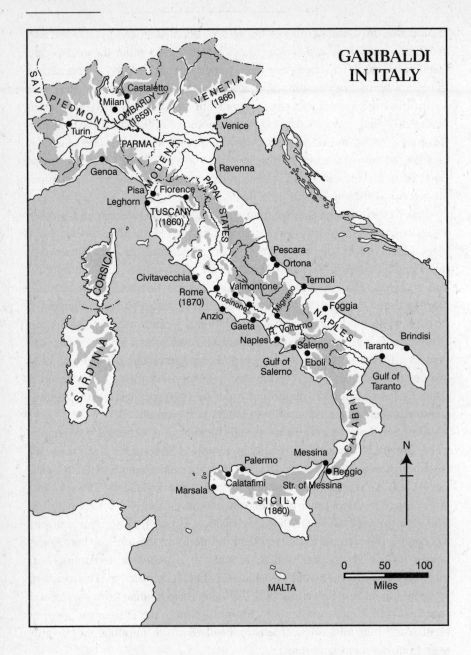

GARIBALDI IN ITALY

SAVOY

PIEDMONT

Turin

Milan

LOMBARDY (1859)

Castaletto

VENETIA (1866)

Venice

PARMA

Genoa

MODENA

Ravenna

Pisa

Florence

Leghorn

TUSCANY (1860)

PAPAL STATES

CORSICA

Civitavecchia

Rome (1870)

Valmontone

Frosinone

Anzio

Gaeta

Naples

Pescara

Ortona

Termoli

Mignano

R. Volturno

NAPLES

Foggia

Brindisi

Salerno

Eboli

Taranto

SARDINIA

Gulf of Salerno

Gulf of Taranto

CALABRIA

N

Messina

Palermo

Calatafimi

Reggio

Marsala

Str. of Messina

SICILY (1860)

0   50   100

Miles

MALTA

legion, returned to Italy to offer their services to the cause of liberty. During his service in Uruguay he had mixed easily with the top political and military leaders, and he was not daunted by the prospect of dealing with the establishment figures in Italy. Although he had spent much of his life in making war, he strongly criticized the futility of war and of nationalism. Decades ahead of his time he looked forward to the unity of Europe, and he espoused many liberal issues like the position of women in society, and the rights of working people.

By the time he and his band arrived in Nice in the spring of 1848, Europe had been rocked by widespread revolution. Austria, the occupying power of much of northern Italy, had been challenged by the creation of a republic in Venice, and by the uprising in Milan, which drove out the hated Radetzky. Then another uprising drove Metternich, the archetypal reactionary figure, out of Vienna. These events caused a surge of excitement for Garibaldi and his veterans. He offered his services to Charles Albert, King of Piedmont, but he was ignored, and when he conducted some guerrilla activity against Austrian troops in the Alps, he achieved little and there was minimal support for his actions. His high hopes were swiftly dashed.

This setback tested his powers of leadership, but a new opportunity arose when a popular uprising drove the Pope out of Rome and set up a republic. Suddenly, many strands of Italian patriotism came together. Garibaldi and his volunteers rushed to Rome and joined with Mazzini and many of the leaders of Young Italy. At the same time, the Pope appealed to the Roman Catholic powers. France, hoping to outmanoeuvre Austria, hurriedly sent a military contingent, which landed at Ostia and marched on Rome to restore the Pope.

The French regulars rapidly dispersed the Young Italy defenders, but then Garibaldi took control of the battle. All his experience in South America seemed to lead to this point. With firm leadership, he drove back the French attack, killing 500 and capturing 300 prisoners. Mazzini and the political leadership then dithered about the next step, while Garibaldi and his veterans routed a large body of Neapolitan troops advancing from the south.

He was about to discover the ruthless and unprincipled cynicism of European power politics. He was commanding a section of the Roman defences while Mazzini negotiated with the French. They duped Mazzini and, during a truce, captured a key building in the defensive line. Garibaldi, at the cost of hundreds of young lives of Italian patriots, counterattacked. He clashed bitterly with Mazzini, because, from his experience in Montevideo, he saw that it would be impossible to hold Rome against the disciplined firepower of the French regulars. He therefore proposed that the volunteers should fight their way out of Rome and disperse in order to wage guerrilla war against the French, Austrian and Neapolitan armies. While this proposal was being considered Garibaldi led the volunteers often in hand-to-hand fighting against the French. The situation in Rome highlighted serious diplomatic differences between the powers, and while the French carried out a ruthless repression of the revolt, the British and US embassies did their best to help people to escape. Eventually, Garibaldi's plan was accepted, and before he led out his volunteers he made his famous speech: 'I offer hunger, cold, forced marches, battle and death', a speech effectively adapted by Churchill in 1940.

About 3,000 volunteers escaped from Rome with Garibaldi, and he called upon all his guerrilla skills to evade the French and Austrian troops who were pursuing him. Although he succeeded in avoiding the main enemy units, his supporters rapidly melted away. They were frequently betrayed to the Austrian forces by priests – whom Garibaldi called pestilential scum – and the Austrians shot any volunteers they captured. At last Garibaldi, with Anita who had accompanied him on the retreat from Rome, reached the Adriatic coast. Anita was desperately ill, and, given brief sanctuary in a loyal farm, she died in Garibaldi's arms. After her death, he fled. He managed to get to Genoa, then Tangier – at that time a British territory – and finally reached New York. He was depressed and dismayed by the failure of the high hopes of the spring of 1848, and the failure of the Italian people to respond to his call to arms. He spent a wretched decade, eking out a dismal existence doing menial jobs, but never giving up hope of a united Italy.

Garibaldi's guerrilla leadership had achieved little in 1848, and the next development seems to support the theory of Clausewitz that guerrilla forces alone cannot win a war. Three other characters then took the lead in what was the prime purpose of the patriots – to remove the power of Austria from Italy. Austria ruled Lombardy and Venetia and had a powerful influence in the three duchies of Parma, Modena and Tuscany. Victor Emmanuel, King of Piedmont, and Cavour, his ruthless and scheming prime minister were eager to remove the Austrians. Cavour, ever the realist, realizing that Piedmont alone could not defeat the might of Austria, managed to beguile Louis Napoleon, Emperor of France, into supporting their cause.

Cavour masterminded the next step when, due to his scheming, Austria attacked Piedmont in April 1859. Cavour had realised the value of Garibaldi's popular appeal and had encouraged him to return to Piedmont, and to raise volunteers. He raised two brigades and, with growing support from the people, waged a successful guerrilla campaign against the Austrians in the area of Lake Como and Lake Maggiore. While this campaign was proceeding, the French army under Louis Napoleon defeated the Austrians in two major battles at Magenta and Solferino. The very heavy casualties in these battles – a significant step forward towards the carnage of war with modern weapons – led to the formation of the Red Cross and also encouraged the warring parties to make peace.

The peace of Villafranca, 1859, was to have violent repercussions. Austria withdrew from Lombardy, but, to the fury of the Italian patriots, not from Venetia. Cavour in an initially secret agreement ceded Savoy and Nice to France in return for its help in the defeat of Austria. When this agreement became public, Garibaldi was outraged, and claimed he had been made a foreigner in the land of his birth. He sent an insolent message to King Victor Emmanuel, and then decided to take action himself. He went to Genoa, where he was well known in the seafaring community, obtained two old steamers, a fair supply of rifles, and set out for Sicily. Sicily and southern Italy, part of the Kingdom of Naples, were ruled by a reactionary, corrupt and priest-ridden regime, and by going to Sicily, Garibaldi hoped to gain the support of the people. This started the expedition of Garibaldi and the Thousand, the most successful guerrilla campaign of the nineteenth century.

After a series of almost ludicrous incidents, Garibaldi and the Thousand landed at Marsala in May 1860. At first the people were so cowed by the regime that they appeared indifferent, but gradually armed bands of Sicilians began to join up with the volunteers. Even with some local support, Garibaldi and the Thousand faced a daunting situation – there were 25,000 Neapolitan troops on Sicily, and in the first clash at Calatafimi, they themselves mustered only 3,000.

At this time, no one else had Garibaldi's experience both of seafaring activity and of guerrilla war, and at Calatafimi he needed all his bravery and leadership skills in the battle against a strong unit of the Neapolitan army. The battle raged for several hours on a hill covered with vines and olives, and the volunteers, ill-prepared for a prolonged action, were gradually pushed back by the enemy. Close to defeat, Garibaldi using his amazing powers of leadership, gathered 300 men and led a grim charge up the hill, and routed the enemy. The victory was won at a high cost in killed and wounded, but it had immense significance for the future of the Thousand, proving that they could challenge and defeat the Neapolitan regulars. This was still the age when journalists or the crews of warships anchored offshore could wander into a headquarters to find out what was happening. From Calatafimi onwards, there are many eyewitness accounts from British writers and sailors who attest to Garibaldi's leadership and bravery, and who strongly supported his cause.

The Neapolitan forces retreated towards Palermo, and here again Garibaldi needed to show his bravery and his guerrilla skills. When the Thousand reached Palermo, Garibaldi received information that there was an unguarded gate leading into the city. He acted quickly, personally led the advance through the gate, and ordered his men to spread out across the city. The Thousand were gravely impeded by the ill-disciplined and volatile Sicilian groups, who frequently gave warning of their presence by indiscriminately firing their weapons and running away when they met strong opposition. In the struggle for Palermo there was prolonged fighting and the Thousand sustained heavy casualties. The Sicilian bands proved hopelessly unreliable, and Garibaldi, as at Calatafimi, faced a crisis where defeat appeared inevitable. At this critical moment, to his amazement, the Neapolitan commander requested a truce. Discussions were quickly arranged on the flagship of Admiral Mundy RN, who was to play a remarkable role in the progress of the Thousand. Mundy and Garibaldi dominated the discussions, and, as the truce continued, more and more people came out in support, even though the Neapolitan naval ships bombarded much of the town. Garibaldi's charisma and leadership, coupled with the pathetic weakness of the Neapolitan commander, prolonged the truce, during which Garibaldi did manage to restock his forces with explosives and ammunition. Eventually, early in June 1860, the Neapolitan troops withdrew from Palermo. News of Garibaldi's success spread rapidly across Italy, and soon over 2,000 well-armed volunteers arrived to support the cause.

The advance of the Thousand was next seriously held up at Milazzo, a small town on the north coast of Sicily. Here there was a serious fire fight in which the volunteers suffered 800 killed or wounded. When the advance had stopped, Garibaldi heard about a small ship, with ten guns, which had defected from the Neapolitan navy. He rowed to the ship, gained the support of the crew, and then bombarded the enemy positions, which surrendered. This single incident had profound repercussions, since the Neapolitans increasingly felt that they could not stop Garibaldi. Their dithering was compounded by the ineptitude of King Ferdinand in Naples and, to Garibaldi's amazement, Neapolitan forces agreed to withdraw from Sicily at the end of July 1860.

In three serious and very different actions at Calatafimi, Palermo and Milazzo Garibaldi had shown his phenomenal bravery, powers of leadership and calmness under fire. But he also revealed an ability to handle the diplomatic situation which his victories created. The withdrawal from Sicily of all the Neapolitan forces – which surely should have been able to defeat Garibaldi in the larger city of Messina – created a totally new situation in which, once again, the politicians decided to intervene.

Cavour was the first to see that if Garibaldi advanced though southern Italy, there would be a serious danger of him attacking the Pope in Rome, which was still protected by French bayonets. Louis Napoleon suggested a French naval blockade of the Straits of Messina to prevent Garibaldi crossing to the mainland, but the British, ever sympathetic to Garibaldi's cause, prevented this. Cavour – always loyal to Victor Emmanuel – remained apprehensive about a strong republican movement sweeping across Italy, but Garibaldi assured King Victor Emmanuel that if the cause succeeded he would lay down his sword at the king's feet.

In a matter of a few weeks, he was able to assemble a force of over 3,000 volunteers, to acquire two steamers in a little port near Messina and, on 18 August 1860, he crossed to the mainland on a moonless night, easily avoiding the Neapolitan navy. He landed east of Reggio, just where Montgomery was to land in 1943. After the successful landing, hundreds more volunteers crossed the Straits in small boats. Two days after the landing they made a sudden surprise attack on Reggio. They were held up by a sturdy fortress defended by artillery, but Garibaldi, in the very front of the attackers, called up snipers to pick off the gunners and very soon the fortress and the whole town surrendered. The pace and the pattern of Garibaldi's guerrilla attacks now changed dramatically.

As the news of the volunteers' victory spread across Italy, the people readily supplied information about the Neapolitan forces, and provided food and shelter. Even priests and nuns, who had considered Garibaldi as the devil incarnate, now rallied to the cause. As his forces advanced towards a town, Garibaldi would go forward, and effectively using his splendid voice, demand its surrender. He rarely met any serious opposition. After the enemy troops had surrendered their weapons, he addressed them and gave them the alternative of joining the volunteers or walking home. Having learnt his lesson in Uruguay, he now established strict discipline among veterans and new volunteers alike.

As his forces swept northwards, Garibaldi still suspected Cavour of some underhand trick, and was determined to reach Naples before this could happen. As he approached fairly close to the city, he commandeered a train, filled it with volunteers, and, riding on the front, directed it to Naples railway station under the very guns of the Neapolitan forces. Outside the station, in what is now Piazza Garibaldi, in an emotional speech he assured the people that on this very day they had become a nation. He then bravely walked on, about a mile, to the fortress where the Neapolitans still manned the guns which could have destroyed him at any time. Instead, they surrendered. Today, cruise ships anchor almost in the shadow of the fortress, largely unaware of the drama played out on the very spot.

Garibaldi had won a dramatic victory of guerrilla forces over regular troops, but then – like the Allies in Iraq in 2003 – when the victory was won, he faced desperate social problems as criminals and thugs moved in to exploit the general chaos and the breakdown of law and order. These serious local problems were overshadowed by the wider political issues. Garibaldi still intended to march on Rome, and this seriously worried King Victor Emmanuel and Cavour, and most European leaders, who feared that if Garibaldi reached Rome and was defeated by the French garrison, it could lead to a general European war. Cavour then acted decisively and with the prior agreement of the French, he sent Piedmontese troops to invade the Papal States, thus effectively preventing Garibaldi from marching on Rome.

The Neapolitan forces withdrew northwards after their defeat in Naples and a force of about 40,000 drew up on the line of the Volturno river – an ideal defensive position concentrated on a fortress designed by the great French military engineer Vauban. At the beginning of October 1860, Garibaldi's volunteers, numbering about 20,000 drew near to the Volturno defences. When the battle started, the Neapolitans were strong enough to push back the volunteers. Then Garibaldi arrived on the scene, rallied his troops and led attack after attack on the enemy. A hard-fought battled continued through the whole day, and once again incompetence or cowardice among the Neapolitan commanders contributed to Garibaldi's victory. He had the support of some Hungarian cavalry and a number of eccentric English colonels, and they all testified to his amazing leadership qualities.

The battle on the Volturno, in which the volunteers lost 2,000 killed or wounded, was Garibaldi's last and his greatest victory, but its results were less clear than those gained during his earlier battles in Sicily. The Neapolitans had not been destroyed, the Piedmont troops under Cavour held the Papal States, and there was no realistic prospect of capturing Venetia or Rome. Passions ran high in a welter of excited political discussions. Mazzini, the arch republican, and many of his followers, strongly opposed the idea of unity under King Victor Emmanuel, yet Garibaldi slowly and reluctantly accepted it. Then Cavour again outsmarted his rivals. He hastily organised a referendum asking, 'Do you want a united Italy under Victor Emmanuel?'. Phrased in that way the answer was exactly what the wily Cavour had intended. Very few answered 'No'.

Garibaldi, having kept his word to King Victor Emmanuel, refused all honours and wealth, returned to his modest farm on the tiny island of Caprera which he had bought some years before. Despite his isolation on Caprera he remained a figure of great interest to the world. President Lincoln offered him a high command in the Union forces, and in 1864 he was invited to London where society lionised him until Queen Victoria realised he was a potential threat to her relations scattered across Europe on their shaky thrones. He made one or two forays into Italian politics, and he even commanded a guerrilla group near Dijon in the Franco-Prussian war, but that and various unsuccessful escapades did not detract from his towering achievements.

Many European biographies have tended to ignore the crucial period of his life in South America. G. M. Trevelyan, the great Cambridge historian did so in his monumental three-volume work, which for decades set the pattern for studies of Garibaldi. This is unfortunate, because he was clearly the most successful guerrilla leader of the nineteenth century, and he developed his military skills during the decade of war in the Rio Grande do Sul and in Uruguay. His experiences there both on land and sea and in his many campaigns on the River Uruguay and River Parana were the perfect preparation for the dramatic years, 1859 and 1860, when his achievements laid the foundation of a united Italy.

The final accomplishment of his hopes came, not from Italian patriots, but from the Prussian chancellor, Bismarck. He defeated Austria at Sadowa in 1866. In this brief war the Piedmontese army performed lamentably but Garibaldi, already an invalid, directed some successful attacks on the Austrians in the hills around Lake Garda, and when the war was over Bismarck forced Austria to hand over Venetia to the Italians. In 1870 his attack in the Franco-Prussian war forced France to withdraw its garrison from Rome and Italian troops were at last able to march into their rightful capital.

Bismarck was the final power broker, but the foundation of a united Italy had been laid by the guerrilla skills and leadership of Garibaldi at Calatafimi, Palermo, Milazzo and the Volturno. These skills had been developed and perfected at Costa Brava, Salto and San Antonio.

THE BOER COMMANDOS: GUERRILLA WAR IN AFRICA

In July 1899, after difficult and protracted negotiations, the British Cabinet leaders, Salisbury, Balfour, Lansdowne and Chamberlain, had received an offer from Paul Kruger, the president of the Transvaal. He agreed that 'outlanders', i.e., the 100,000 men, predominantly British, who had flocked to the Transvaal for the rich pickings of the gold and diamond fields, would be given the vote after five years' residence. This was an immense concession from the dour and rugged Kruger, who as a boy had taken part in the Great Trek of 1837 and who personified the severe and puritanical outlook of his people. Indeed in earlier discussions he had said 'It is not the vote you want, it is my country'.

Having received this concession, the cabinet, delighted to have achieved peace, went off to their stately homes for their four-month summer recess. They had reckoned without Sir Alfred Milner, High Commissioner for South Africa and Governor of Cape Colony. Arrogant and contemptuous of the Boers, he was horrified at the suggestion of peace, and by Machiavellian intrigue – helped by daily leaks from his Balliol friends in Whitehall – he deliberately engineered a declaration of war.

Initially, the clash had centred on Kruger and the Transvaal, but, because of Milner's machinations, the Orange Free State under President Steyn, agreed to fight. Thus the two Boer republics faced the might of the British Empire at its height. Their forefathers, the Voortrekkers, had left the Cape because of the arrogant attitude of the British towards their customs, their religion, and their laws. The final straw had been the abolition of slavery by Britain in 1833, which undermined their whole way of life. Setting out with all their possessions on ox-wagons, they sought freedom and independence in Natal, and north of the great Orange and Vaal rivers, in open veldt, which they, erroneously, assumed was empty.

Major factors in the build-up to war in 1899 were the massive discovery of diamonds in the 1870s at Kimberley, the discovery of gold in Johannesburg in the 1880s and the scheming of Cecil Rhodes – a visionary idealist or a cowardly blackguard, depending on your point of view – who envisaged a Cape to Cairo railway through British territory. Finally came the Jameson Raid of 1895 when, with the backing of Rhodes – then prime minister of Cape Colony – Jameson set out from the Bechuanaland border near Mafeking on a madcap scheme to overthrow Kruger. The raid was a fiasco and a disaster. After it Kruger prepared to defend his country and, with the immense revenue from the gold and diamond industries, he purchased millions of pounds' worth of weapons – notably Mauser rifles and Krupp artillery – and sent young officers to be trained in Germany in their use.

When the war actually started in October 1899, the Boers had over 50,000 men in their commandos. Their organisation was remarkably similar to the Landwehr of Scharnhorst and Clausewitz in Prussia. Each burgher in the republics had to be ready to report to his commando with a horse, a rifle, ammunition and biltong or dried meat for basic rations. The commandos had really been intended to protect the frontier communities against occasional clashes with African tribes, rather than take part in a major war. The British had 50,000 troops in Natal, and because of squabbles between the War Office and the Government, a reinforcement of 10,000 was delayed and did not set out from Southampton until September.

Although the British had fought wars in Africa for decades – including defeats by the Zulus at Isandhlwana in 1879 and by the Boers at Majuba in 1880 – this was a new type of war, and the British commanders on the ground were incompetent and ill-prepared for it. General White, the Commander in Chief who landed in Natal in October 1899 to take over, was described by Chamberlain as 'old, doddery, weak and vacillating.' On the Boer side, the two senior commanders were equally inept. Cronje was old and slow, and Joubert, known as Kruger's crony, was totally inadequate.

The issue of guerrilla or traditional war was highlighted almost from the start. The briefest glance at the map of this vast country would show that the war would centre on the railways, and particularly the railway from Durban over the Tugela river, past Colenso, Ladysmith, Spion Kop, Elandslaagte and Majuba to Johannesburg. The Boers' younger, aggressive and competent commanders, like de Wet, Botha, Smuts, de la Rey and Reitz, who knew the potential of their units, were strongly in favour of swift action. They planned to invade Natal, make a dash for Durban, where there were few British troops, and seize the port to prevent British reinforcements from landing. They argued for a simultaneous and powerful incursion into Cape Colony to rouse the predominantly Boer farming population. That was certainly what Milner, cowering in Cape Town, feared most.

Instead of these rapid moves, using their greatest asset, mobility, which could have achieved success against the ill-prepared British, the Boer commandos, under the feeble leadership of Joubert and Cronje, allowed

71

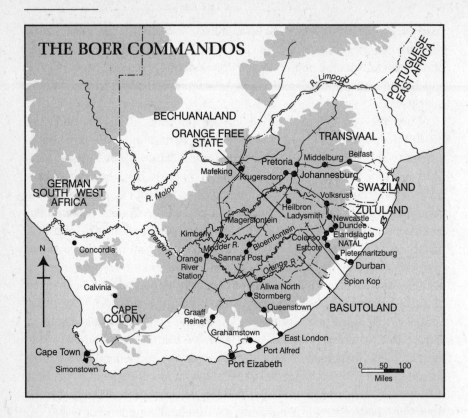

THE BOER COMMANDOS

themselves to be dragged into the most static type of warfare – sieges. By the end of October 1899, British garrisons of about 500 troops were besieged in Kimberley and Mafeking, two small towns on the isolated railway from Cape Town running north to Rhodesia. A larger garrison of 2,000 was encircled in Ladysmith.

Even before the war started, competent British officers like Rawlinson and Buller, who later was unjustly blamed for many of the disasters, had argued that it was courting disaster to try to hold Ladysmith, and that the garrisons should be withdrawn to the line of the Tugela River. Many in the British army did feel uneasy about fighting sturdy farmers, whose religious and moral ideas they supported, but there were others in, for example the Imperial Yeomanry, who thought they would give up their foxhunting and hunt Boers instead. A few, seeing the baleful figure of Rhodes in the background, pondered whether it was a new war for big business and high finance.

In the western region, Cronje had invested Mafeking by 14 October 1899. Thereafter it was a dilatory siege, with Cronje, who like Joubert was accompanied by his wife, on the outside and, on the inside, Baden-Powell, who cancelled military activities on Sundays and held cricket matches instead and Gilbert and Sullivan concerts. The British tried to justify this siege because it tied up large numbers of Cronje's troops. There was rather more point to the siege of Kimberley, because there lay the wealth of the de Beers diamonds, and inside was Rhodes himself, whose behaviour throughout the siege was cowardly and despicable.

One of the earliest actions by the commandos took place in October, 1899 near Colenso, when Botha's forces ambushed an armoured train. The action became famous because it was described by the war correspondent Winston Churchill. There were further brisk and serious clashes in the area beyond Ladysmith. The British were worsted near Dundee, when their blimpish commander complained that the Boers had had the impudence to attack before breakfast. Then at Elandslaagte the British suffered further heavy casualties from the accurate and disciplined fire of Botha's commandos. By 29 October, Ladysmith was cut off.

In the western theatre at the same time, Lord Methuen, under pressure to relieve Kimberley, advanced to the Modder River. A position near the river was defended by 8,000 Boer commandos under de la Rey, who deployed his well-armed troops in slit trenches. On 23 November 1899, Methuen ordered a fontal assault and suffered terrible casualties from the withering Boer fire. The Boers then retreated to an even better position at Magersfontein.

Meanwhile, General Gatacre – nicknamed 'Backacher' – advanced up the railway line from East London to Stormberg and, in a clash with a Boer commando, suffered heavy casualties and lost over 500 prisoners. He retired back down the railway. These actions were merely the prelude to 'Black Week', 10–15 December 1899.

After the disaster at the Modder River, Methuen advanced to Magersfontein and approached a carefully prepared Boer position. Here again almost everything went wrong. The attack started on 11 December. The artillery bombarded a hill empty of Boers, whilst the Highland Brigade – The Black Watch, Seaforths and Argyll and Sutherland Highlanders – and the Guards Brigade, advancing with no supporting fire, were mown down. They sustained over 1,000 casualties. A British colonel wrote, 'Methuen sticks to his suicidal idea of frontal attacks.'

By 15 December, Buller was advancing to the relief of Ladysmith. Fortunately for the Boers, Joubert had a riding accident, and was replaced by Louis Botha, and he was in command at Colenso. As Buller approached

Colenso, he heard the news of Methuen's defeat at Magersfontein. There-fore, hoping to avenge that defeat with a quick victory, he abandoned a proposed flank march of about 40 miles, and decided on a frontal assault with his 16,000 troops. Unbelievable blunders followed. The commander of the artillery placed his guns right forward, as he had done at Omdurman, and they were unable to give support to the Irish Brigade, whose guide blundered and led them into a loop of the Tugela River, where almost defenceless, they were mown down by accurate Boer fire. On the following day, having made no progress, Buller advised General White in Ladysmith, to seek the best terms he could get. This caused an outcry from the government in London and, on 17 December, Buller was replaced as commander in chief by Lord Roberts, but retained his command in Natal. Buller was always blamed for the disasters of the Ladysmith campaign, but, in fairness to him, he had strongly advised before he left England that the British forces should be withdrawn from Dundee and Ladysmith to the Tugela River at Colenso.

In the early battles with the British the Boer commandos under Botha, de Wet and de la Rey had acquitted themselves well, and had proved the value of attacks on the British lines of supply and communication, but because of the supine leadership of Joubert they had been denied their one real chance of victory. This might have been achieved if, as they wished, they had advanced rapidly into Natal and seized Durban, while other commandos mounted a swift attack into Cape Colony, to rouse the Boer farmers and threaten the government in Cape Town. Joubert and Cronje condemned the commandos to the heartbreaking stalemate of sieges at Ladysmith, Mafeking and Kimberley, and as well the necessity of fighting set-piece battles instead of using mobility and guerrilla tactics. After the Boer victories of Black Week – Stormberg, Magersfontein and Colenso – there were still set-piece battles to be fought.

The Boers, heartened by their successes, decided to launch an attack on Ladysmith, and this caused heavy casualties to the Rifle Brigade manning the defences. Worse was to follow. Buller, outmanoeuvred at every turn by Botha, decided to try to outflank the Boer position. On 22 January 1900, he ordered General Warren to attack the defended hill of Spion Kop. Warren's troops scaled Spion Kop in fog and then found themselves unable to dig-in because of the rocky ground. They came under murderous fire from the Boers. A desperate fight continued all day. Both sides felt it was a disaster, and withdrew from the hill. Botha, who had constantly rallied his troops during the prolonged battle, was close to the front, and when he realised that the British had withdrawn, he rapidly re-occupied Spion Kop. Warren, who failed to move the main body of his troops to the battle, was the chief architect of the disaster. It was said of him that he snatched defeat from the jaws of victory, and that he brought tragedy to the verge of farce.

While the British troops under the savage military discipline of the day, had to suffer and die because of the incompetence of their commanders, the situation on the Boer side was different, but not without its problems. Deneys Reitz in *Commando* has described how, after a boyhood of hunting, riding and camping, at the age of 17, partly because his father knew Kruger, he was given a new Mauser rifle and allowed to join the commando in Pretoria. The unit embarked on the train with horses, guns and supplies, and made for the Natal border. Already 'Nice old Joubert', appeared totally bewildered at the situation. When they reached the border, each commando was divided into three groups of about 200 men, and these were sub-divided into fighting units of 25 men – similar to an infantry platoon.

In the commandos, strong criticism soon built up because their strength was frittered away in meaningless sieges, when their only hope of victory lay in using their mobility in rapid advances. The commando, in which Reitz served, had several fights with British patrols and then attacked and captured Dundee, just north of Ladysmith. The men in the commandos, who received no pay, and had to survive on basic rations, were amazed at the mountains of luxuries and tinned food they captured in Dundee. Already Botha and de Wet were making their name as resolute commanders, and they shared the feelings of their men that the splendid guerrilla fighters in the commandos should not be allowed to stagnate in ruinous sieges, when they could have been riding rapidly to the sea.

Static warfare centred on sieges and set-piece battles created serious problems for the commandos. They were entirely democratic, and after a reverse or during a pointless siege, large numbers would ride off home. In one attack at this time only half of a commando took part, and many poor whites, who had joined up, now slunk away. Some Boers did argue that it was right to invest the three towns and prepare to ambush the forces coming to their relief, but this view ruined any hope of a short and successful war. What could have been achieved was illustrated in November 1899, when President Steyn, after initial hesitation, sent a small commando to the border of Cape Colony and it captured Aliwal North, close to where the Orange River crosses the border. This caused serious concern to Milner, although it was only on a small scale. When the war started the commandos mustered 40,000 men and if these had been launched in a swift drive to Cape Town there was little to stop them.

Lord Roberts, who, after Colenso, had been appointed commander in chief, received substantial reinforcements and, early in 1900, decided on his strategy. He felt strong enough to advance northwards from Cape Town along the western railway as far as the Orange River Station, and then, like Stonewall Jackson marching on Washington, to move across country to Bloemfontein, the capital of the Orange Free State. This plan was altered slightly because of the shrill squealing of Rhodes in Kimberley, and his insistent cries for help. Roberts decided that, while keeping up his momentum towards Bloemfontein, he could also relieve Kimberley. During this advance, one of the outstanding commando leaders – Christian de Wet – demonstrated how effective guerrilla tactics could be. During February 1900, he shadowed Roberts' main force, and had several brisk skirmishes. Then he saw an opportunity to capture a substantial part of the mountainous British baggage train. It had been bogged down, and before it could be moved away de Wet made a sudden attack. He captured over 200 ox-wagons and more than 1,000 oxen. The Boers drove off the wagons and destroyed all the supplies they could not cart away. De Wet described their 'enormous booty', and regretted that they could not take more. On 15 February, Kimberley was relieved by the advance of a cavalry division under General French, which had galloped across the open veldt. The manoeuvre succeeded, but it killed nearly all the horses, thus adding to an already serious problem.

The relief of Kimberley was followed in days by a battle which illustrated grievous blunders on both sides. After the relief of Kimberley, Cronje had set out with a huge retinue including women and children to move towards Bloemfontein. He reached Paardeberg on the Modder River before the advancing British caught up with him. His ineffective force was soon surrounded and held, while artillery was brought forward. De Wet, with his strong and mobile commando ranging widely across the open country beyond Paardeberg, cleared a route through a weakly held sector where Cronje could have broken out. After Cronje failed to move, de Wet then begged him to fight his way out.

The British commander, Kelly-Kenny, had a sensible plan to complete the ring around Cronje's forces, and to bombard them until they surrendered. Then Kitchener arrived – eager to make his mark – took over command, over-ruled Kelly-Kenny, and demanded a series of large-scale infantry assaults. Inside Paardeberg, although Cronje was supine, his force still had large numbers of Boer commando members who were fighting for their lives, and wherever the British attacked they were met by accurate Boer fire. Usually the attacks petered out with horrendous losses. Kitchener became increasingly reckless and ordered that the forward divisions rush the laager at all costs. These attacks caused the heaviest casualties of the war – 1,200 in one afternoon – and they were all entirely unnecessary because Cronje would shortly have had to surrender anyway. Kitchener's approach to the Paardeberg assault was a gigantic blunder, which threw away the lives of thousands of men and has been called 'a study in how not to fight a battle'. On the Boer side, de Wet had done his best, unsuccessfully, to rouse Cronje from his lethargy and watched, horrified, when, on 27 February 1900, Cronje surrendered. De Wet considered this a devastating blow to all Boer hopes.

After Paardeberg, there was little opposition to the massive advances of the British forces, and on 13 March Bloemfontein fell. At the same time news came through that Ladysmith had been relieved on 28 February. De Wet considered this further blow to be the result of Cronje's inadequacy, and merely commented, 'It would break your heart.'

There is an image on the British side of Boer commandos composed of 100% dedicated loyal men, but this is far from the truth. At a siege, or after a reverse many burghers melted away, and in one skirmish, even in de Wet's own unit, men broke and fled before a British advance. De Wet's description, during these difficult days, of the large numbers of burghers coming forward with doctors' certificates for heart problems might bring to mind jokes but it wasn't amusing for Boer commanders. De Wet, who had always been critical of Joubert and Cronje, both of whom allowed women and families to accompany the commandos, now insisted that the commandos must be made into more effective and well-disciplined military units, without families and hangers on. He also ordered that wagons, which had always impeded effective movement, must be abandoned.

After the fall of Bloemfontein, Roberts expected the war to be rapidly concluded. There were discussions about peace, but when the British government demanded complete surrender, the Boer leaders President Steyn, Botha, de la Rey, de Wet and Smuts all agreed to continue the struggle. Although there had been guerrilla-style attacks in the first six months of the campaign, it was now to become all-out guerrilla war.

De Wet very rapidly started his new campaign. With 350 men he attacked and overpowered the small British unit, which was guarding Sanna's Post, the main waterworks for Bloemfontein. When a British column advanced, unaware of any trouble, he was able to take more than 200 prisoners without firing a shot. In the ensuing battle, his commando captured five artillery pieces and as many weapons, food and ammunition as they could carry away. De Wet considered the conduct of his burghers to be beyond praise. He also commented that it was extraordinary for Roberts not to send help to Sanna's Post, which was vital to his water supply, and was only 16 miles from the city.

After capturing Bloemfontein, the large British forces advanced inexorably northwards towards Johannesburg and Pretoria, while Buller, after the relief of Ladysmith – 28 February – advanced from the east. Although this provided the Boers with opportunities to attack the British supply lines, it put them under immense pressure. Deneys Reitz, who took part in the retreat after Ladysmith, described the Boers as 'a demoralised rabble, fleeing blindly'. The commandos lacked any overall discipline, and many burghers merely rode off home. It was only the 'invincible determination of Botha and de la Rey' which kept the commandos in being. De Wet, as he retreated northwards before the advance of Roberts, voiced particularly vicious criticism of those Afrikaaners who had gone over to the British side, 'for a paltry five shillings a day'. He argued strongly that Boer tactics 'Demanded rapidity of action more than anything else. We had to be quick at fighting, quick at reconnoitring, quick (if it becomes necessary) at flying'. He believed that if so many burghers had not proved false to their own colours, England would have found her grave in South Africa. While desertion was a problem for all the commandos, de Wet felt that Roberts's ineptitude in handling the Boer people under his control was the best recruiting factor for the commandos.

Despite the general retreat, de Wet was still strong and forceful enough to undertake major attacks against the British. At the end of May 1900 he made a successful attack near Heilbron, which had become the temporary capital of the Orange Free State. When he received details of the movement of a very large convoy, he surrounded it with about 500 men, and demanded its surrender. The white flag soon went up, and the commando took over. Then, after some fierce skirmishes with other British units in the area, de Wet took over one of the biggest hauls of loot in the entire war. His men carried away what they could, but he wisely buried a huge cache of weapons and ammunition, thinking correctly that it might be useful later on. He gave an amusing description of burghers, who had loaded their horses so heavily with loot that they themselves had to walk. Again at this time, some fairly senior commanders defected, and de Wet commented bitterly that it was easier to fight the English than treachery among his own people.

Early in June 1900 Roberts entered Pretoria and assumed that the war was virtually over. He told Queen Victoria that it was, and, foolishly, allowed Botha to march off with his best units, weapons and gold. The Boer leaders then held grave discussions. Kruger, now old and exhausted, went off into exile down the Delagoa railway to Mozambique, but Botha, de la Rey, and President Steyn, who travelled with de Wet's commando, determined to fight on. By this time Mafeking had been relieved – 17 May 1900 – by a force of English, Scottish, Welsh, Irish, Australian and Canadian troops, but the Boers believed that the rest of the world, and especially Germany, Holland, France and the USA, were behind them in their fight for justice and liberty. A famous German cartoon shows Queen Victoria feeding a Tommy with chocolate, while at the other end he is being spanked by Kruger.

Botha now emerged as the most forceful organiser of the commandos, and he assembled a force of several thousand which, in a hard-fought battle at Diamond Hill, challenged a pursuing British division before dispersing to continue the guerrilla war. The Boer leaders all felt that the surviving commandos would be far more effective because the weak members had been weeded out, and they were no longer inhibited by the dithering leadership of Cronje and Joubert.

In the confused period after the fall of Pretoria, Botha, Smuts, de Wet and de la Rey dispersed widely across the Transvaal and the Orange Free State. They moved about for much of the time with relative impunity, since most British units were loath to move far away from the railways and into the trackless and map-less bush. De Wet moved with a commando of 2,500 escorting President Steyn, the Orange Free State government and 400 wagons. Even after weeding out the less resolute burghers, de Wet still had serious setbacks. One respected leader, Prinsloo, after he was put in charge of a commando, instantly surrendered to the British together with 3,000 troops. De Wet moved south into the Orange Free State, and at first was able to keep his force supplied by raiding large British store depots, and by ambushing supply trains coming up the railway. One ambushed train had over 50 wagon-loads of food. As usual, the Boers took what they could and destroyed the rest. The widespread and successful attacks on the railways, and the destruction of bridges and supply depots, made the leaders realise what they could have achieved in the early months of the war if only they had been given a free hand to gallop into Natal and Cape Colony, before British reinforcements arrived.

De Wet, because he was escorting President Steyn, came under particular pressure from the British, but he was still able to mount serious counter-attacks. In November 1900 he led 1,500 men and captured De Wetsdorp, a small town which had been named after his father. Here he took 400 prisoners, together with massive supplies. In many of the Boer raids, the most valuable capture were the horses, because their own horses were often driven to death by their urgent and constant movement.

Throughout history, from Roman times onwards, guerrilla activity has usually brought savage reprisals on the local population, and Roberts initiated this policy. He ordered that every building within ten miles of a railway would be blown up or burnt, grain destroyed, and sheep, cattle and horses taken away or slaughtered. Devastation spread across the whole country. Increasingly, the women who had been let behind to run the farms, had to load any grain, together with their few precious possessions, on to a wagon and drive off. De Wet commented bitterly about the shameful history of barbarities committed against their women and children. In January 1901 he wrote that 'South Africa was stained with the blood of burghers and defenceless women and children, and with the blood of English soldiers, who had died in a quarrel for which they were not responsible, and which could have been avoided' (C. R. de Wet, *Three Years War*, 1902, p.250).

To accompany the policy of burning and destruction, Roberts ordered a wide sweep, with over 50,000 troops, to clear the Boers away from the Natal to Johannesburg railway, and to clear the eastern Transvaal. Deneys Reitz was caught up in this campaign, and he described the horror of realising that in addition to the destruction of farms, crops and animals, the families were to be taken away to concentration camps. In this he believed that Roberts made a serious error of judgement, for instead of undermining the morale of the fighters, it strengthened their resolve.

The success of the Boer commandos depended to some extent on the personality and drive of the different British commanders. Buller, who was shortly to go home in undeserved semi-disgrace, had proved himself one of the best British commanders in the new type of war against the commandos, and he refused to implement the policy of farm burning. In the western sectors, Roberts' policy appeared capricious and ineffective, yet he went home to an earldom and a gift from a grateful country of £100,000. Kitchener, who succeeded Roberts, was universally disliked by his British colleagues, one of whom wrote 'All combine in cursing Kitchener'. By the time of his disastrous intervention at Paardeberg, Kitchener became known as 'king of chaos'. With Ian Hamilton, who had been responsible for several disasters around Ladysmith, and who was to prove his incompetence more fully at Gallipoli, Kitchener signally failed in his attempts to capture de Wet and President Steyn.

In February 1901 de Wet and a large commando drove south and, after many dangerous clashes, managed to evade the British patrols and advance into Cape Colony. He had to move constantly to avoid his pursuers, and shortage of horses became his most urgent problem. What a different situation it would have been if his advance had taken place in October 1899, when the commandos were fresh, and when the British had few defences and hardly any troops in the northern part of Cape Colony.

In response to aggressive British pursuit, de Wet evolved a sound tactic. If the pursuing troops approached too close, he left a group of burghers, with the best horses available, to hold up the enemy advance. When they opened fire, the British normally halted, brought forward some artillery pieces and then sent infantry units out to either flank. This manoeuvre often took several hours, and the burghers then rode off before an attack went in. After he advanced into Cape Colony, although he was harassed by the British, de Wet divided his force into six commandos, so that these smaller groups could move more easily, keep themselves supplied, engage in more frequent attacks, and inflict disproportionate losses on the enemy.

De Wet is rightly revered as one of the great guerrilla leaders in the Boer War, yet, in his book *Three Years War*, he argues strongly that, although the capital Pretoria had been captured, his troops were the legitimate forces of the Orange Free State, and should not be called guerrillas. He considered that the term guerrilla should only be used when a nation has been totally vanquished and fully occupied, which was not the case.

In March 1901 Kitchener sent messages suggesting a truce to President Steyn, who was still with De Wet's commando. This prompted discussions between de Wet and Steyn on the one hand, and Botha, who was ranging across the wider spaces of the Transvaal. Botha argued that the whole Boer position was now hopeless, but Steyn and de Wet – although they were on the run and had nearly been captured – rejected the idea of truce, and reminded Botha that when the war started the Orange Free State had come to the aid of the Transvaal. During protracted discussions, the odious Milner, who was still terrified of a Cape uprising, was now determined to prolong the war until the Boer commandos were completely crushed.

During 1901, while guerrilla attacks from the commandos continued across the Orange Free State and the Transvaal, and with incursions into Cape Colony, Kitchener decided on a more severe and draconian policy. He rapidly increased the establishment of concentration camps for Boer women and children, and swept the country clean of farms, people, livestock and crops, so that there would be nothing left which could assist the commandos. At the same time he established blockhouses along the railways, and connected these with hundreds of miles of barbed wire. The blockhouses – built of stone, wood and corrugated iron, and manned by six or seven soldiers – were sited about 1,000 yards apart, within sight of the next one, and connected by trenches three feet deep and covered with barbed wire. Some 8,000 blockhouses were manned by 50,000 troops. The Boers considered that the blockhouse system was the most effective British counter-measure in overcoming their resistance.

The establishment of concentration camps, which peaked early in 1901, had unexpected repercussions. It infuriated the Boer fighters, but it did relieve them of the responsibility of protecting and providing for the families back on the farms. News of the disasters in the camps, mostly caused by epidemics of typhoid, enteric fever and measles, and always exacerbated by massive incompetence, gradually leaked out. By October 1901, it was known that there were over 3,000 deaths per month in the camps. Some reorganisation improved things, but the key person in resolving the tragedy was an intrepid English lady, Emily Hobhouse. She visited the camps, interviewed the Boer women – usually the wives of the commando fighters – and returned to England to fight an effective campaign against the concentration camp policy. She was strongly supported by the Liberals under Lloyd George and Campbell-Bannerman, who criticised 'this barbarous war'. It must also be remembered that there were an equal number of Africans in concentration camps with a similar death-rate. Before the end of the war 27,000 Boers and 14,000 Africans had died in the camps.

Kitchener's policies of concentration camps, of blockhouses and wire, accompanied by aggressive sweeps across the country leaving total devastation in their wake, was extremely unpopular with his own staff. Several young officers, who were to reach high command in the 1914–18 war – Allenby, Byng, and Haig – believed that Kitchener was out of touch with reality, and they strongly criticised 'this sickening campaign'.

To back his military strategy, Kitchener kept up the diplomatic pressure. In August 1901, he sent an imperious summons to President Steyn and de Wet demanding their surrender, and threatening that anyone who remained in arms after 15 September 1901 would be exiled forever from South Africa. Steyn and de Wet sent dignified replies stating that they were fighting for their liberty and independence, which they would never sacrifice.

Further north in the Transvaal, the bitter struggle continued, and there are heart-rending accounts of the agony the fighters faced over what to do with their families while the fight continued. The alternatives were often to leave them on the farms hoping the British would not come, or send them away to Swaziland, or down the Delagoa railway to Laurenco Marques in Portuguese territory – perhaps never to see them again. The British destroyed over 30,000 farms. Deneys Reitz served in a commando, which rode for days through country devoid of human beings and with every farm and every building in ruins. Tens of thousands of sheep had been clubbed to death and left to rot. The burghers lived on biltong and maize, and had forgotten the taste of coffee or sugar or vegetables. On the high veldt they suffered sometimes from heavy and prolonged rain, and at others from intense cold, where every pool was frozen solid, and if a man had a wet jacket, by morning it was frozen to him like a suit of armour.

After serving in the Transvaal, Reitz met Jan Smuts, who was leading a commando of 3,000 men making an incursion into Cape Colony. *The Times History of the Boer War* recorded, 'This handful of resolute men forms one of the most interesting episodes in the course of the guerrilla war' (Vol. 5, p.302). Initially, the Smuts commando was very much on the defensive, and was harried by strong British forces. To reach Cape territory, the commando, guided by a helpful local farmer, climbed in the dark down a precipitous cliff, and had to cross the foaming current of the Orange River. They were on the border of Basutoland, and soon after crossing, they were approached by a large group of mounted Basuto warriors, but they did not attack the main Boer party. They did harass the rear of the column as it moved off, and there were several sharp clashes.

When the commando moved away from the Basuto border and into an area of European settlement, they generally received help and hospitality from the farming families – mostly of Dutch extraction. One thing favoured the commando at this time, that in Cape Colony, Kitchener could not enforce his policy of farm destruction. As they moved further into the Cape, the rainy season started and they suffered severely from both the wet and the cold. They managed to elude the strong British detachments, which had been sent to capture them, but the constant movement, and the storms and bitter cold, with their horses often dying from exposure, tested the burghers to the limit. On one occasion, the commando was actually surrounded, but were led on a secret path through a bog by a crippled farmer who hated the British. In this phase of the operation, they were not an aggressive guerrilla force, but just an exhausted group of men fleeing for their lives. Reitz described how, after one particularly cold night up in the Bamboo Mountains, fourteen men and nearly fifty horses died of cold.

In September, 1901, when the whole group were exhausted and nearly starving, a friendly Dutch farmer warned them of a strong British patrol, 200 strong with many weapons. The commando, under the control of Smuts, fought off a small enemy unit, and then found themselves on the edge of a fairly large military camp. Smuts, showing shrewd and brave leadership, led the attack, and after a fierce fight in which the superior Boer marksmanship carried the day, they forced the garrison to surrender. The unit they had defeated was a squadron of the 17th Lancers, whose Commanding Officer was Douglas Haig. The British defences were casual and incomplete, but for the Boers it was an absolutely crucial victory at the cost of one man killed. Reitz described how they rode into action that morning at their last gasp, and then emerged later, refitted, with fresh horses, new rifles, saddles, boots, ammunition and food. We were 'like giants refreshed ... and our confidence in Smuts reborn.' The Lancers' defences, while disgracefully casual, had genuinely been confused because the Boer attackers were wearing British uniforms. This was not a deliberate act of deception, but, merely that after their prolonged privations, the only uniforms they had were those they had captured along the way.

After this incident, Kitchener repeated his warning that any Boer found wearing British uniform would be shot, but the victory gave the commando a great boost, and after it they were generally welcomed by the local farming fraternity. Passive help was one thing, but there was never any sign that the rural population would rise in their support.

The commando was eventually able to break away from the British cordon, and they gained some respite by moving into thickly wooded hilly country, where, in relative security, they were able to build huge fires to protect themselves against the cold. Smuts then divided his group into two commandos of about 1,500 men, and they set out to move westwards into the remote country that borders the Great Karroo Desert. Here they again suffered serious privations because there was little food or fodder available, but they finally reached the coast of the South West Cape, Here there were no railways, almost no British troops, and the local community was friendly and supportive. By December 1901 the commandos were well established and Reitz became a staff officer at Smuts' headquarters. He had to ride across many miles of pleasant country, keeping contact with the different commando units.

By the start of 1902, Smuts had established a firm base, which was not attacked by the British, and from which he was able to send out formidable fighting patrols. They were strong enough to ambush and capture British supply convoys, and during January 1902 they 'were able to feed, re-clothe, re-arm, and re-mount in luxury'. Smuts planned to move north to a copper-mining area around Concordia, in order to draw off British forces from both the Orange Free State and the Transvaal, and then to drive southwards towards Cape Town hoping for support from the old settled districts west and north of the city. Reitz worked with these powerful commandos, and he felt that they had virtually unchallenged control of a large area of the western Cape up to the Orange River.

Meanwhile, de Wet had established his commando in the north-east of the Orange Free State and, on Christmas Day 1901, he attacked and captured a British position near Bethlehem at the end of a spur of the Durban railway. He sustained 40 casualties, but killed 100 enemy, took 200 prisoners, and captured a greater volume of supplies than he could deal with. In spite of this success, the morale of his men was low, and often when he ordered an attack, half or more refused to charge.

Kitchener was severely criticized for failing to destroy the guerrillas when he had 200,000 men under his command, and he was seriously frustrated by the continuing attacks of the commandos. While Smuts continued to campaign in Cape Colony, and de Wet in the Orange Free State, Botha and de la Rey were operating in the Transvaal. Kitchener determined to put an end to these activities, and early in 1902 sent powerful patrols with field guns to catch de la Rey. Undaunted, de la Rey was strong enough to attack a supply convoy and, for the loss of 50 men, inflicted 400 casualties. Encouraged by this success, he attacked an even larger force and captured General Lord Methuen, the man who had blundered at Magersfontein at the start of the war.

Kitchener nearly had a breakdown over this humiliating setback, but in fact it was the last flicker of the Boer revolt. In April 1902, peace negotiations started and, under flags of truce, the Boer leaders were invited to Vereeniging, a small town on the railway just south of Johannesberg. Smuts and Reitz were taken to Johannesberg, and there they met with Botha and the other leaders. Botha's men had captured General Gough near Dundee at the end of 1901, but in spite of this success, they were now ragged and starving. Reitz commented, 'If these were the pick of the Transvaal commandos, then the war must be irretrievably lost? Almost every delegate had the same story of starvation, and lack of ammunition, horses, food and clothing. They agreed that the blockhouse system, together with aggressive sweeps by British cavalry patrols had finally strangled their efforts. They were further disheartened by the reports of the heavy death-toll among their women and children in the concentration camps. De Wet wrote 'Every homestead was burnt, all crops and livestock were destroyed, and there was nothing left but to bow to the inevitable ... Already our women and children are dying by the thousand, and starvation is knocking at the door?

Eventually, despite prevarication by the vindictive Milner, who even now wished to prolong the war, terms were agreed in May 1902 at Vereeniging. There were deep divisions on the Boer side, and charges of betrayal. De Wet never fully accepted the peace terms and Deneys Reitz, with his father, refused to live under British rule and left for exile in Mozambique. Reitz illustrates the depth of bitterness in defeat, but also the leadership qualities of Botha and Smuts. Smuts eventually persuaded Reitz to return and serve the new South Africa. He did this and in 1918 was commanding a British regiment, the Royal Scots Fusiliers, in the advance to the Rhine.

In the negotiations, Botha argued strongly that the continuing existence of the commandos meant that the Boers could obtain a negotiated settlement instead of unconditional surrender as demanded by Milner. Both Smuts and Botha realised the perilous state of their troops, and the devastation of the whole region, and believed that a prolongation of the war would be a catastrophe.

In the end, the treaty of Vereeniging was accepted by a large majority. Although many 'Bitterenders' were appalled, and would never accept British sovereignty, the terms were generous. All Boer prisoners were repatriated from the far-flung islands of the British Empire – notably Ceylon and St Helena. A general amnesty was granted, together with generous offers of economic relief. Self-government for the former Boer republics – envisaged in the treaty as a very long way in the future – happened much more quickly than expected. In 1905, the new Liberal government, which had been highly critical of Kitchener's policies, honoured the promise of self-government. In these territories after 1905, Botha and Smuts gave further evidence of their mature leadership, took their followers into the Union of South Africa in 1910, and became revered Empire statesmen.

The successful Boer commando leaders adapted quickly to new elements in guerrilla war – notably a completely new terrain and new accurate long-range weapons. The Boers had a cause – their religion and their whole way of life. They had the dedicated support of their people. They had leaders who understood the guerrilla principles of swift movement, surprise attack, swift dispersal and the use of the open veldt as their secure base. Their new weapons – especially the Krupp artillery and Mauser rifles – shrewdly purchased by Kruger, played an important part in their early successes in the autumn of 1899. The commando leaders quickly realised that the rail-ways and the telegraph system provided valuable targets for guerrilla attacks, which could have stifled any British advance. With all these factors in their favour, the real tragedy for the Boers, which denied them their chance of a quick victory, was the initial dead-hand control of Joubert and Cronje, who tied the commandos to the three great sieges. Joubert and Cronje also rejected the twin plans of Botha and Smuts for a rapid dash through Natal to seize Durban, and, simultaneously, a powerful incursion into Cape Colony, to rouse the majority of Dutch burghers to support a drive to capture Cape Town, before any reinforcements arrived.

In terms of guerrilla war, there is an ironic footnote to the achievements of Smuts, who at the end of the Boer war was rightly respected as one of the great guerrilla leaders. By 1914, he was admired as a statesman as well as a military leader. In 1916 he was given command of 45,000 troops in German East Africa (Tanzania), in order to eliminate Colonel Paul von Lettow-Vorbeck, who in 1914 had set out on his guerrilla campaign with about 2,000 troops. His aim as a guerrilla leader was to occupy as many Allied troops as possible, to prevent them fighting Germany on the western front. Von Lettow-Vorbeck proved himself a brilliant guerrilla leader, who for four years eluded the clutches of 137 generals and over 300,000 Allied troops. On 11 November 1918, he was cycling off to organise another attack, when he received the message that the armistice had been declared. Smuts' lack of success against Von Lettow-Vorbeck shows perhaps that well-led guerrillas always have an advantage against the more ponderous move-ments of regular troops.

MICHAEL COLLINS: GUERRILLA WAR IN IRELAND

In the Easter Rising of 1916 – that defining moment in Irish history – Michael Collins, aged 26, took part in the occupation of the Dublin General Post Office. He gave brave and cheerful leadership during the siege, and then, when the surrounding streets were ablaze from British shelling, he led his group out of the burning building, only to find that they were surrounded. He surrendered.

Collins was universally known as Mick during his life but, perhaps because of the horror at his tragic death in 1922, was always thereafter referred to as Michael. Before the Easter Rising he had done little to presage his sudden rise to fame. Born in Cork in 1890, when his father was 75, he was spoiled as the youngest of seven siblings. The family, strongly influenced by the older sisters, followed the Irish tradition of protest against British domination. The family lived in west Cork and fairly close to Skibereen – a name forever associated with the Irish famine and the callous English reaction to it. Collins was brought up in a home where strict parental control was lacking; it was a generous and hospitable atmosphere. He developed into a boisterous, powerful and humorous young man, much given to wild practical jokes. One of his sisters encouraged him to read widely, and before he left home he had studied with admiration the exploits of the Boer farmers whose commandos had fought so successfully against the British. His particular hero was Christian de Wet, one of the most successful commando leaders, who showed what a determined man could do against the might of the British empire.

Collins left home and went to London in 1906, aged 15, living with a sister while he worked in the post office in Kensington. He had little formal education, but a great innate intelligence, and he passed examinations quite easily. After his time in the post office, and a useful stint working for a stockbroker, he took the civil service clerical examination, and worked for the Board of Trade. In 1915, he left the civil service and took a job in the London branch of a New York bank. During these years he read voraciously: Shaw, Wilde, Yeats and much Irish revolutionary literature. He followed Gaelic football enthusiastically, and soon joined the Irish Republican Brotherhood (IRB) which, in the new century, had revived the revolutionary traditions of the Fenians. Early in 1916, through the IRB, he heard rumours of a possible uprising and he returned to Dublin.

In the 1960s, the inimitable entertainers Flanders and Swann made a light-hearted quip about the Irish troubles:

They blow up policemen, or so I have heard,
And blame it on Cromwell and William the Third.

There was an element of truth in that jingle. But the tradition of Irish protest goes back even further. Right back, in fact, to the guerrilla activity against the Norman invasion in the eleventh century. Then there were the Wild Geese, those Irish men who fled the country and, in the eighteenth century, fought in large numbers for the continental powers against England and the English Protestant domination of their country. Wolfe Tone kept up the tradition and, in 1798, tried to gain French support for the United Ireland movement. In the nineteenth century, Daniel O'Connell gave distinguished leadership with his skilful attempts to repeal the Act of Union of 1800.

In the decades after O'Connell, the demand grew for 'Home Rule' for Ireland. Parnell – a Protestant like Wolfe Tone – led the parliamentary move-ment. During the 1880s Parnell gained the support of Gladstone, who needed the backing of the Irish MPs, and who saw the justice of Home Rule. Even as early as that, Joseph Chamberlain voiced the fears of Ulster, with its Protestant majority, about Home Rule, and had suggested a separate parlia-ment for Ulster. Parnell's efforts failed.

By the time Home Rule again became a possibility, under the Liberals in 1912, the situation had changed dramatically. Edward Carson and James Craig had organised the Protestant working classes and had created massive opposition to Home Rule. Nevertheless, the Home Rule Bill was introduced by Asquith and passed on 18 September 1914. Because of the outbreak of war, the bill's introduction was suspended until the cessation of hostilities. During 1914, the intensity of popular feeling about Home Rule was shown by the Curragh Mutiny, when 60 British cavalry officers resigned their commissions rather than agreeing to force Home Rule on Ulster. Irish resent-ment simmered on.

From the start, bungling and incompetence doomed the Easter Rising of 1916 to failure. The planners had arranged with an agent in New York for a shipment of German arms, unaware that the British had broken their secret code. The German ship, the *Aud*, bringing the arms, was intercepted off the coast of Kerry, and then it was scuttled in Cork harbour. Roger Case-ment managed to land, but he was captured and, later, executed. This disaster, coupled with conflicting orders from the Irish leaders, caused many to call off the planned uprising, with the result that virtually the only rising took place in Dublin, and not across the whole country as intended. Collins was present at the General Post Office when Patrick Pearse read the proclamation of the Irish Republic, concluding his statement with the words 'Ireland unfree shall never be at peace' – a statement echoed years later by Bin Laden referring to Palestine.

The rebels seized the General Post Office, St Stephen's Green, Jacobs' biscuit factory and just a few more buildings but, from the start, they had little chance of success against the overpowering British military force stationed in Dublin. Collins gained respect as the ablest and most resourceful military leader during the siege, but when a cease-fire was called on 9 April 1916, he, along with all the others, was taken prisoner.

Fortunately for him, he was not identified by the British counter-insurgency forces. In May 1916 he was taken to Stafford detention centre, and, in June, from there to Frongoch in north Wales. These centres – known in Irish folklore as the Republican Universities – were poorly controlled and enabled Collins and many of the future leaders to discuss and plan future strategy. At Frongoch Collins began to show his wider leadership qualities. He had a sudden and aggressive temper, but his boisterous humour and his innate kindness and consideration for others enabled him to gain favours from the prison staff. He spent days pondering over the tragic details of the Easter Rising and he concluded that from the start it had been completely bungled.

During the post office siege, Collins had met John MacBride, who had fought against the British in the Boer War, and who was able to give him graphic details about de Wet – already Collins's hero – and the operation of the Boer commandos. What Collins learnt from MacBride formed the basis of his plans to wage the guerrilla struggle against the British. MacBride stressed the importance of constant mobility, which had been the key to the Boer success. Referring to the bombardment of the General Post Office, MacBride made the obvious point that you should never be trapped in a single building when your enemy has superior firepower.

Considerable detail is known about life in Frongoch, where Collins was held until December 1916, from the surviving letters the prisoners wrote to their families. Collins emerges as a natural leader, who imposed his powerful personality on staff and prisoners alike. He had an uncanny flair for persuading the most unlikely people to give him help and loyalty. From Frongoch, using such help, he was able to communicate with other rebel leaders, including de Valera who was in Lewes jail. Both inside and outside the prison, Collins actively developed links with the Irish Republican Brotherhood, and started to build up his system of cells, i.e., small groups of dedicated men who could operate independently, but had no knowledge of other cells.

Two issues preoccupied the prisoners at this time. They claimed from the beginning that they should have the status of prisoners of war, and should not be treated as common criminals dressed in prison garb – thus echoing the demands of the imprisoned suffragettes. Secondly, they feared that if Britain introduced conscription to Ireland, they would be among the earliest cannon-fodder for the hated Empire. Collins frequently gave a lead in these protests, and also protests about the appalling conditions in the prison camp. The British press publicised this, and it caused an outcry in the US where the Irish lobby had already been outraged at the executions of the Easter Rising leaders. Because of the adverse publicity, and British hopes of America coming into the war against Germany, the prisoners of the Easter Rising were granted an amnesty in December 1916. Collins reached Dublin on Christmas Day.

The IRA leaders were re-united in Dublin early in 1917, with Collins prominent among them. They quickly faced a political challenge. John Redmond was the official leader of the Irish parliamentary party, but his policy of imperial loyalty – hoping, foolishly, that in return there would be better treatment for Ireland after the war – was anathema to Sinn Fein. A by-election in January 1917 clarified the situation. Collins and Sinn Fein put up a candidate to oppose the official Redmond nominee, and Sinn Fein won, on a policy of continuing the fight, not for Home Rule, but for full independent sovereignty.

Collins now began to emerge as the most effective leader of the anti-British struggle. In February 1917 he became secretary of the Irish National Aid Fund, which raised very substantial funds – mostly in the US – for the dependents of those killed or imprisoned at the Easter Rising. He quickly proved to be an outstanding administrator, operating with efficiency and compassion, using his role to establish contacts in Ireland, Britain and the US, and to strengthen his links with the IRB and Sinn Fein supporters.

In 1917, de Valera won a by-election, and brought together several rival factions to agree that Sinn Fein should campaign for the whole of Ireland to be an independent republic. De Valera became President of Sinn Fein with Collins as Director of Organisation. Assuming that there would be a general election as soon as the war was over, Sinn Fein decided to contest every seat in Ireland, and, if successful, to form the Dail Eirrann, or Irish parliament.

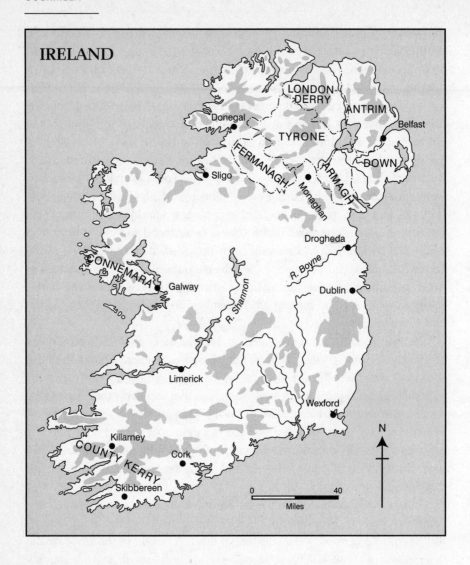

IRELAND

The government in Dublin Castle became alarmed at the rapid spread of Sinn Fein activity, and interned several IRA leaders for making inflammatory speeches or organising drilling. Collins, who increasingly needed to keep his identity a secret, always went around Dublin wearing a grey suit and collar and tie – assuming, correctly, that the security services would not suspect someone so well-dressed. This disguise served him safely for years.

At this time, the IRA started to use the weapon of the hunger-strike as a protest against their imprisonment. Thomas Ashe, a personal friend of Collins, was visited in hospital during his last days by nearly 30,000 people.

When he died, even more attended his funeral. Collins made a graveside speech and three volleys were fired – starting a tradition which has continued into the twenty-first century.

An important part of Collins's success as a guerrilla leader lay in the system he established to obtain secret information at the very highest level from the British security forces. Early in 1917, he had recruited several key men in the Dublin Castle security apparatus, and they were the nucleus of his amazingly successful system, based on the personal loyalty to him of both men and women. His intelligence gathering included all military units as well as ports, docks, railways and trains. He was notorious for luck and his brilliant use of the opportunities which came his way. This was shown when Nancy, his cousin, was put in charge of all the top-secret codes in the Castle. This led to the death of many British security agents in Dublin. On another occasion a woman supporter became personal assistant to a British divisional commander and was able to pass on critical intelligence for the whole of south-west Ireland about troop movements, convoys, counter-agents and all the activity of the security system.

Collins's activities had not passed unnoticed, and early in 1918 he was briefly in prison in Sligo. As the demand grew for an Irish republic, or, at least Dominion status for the whole of Ireland, it became clear that the work of Lord Carson and James Craig – to create a separate state in Protestant-dominated Ulster – was going to make this the insoluble problem of Irish unity. And so it has been from that time to the Good Friday Agreement of 1998 and beyond. At the start of 1918 the other great issue – less fundamental but more urgent – was the fear of conscription, which again came to the fore. It aroused very strong feelings not only in Ireland but also in the US. The idea was pushed hard by Sir Henry Wilson, showing his Ulster, Protestant intransigence. The Conscription Bill actually passed the House of Commons in April 1918 and the Irish members walked out, some seeing it as a declaration of war on the Irish nation. The Conscription Bill had an immediate effect in Ireland, where the Roman Catholic Bishops led the protest, and Sinn Fein gained massive support. The Irish Volunteers – set up to counteract the Protestant Ulster Volunteers – responded to conscription by planning the assassination of members of the British cabinet, since conscription would mean the killing of Irish citizens. Although conscription was never enforced, its threat played into the hands of the IRA. The British responded by a severe crackdown on IRA activity and even Gaelic football.

The post-war election took place in December 1918, and Collins campaigned for Ireland as an independent nation, and to break the connection with England, 'the unfailing source of all our ills'. Ireland had high hopes from the election and from the peace conference, but found that for President Wilson, as well as Lloyd George, other issues at the conference tended to push the Irish question to one side, in spite of the Sinn Fein election victory across the whole of Ireland except for Ulster.

Sensing the frustration of his hopes for an Irish republic, Collins now concentrated on setting up his guerrilla organisation. He built up and strengthened his already formidable intelligence network, and used the information to smuggle arms into Ireland. He realised that arms would be cheap and plentiful in 1919. At the same time, he built up his organisation across the whole of Ireland, and backed up their activities with carefully controlled bomb-making factories. He showed phenomenal energy and attention to detail, and even organised classes in the Irish language, which were in fact a cover for training guerrillas. Such activity needed much financial back-up, for often his supporters were virtually penniless. He recognised that a crucial part of the training was to convince the poor Irish lads who came forward as volunteers that they could take on both the police and the British army.

Early in 1919, at a Sinn Fein meeting, Collins made a vital speech arguing that the struggle for independence should be led by the Irish Volunteers who were prepared to lay down their lives and to carry out the violence by which alone the British could be removed. De Valera opposed this, arguing that the Irish people were not ready for violence.

The first historic meeting of the parliament, or Dail, took place in April 1919 and the Declaration of Independence of the Irish Republic was read along with demands for the withdrawal of the British military occupation. A major factor in the deep seated tragedy of Ireland, is that, on the one side are leaders like Collins and their loyal supporters, who look back to what they see as centuries of British injustice and oppression, and to the horror and suffering of the famine. On the other is the British establishment, who at the time found it inconceivable to contemplate what they saw as the break up of the United Kingdom and of the British Empire at the hands of what they saw as a few ill-organised ruffians.

That chasm of misunderstanding has never been effectively resolved, and has been reinforced by religious bigotry and prejudice on both sides. Religious control of education – which Collins was shortly to discuss with Craig – has deepened the division still further, so that in the twenty-first century, the world can witness a howling mob of Protestants threatening little Roman Catholic girls as they go to the Holy Cross primary school in Belfast.

At this crucial time when the Dail first met and Collins was a major figure, a sinister event took place which introduced another fairly permanent element into the Irish imbroglio. A group of volunteers ambushed a police patrol, captured a large supply of explosives, and killed two of the police escorts. The attack was led by Tom Barry, who later wrote *Guerilla Days in Ireland* (Irish Press, Dublin, 1948). In his book, Barry, who later became Commandant General of the Irish Army, gives a vivid description of the early days of the IRA. He was serving in Mesopotamia in the British Army in 1916 when he heard of the Easter Rising and the proclamation of the Irish Republic. His recollections of the West Cork Brigade illustrate clearly how the savage brutality of British forces brought almost universal support for the IRA. Barry took part in the early raids, which aimed to capture a few weapons. Like Collins, he soon saw the value of the Flying Column.

Because of the interest in the Irish situation, this raid gained massive publicity, and embarrassed Collins, who had not given the order for the attack. This incident pre-empted what was to be Collins's main campaign for an Irish republic, and it illustrated the need for discipline and control in guerrilla war. At the same time he became finance minister and had the burden of trying to raise a loan of £1,000,000 for the new Irish state.

During 1919, Irish leaders had high hopes of support from President Wilson, who was under considerable pressure from the Irish lobby in the US, and who came to London on his way to the Versailles Conference. Wilson was generally sympathetic, but soon showed that he was not prepared to fight the Irish cause and offend the United Kingdom, his major wartime ally. In the Dail, Collins proposed a motion supporting Wilson's plan for a League of Nations, designed to support the rights of small nations. The hopes of an Irish republic, now aired on the world stage, appeared to be getting closer to realisation.

While Collins was involved at a high level dealing with the political issues, and attempting to raise large loans, he was at the same time busy setting up his terror campaign. He had already lost a number of able and loyal colleagues, who had been snatched by British counter-insurgency agents. This led him to another of his original contributions to guerrilla war. From his penetration of the British system, he was able to discover where his colleagues were imprisoned. With almost boyish enthusiasm, he used the information he gained to rescue men from prison. Across both Ireland and England, often helped by sympathetic warders or other staff, Collins organised a number of spectacular rescues of IRA prisoners. The most spectacular was his personal raid on Lincoln jail to rescue de Valera, who had again been apprehended. While he was in prison, de Valera had offered to serve as an altar assistant when Mass was said by the prison chaplain, and he had used this opportunity to make an impression of the jail keys from the warm wax of the altar candles. In the middle of the break-out, the key broke in the lock, but somehow it was pushed out, and de Valera, Collins and the other rescuers hurried off into the night.

Collins's personal involvement in the rescue of de Valera did not lead to feelings of warmth and gratitude. Almost at once there was deep disagreement between these two powerful characters. Collins believed passionately that only the ruthless prosecution of his clandestine attacks on British agents and on the police could force Britain to consider independence for Ireland. De Valera, who had plenty of time to formulate his plans while sitting in Lincoln jail, had decided that his most useful role was not to get involved in Collins's campaign, but to go to America to raise money from the large and supportive Irish community. He could thus raise the profile of the demand for an Irish republic by approaching both the Democratic and Republican parties, and even President Wilson himself. Thus began an intensely personal feud between Collins and de Valera. It erupted again and again until Collins's death, and did immense damage to the Irish cause. Collins strongly opposed the idea of de Valera going to America, and then, to his added chagrin, having rescued him from Lincoln, he had to make all the arrangements for getting de Valera to New York as a fugitive.

De Valera left for America, and stayed for more than a year, just when the division developed in the IRA between those seeking a peaceful solution and those, like Collins, who believed that only fighting and violence would achieve their aims. While this bitter division increased, Collins made one of his distinctive contributions to guerrilla-war philosophy. In September 1919 he set up the Squad. This was a group of twelve men, fiercely disciplined, directly controlled by Collins himself, and trained to carry out assassinations. His inside information enabled him effectively to target key British agents – especially the notorious G division. The result of the early assassinations had been the suspension of the Dail and the proscription of the IRA.

Before the end of 1919 Collins had illustrated his ruthless grip on the key issues of guerrilla war. He had his highly disciplined Squad, which could eliminate a chosen British agent on his sole command. He had his intelligence service with loyal supporters, including many women. Some of these held secretarial posts under high-ranking British officers, and passed on timely and critical information – often hidden in their corsets. One agent worked in the top British security office and had to type top-secret instructions about attacks on senior IRA members including Collins himself.

Collins inspired remarkable loyalty in ordinary people, and a pub in Dublin run by a family called Devlin became his unofficial headquarters. Despite his boisterous behaviour, which included pillow fights with his friends – all part of easing the dreadful tensions in their lives – the Devlins never let him down. He combined ruthless determination and efficiency with a great sense of humour. At the same time he always showed a deep compassion and kindness to those who risked their lives with him. The total commitment of all his team assured his success.

The assassination activities of the Squad were accompanied by the wider campaign of the IRA. This was launched in January 1920 with an attack on the British barracks in Cork. In the following days the IRA attacked barracks across the country, and the British retaliated by imposing martial law across much of the south from Wexford to Limerick.

In the same month, local elections were held across the whole of Ireland, and the results of these should have given pause to the British regime. Sinn Fein won majorities on most councils and, significantly, in the city of Derry and in Fermanagh and Tyrone. Many new councillors were IRA members, including the Lord Mayor of Cork, and the councils rapidly transferred their allegiance from the British to the Dail.

British reprisals followed swiftly. In March 1920, the Lord Mayor of Cork was murdered by British agents, who clumsily and ineffectively tried to show that the murderers were a rival IRA gang. The jury that tried the case produced, despite official pressure, a verdict of wilful murder against the whole British establishment from the British Prime Minister, Lloyd George, downwards. Other mayors were murdered soon afterwards, and General Gough, who had led the cavalry officers in the Curragh Mutiny, commented that Ireland had fallen into bloody and brutal anarchy. The British, in reply to the deliberate murder of its agents, set up two forces – the Black and Tans and the Auxilliaries. The Black and Tans were former soldiers – many now unemployed – who kept their khaki uniforms, but wore in addition the hat of the Royal Irish Constabulary (RIC). The Auxilliaries were a smaller, more disciplined force of ex-officers. The Black and Tans, in addition to killing selected targets, appear to have been encouraged to cause destruction and mayhem all over Ireland, and became a byword for brutality.

One of Collins's contributions to the development of guerrilla warfare was the idea of the Flying Column. This term creates the image of highly armed groups transported across the country to major targets. The reverse was true. The type of Flying Column which proved most effective was a group of about a dozen men, who would lie up, sometimes for days – knowing they had the support of local people – before carrying out an ambush or attacking a police barracks. Their local knowledge, and the fear they instilled in the local police for the safety of their own families, enabled the Flying Columns to close down police barracks across Cork, Tipperary, Connemara and much of the south and west of Ireland.

Collins's deliberate elimination of spies and British agents, who were a far bigger threat to his organisation than large military units, was disapproved of by many senior leaders in the Dail, like Cathal Brugha, who took a legalistic attitude, and who did not take part in the actual fighting. Brugha was ridiculed by Collins's supporters for suggesting that in Dublin, ambushes should not take place on Saturdays, because of the danger to families out shopping.

In 1920 the British government passed the Government of Ireland Act, which partitioned Ireland and set up a separate state in Ulster. At the same time, the government faced the dilemma of publicly supporting killings and reprisals. As a result, the cabinet in London agreed on the policy of destroying creameries – where the dairy products of an area were collected – as reprisals for IRA attacks, since this would cause widespread damage, unemployment and the maximum suffering to the local people. While the Black and Tans were notorious for their brutality, the RIC were equally destructive. In one notorious incident, after an RIC officer was killed in Sligo, the Auxilliaries and the RIC went berserk and destroyed much of the town centre including the creamery. In another incident, near Dublin, a large group of Black and Tans went on a drunken rampage after a shooting incident. They destroyed a factory, nearly fifty houses, and killed or wounded many people. With the breakdown of law and order, criminal gangs on both sides often took the law into their own hands – as they still do in Ulster – and reprisals became more and more brutal. The British authorities were drawn into this spiral of violence, and increasingly sanctioned the widespread use of torture to gain information about the IRA, and because of the danger this posed to his whole campaign, Collins was ruthless in eliminating those who betrayed their comrades.

In June 1920, a British commander spelt out to his garrison what he expected them to do under martial law, in order to beat Sinn Fein and the IRA at their own game. He ordered his men, when they were attacked, to go into the area, commandeer the best house and throw the occupants into the gutter. He advised that, when rounding up suspicious characters, his men should shoot to kill: ' The more you shoot the better; if people go on hunger strike let them die; Sinn Fein must be wiped out.' As the killings and retribution spread across Ireland, the Ulster Volunteers began their campaign of retaliation in the north-east. Collins played the major role in the IRA campaign in Ireland, but Cathal Brugha directed the campaign in England, with the burning of factories and attacks on the homes of the more notorious Black and Tan leaders.

As 1920 – a year of murder, destruction and suffering – drew to a close, two events took place, which brought the Irish struggle to a world audience. Kevin Barry, an 18-year-old Dublin student who supported the IRA, was captured, and in spite of widespread protest, the British cabinet decided he should die. At the same time, several IRA prisoners went on hunger strike. Terence MacSwiney, who was in an English jail, died. When his body was returned to Dublin, the Dail called for a national day of mourning, which was massively supported.

Sinn Fein became increasingly aware that the British intelligence system had considerably improved and, certainly in Dublin, several of Collins's senior colleagues were apprehended. Some were released after brutal interrogation and torture, but some were shot. In this tense situation, Collins was once again saved by his ability to gain the loyalty of a wide range of generally unremarkable people. Early in 1921, he was able to recruit a man who was the hall porter in a house used by several senior British intelligence agents. He provided Collins with copies of all the necessary room keys. In the shadowy cloak and dagger world where Collins operated, it is easy to forget that he was a Minister in the Dail cabinet. In November 1920, when he had final details of the agents he intended to eliminate, he had to have the list approved by the Irish Army Council. The delay this caused was nearly fatal because the British apprehended some members of the Squad who were going to carry out the attack.

Collins had chosen Sunday 21 November 1920 for the operation because a large crowd were expected in Dublin for a Gaelic football final. Early on the Sunday morning, nineteen British agents were roused from their beds and shot. The British reacted swiftly, and soon Dublin was being combed by both the Auxiliaries and by the Black and Tans. During a day of fierce tension Collins cycled round Dublin as usual, visiting his bases.

That afternoon, the British authorities, realizing that the IRA had close links with Gaelic football supporters, decided to surround Croke Park where the match took place. There the military forces, claiming they were fired on first, opened fire on the crowd and the players with rifles and machine guns. Fourteen people were killed and hundreds wounded. Reports reached Collins that, after this incident, the Auxiliaries and Black and Tans, who were holding IRA suspects, tortured them, beat them up, and then shot them. The official version was usually given as 'Shot while trying to escape'. Collins visited the mortuary and then attended the funerals. This event – known as 'Bloody Sunday' – retained its unique place in the annals of Irish warfare until, in the more recent troubles, it was joined by another Bloody Sunday – 30 January 1972. It took over thirty years to decide which side fired first in this latter event. The official version of the Croke Park massacre described how the police were fired on by Sinn Fein including 'some of the most desperate criminals in Ireland', and were forced to fire in self defence.

The ghastly descent into more and more bloody reprisals by both sides continued after the Croke Park incident. Cork had always been a stronghold of the IRA and, in December 1920, the Black and Tans and Auxilliaries destroyed the centre of Cork, including the City Hall, in retaliation for an attack. In his biography of Collins the distinguished writer, Tim Pat Coogan, quotes a letter from a young English infantry officer who took part in the destruction of Cork. He wrote 'In all my life I have never experienced such orgies of murder, arson and looting as I have witnessed with the RIC.' He described how, with no provocation, one RIC man stopped a car and shot a priest and his companion. He added that men who had served in France and Flanders said they had seen nothing to compare to the destruction of Cork.

In spite of the increasingly effective British intelligence system and several very close shaves, Collins – to the near despair of his friends – continued to travel about Dublin and the rest of Ireland with hardly a thought for his own security. This was also the period when he began to suffer from the almost pathological hatred of Cathal Brugha. This feud, which began over a trivial dispute about the presentation of accounts, was to have disastrous consequences for the Irish movement. Brugha argued that the campaign against British agents should now be waged in England as well as Ireland. Collins opposed this on purely practical grounds, since successful operations demanded an immense amount of planning, and he was already fully stretched in Ireland. In 1921, Collins eventually gave in, and work started on a project to kidnap twelve members of the British government and hold them hostage. Such a scheme took months to plan. At the same time British agents were arriving in Dublin in fairly large numbers, and Collins's system was working so well that it was relatively easy for the IRA to identify and eliminate them. Collins planned an operation, similar to the Bloody Sunday scheme, which involved an attack on over fifty newly-arrived agents. Both of these schemes were fairly well advanced when word came from the British government that they were prepared to discuss peace, in order to put an end to the killing and destruction.

Such moments rarely occur in the history of guerrilla warfare but Collins, with no military training and little official backing, had waged a guerrilla war which, in a couple of years, had forced Britain – still at that time one of the most powerful countries in the world – to initiate a move for peace. So he had achieved a very big step towards that ultimate aim of the true guerrilla – to remove an alien or hostile power from your country. Collins's success depended largely on his exceptional intelligence system, which enabled him to have agents at the very top of the British counter-insurgency apparatus. This was backed up by the personal loyalty he inspired, by his fearless and dramatic qualities of leadership, and by a boyish, humorous and rumbustious attitude to life, which masked a totally ruthless streak.

As early as 1920, a document was circulated by Sinn Fein – attempting to achieve a constitutional compromise – which expressed the view that a settlement should be reached which would not diminish the security of the British Isles, or the liberties of Ulster. If Ulster would join, in a spirit of conciliation and co-operation, there was no limit to what could be achieved. After eighty more years of bloodshed, destruction and mayhem, such a view appears naïve or fanciful, but it does illustrate the desire on both sides to achieve an honourable peace.

Although the first tentative peace feelers had been put forward, there was absolute determination on the British side that there could be no direct discussion with Sinn Fein. Clandestine discussions continued, frequently conducted by senior Australian Roman Catholic clerics, who were often in danger of their lives from the ill-controlled Auxilliaries and Black and Tans. Negotiations were bedevilled by deep divisions on both sides. Lloyd George tried to push the peace process forward against the fierce opposition of the Conservatives and Unionists. They were backed up by the intransigent Ulsterman, Field Marshal Sir Henry Wilson, then CIGS, and by army leaders who believed that, given a free hand, they could destroy the IRA for good in a couple of months. On the Irish side, a growing number of people were so sickened by the murder and destruction that they demanded a truce. Collins sought an honourable peace, but saw that the British wanted

101

capitulation. The British also demanded the handover of IRA weapons, an unresolved issue, which was to rumble on until the Good Friday Agreement and well beyond.

As divisions increased, they were exacerbated on the Irish side by renewed clashes between Collins and de Valera, who had returned to Ireland after eighteen months in the US. He had raised money but failed to win serious political support for the Irish cause. Collins believed, correctly, that his personally-led campaign against the RIC barracks and British agents had forced Britain to consider negotiation.

Soon after de Valera's return, there was another fundamental clash between the two leaders. De Valera, who constantly stressed his position as President of the Dail, believed that their cause would be better served if their troops were organised as a regular army, and not as guerrillas. Pursuing this theme, he advocated an attack on the Dublin Customs House, the centre of British administration. Collins, who had to accept de Valera's superior position, was absolutely appalled at the suggestion and opposed it bitterly. It went against every precept he had hammered out in his successful campaign against the British. Once again, Collins had to implement an operation which he personally opposed. The attack on the Customs House was de Valera's idea, but the Dublin IRA, which Collins had built up, had to carry it out. The attack, in May 1921, was dramatic and certainly gained world-wide publicity, but Collins was horrified at the carnage, and heart-broken at the death or capture of so many of his close friends and most experienced fighters.

During the summer of 1921, Collins, as a minister of the Dail, had the responsibility for discussing the steps towards a truce, which his guerrilla campaign had made possible. In the all-Ireland election of May 1921, Sinn Fein won a very large majority, but the Unionists, under the positive leadership of Sir James Craig – assisted by intimidation and vote rigging, particularly in Tyrone and Fermanagh – won a majority in Ulster. After the election, urgent discussions attempted to bring about a truce. The South African, General Smuts, as a respected Empire leader, who had once fought successfully against the British, played an important part. Eventually, a truce was agreed on 11 July 1921.

Hopes of an independent republic for the whole of Ireland rapidly receded as the reality of a separate Ulster emerged, under its prime minister, Craig. King George V, personally distressed by the situation, made a sincere appeal to all the Irish people for a new era of peace, contentment and good-will. Increasingly, in the discussions between Lloyd George and de Valera, the British offer referred to Dominion status for the south. At the same time, there was a widespread feeling that, if the truce broke down, the British were preparing to take over and impose martial law. Tense and tetchy negotiations centred on the amount of Irish independence, and the issue of an Irish republic, which Lloyd George made clear was unacceptable. De Valera deliberately took pride of place on the Irish side during the early negotiations, but then, when a delegation had to be sent to England, he insisted that Arthur Griffith and Collins led the group. Collins was absolutely appalled at the suggestion, and he protested strongly, because the British regarded him as the number one gunman. Nevertheless he had to go, and with a heavy heart he set off with the delegation to London in October 1921.

Michael Collins's achievements place him among the great guerrilla leaders – like Tito and Mao Zedong – who waged their campaign and then took part in the creation of a new state. Collins's activities had brought the British to the negotiating table, but he became increasingly unhappy with his position in the Irish delegation. He wondered, as others have done, whether de Valera deliberately gave Arthur Griffith, the leader of the delegation, and Michael Collins an impossible task – a poisoned chalice. Certainly, as Collins, still under thirty years old, faced the might of Lloyd George, Churchill, Austin Chamberlain and Lord Birkenhead – the most fearsome barrister of his day – his greatest worry was not about his formidable British opponents, but about the attitude of de Valera back in Dublin, and the machinations of his old enemy Cathal Brugha. Collins soon realised that the wily Lloyd George was well aware of the changing moods in Ireland, and was manipulating the situation. The gulf between the two sides made agreement almost impossible. The British were not prepared to compromise on allegiance to the crown, and the idea of an Irish republic remained anathema to them, but Ulster remained the real stumbling block.

The position of Ulster was and is likely to remain the major obstacle to any aspirations for a united Ireland. The problem has deep historical roots. The Protestant plantations under the Tudors and Stuarts, and the immigration of lowland Scottish Presbyterians to Ulster, laid the foundations of this intractable problem. The names of Cromwell, Drogheda and the battle of the Boyne can never be erased from Irish folk memory, but there were moments at the end of the nineteenth century when it seemed that peaceful Home Rule might be achieved. During the 1880s the Irish leader Parnell had the support of Gladstone and the powerful nonconformist lobby in the Liberal party for a Home Rule Bill. In 1890, when most of the obstacles had been overcome, Parnell, who had been living for years with Katherine O'Shea, the estranged wife of Captain O'Shea, was named in a divorce petition by the odious captain. Victorian non-conformist public opinion was horrified, and in the aftermath, the Home Rule Bill was defeated in the House of Commons, though the Tory House of Lords would probably have rejected it anyway. One of the fascinating 'What ifs' of history, is the question what would have happened in Ireland if Parnell had not met Katherine O'Shea?

By the time Collins came to tackle the problem, it was far more difficult, because Sir Edward Carson, using the handy slogan 'Play the Orange card', had organised the Protestant working class – especially in the Belfast ship-yards – with the resulting sectarian bitterness and prejudice. While Collins was working for the truce, he had addressed a massive meeting in Armagh, and had appealed to all Irish people to share in the exciting prospect of government for the whole of Ireland. By then, the work of Carson and Craig, who were determined to establish a separate six counties, together with the destructive work of the Protestant Cromwell Clubs, and the formation of the B Special Constabulary – largely from the Ulster Volunteers – had changed the situation. In his negotiations, Collins was on a tightrope between Churchill and the Ulster Unionists on the one hand and, on the other, de Valera in Dublin making inflammatory and extreme claims. Despite this, there was a strong feeling across Ireland in favour of peace – almost irrespective of what happened to Ulster.

The most advanced constitutional concept the British could envisage was Dominion status for an Irish Free State. Back in Dublin, de Valera, constantly emphasizing his position as President of the Dail, but not directly involved in the negotiations, rejected absolutely any suggestion of allegiance to the Crown. He even made trouble over what were intended as sympa-thetic messages from the Pope and from King George V, and constantly reiterated his demand for independence for the whole of Ireland.

In London, Arthur Griffith and Collins – more accustomed to organizing guerrilla ambushes on the remote roads of Cork – performed brilliantly in the marbled halls of Westminster, Whitehall and Downing Street. Amaz-ingly, and much to his surprise, Collins gained the respect and even affec-tion of Churchill and Birkenhead. As the negotiations dragged on from October through into December 1921, Collins, under immense pressure, increasingly began to feel that Ireland should accept what was practically possible at the time – i.e., an Irish Free State and a separate Ulster – and, from that position, work to achieve more concessions in the future.

Messages to and from Dublin increased the enmity between Collins and de Valera. Both Arthur Griffith and Collins strongly resented de Valera's stand. Roy Jenkins, in his biography of Churchill, wrote, 'With a fine feeling for politics, if not for statesmanship, he [de Valera] decided to stand back, let his lieutenants take the strain, and reserve the right to repudiate what they had done' (Roy Jenkins, *Churchill*, p.365). Jenkins could have added that, during the negotiations, de Valera and Cathal Brugha deliberately set out to undermine and embarrass Griffith and Collins.

Throughout the discussions, a heavy burden fell on Griffith and Collins but, with their tireless energy, they won the admiration of all the British group. Their urgent visits to Dublin led to vicious clashes with de Valera. As the negotiations reached a climax, with added tension coming from Dublin, the pressure on Collins mounted yet further. He was the man whose guerrilla strategy had made the peace negotiations possible, yet now he was fighting for peace and reconciliation against the hawks in Dublin, most of whom had no experience of war at all. There are several contemporary descriptions of his anguish. Churchill said 'I have never seen such pain and suffering in restraint', and another witness wrote 'My heart ached with anguish at the thought of what his mental torture must be.' Right to the end, the British thought that the Irish might refuse to sign the treaty, but on 7 December 1921, Griffith, Collins and the delegation signed the treaty which sealed the partition of Ireland into the Protestant Ulster in the north, and the predominantly Roman Catholic Irish Free State. Lord Birkenhead who, surprisingly, had been supportive of Collins, quipped that he had probably signed his political death warrant, to which Collins, with tragic prescience, replied 'I may have signed my actual death warrant.'

Griffith, Collins and their group returned to Dublin, where they were greeted enthusiastically by the majority, but immediately there were signs of bitter opposition from others. Collins hoped that what they had achieved would be a first step towards what they all hoped for – a republic for the whole of Ireland. De Valera, driven, it would appear, by conceited petulance, called a cabinet meeting and called for the resignation of Griffith, Collins and Robert Barton – the three key delegates – because they had signed the treaty without referring the final draft to him. This was the first crucial step towards civil war. The Irish Republican Brotherhood gave Collins a joyous reception for what he had achieved, and gave him their full support. In a dramatic and acrimonious Cabinet meeting, in which de Valera and Brugha led the attack on Griffith and Collins, the vote went narrowly in favour of the treaty.

De Valera then immediately issued a statement – which was basically untrue and led almost inevitably to civil war – that the terms of the treaty were in violent conflict with the wishes of the majority of the Irish people. Over Christmas 1921 there was a bitter debate in the Dail, which was well portrayed in the 1996 film *Michael Collins*, in which Liam Neeson played the lead. The debate lasted 13 days, much of it taken up by de Valera and Brugha trying to undermine the treaty. De Valera brought the debate to a close with a final venomous attack on Collins, but in the tense and emotional vote – with both men and women openly weeping – the treaty was passed by 64 to 57 votes, a majority of seven in favour.

After this vote, and with general indications that the country favoured the treaty, the Dail should have led the country towards peace and reconciliation. Yet it was de Valera and the Dail which took another big step towards civil war. De Valera threatened to resign, and, when he narrowly lost that vote, he walked out of the Dail followed by his supporters – thus, at that critical moment, leaving the country without a government.

The speed with which these events took place is remarkable. The treaty was signed in London on 7 December 1921, and the delegates returned to Dublin. Then there followed the debate, the resignation of de Valera, the fall of the government, and the installation of a new government under Arthur Griffith and Collins on 16 January 1922. Collins presided at the official take-over of Dublin Castle. Fanned by de Valera, the deep divisions over the treaty now became more prominent, and the pressure fell once again on Collins, who had to cope with the anguished emotions these divisions caused in Sinn Fein, in the IRA and in the new Irish Army.

Collins worked frantically to avoid a permanent split, and to avoid civil war, or even renewed war with Britain. In addition to all his other responsibilities, he had virtually to draft the new constitution for the Irish Free State and, it should be remembered, to negotiate details of the constitution with the British government. Here again his impressive achievements during the treaty negotiations bore fruit. When the bill establishing the Irish Free State was introduced at Westminster, Churchill guided it through the Commons and Birkenhead through the Lords.

Across Ireland from January 1922 onwards, the feud between Collins's supporters in the IRA, and those opposed to the treaty, grew more violent. Now, instead of sending death threats to British agents, they sent them to each other. By April 1922, the rival groups were seizing barracks and ambushing military lorries in the search for weapons. Across the country people agreed that the level of violence and horror was worse than during the struggle with the Black and Tans.

While de Valera's intransigence, and his impractical demands for an Irish republic for the whole of Ireland, provoked the civil war in the south, the situation in the north – a different type of civil war – showed that the concept of Irish unity was unlikely to succeed. During 1922 the Unionists showed that they were determined to keep the British link. Some IRA members had been sentenced to death, and in retaliation the IRA crossed the border and kidnapped a number of prominent Orangemen. Collins knew of the kidnap plans and was embarrassed when Churchill protested. In another incident, typical of the time, some B Specials – whose notoriety lasted into the 1980s – went over the border from Ulster into Monaghan, and shot an IRA commander. When four of the B Specials were killed it created an uproar in Belfast and led to widespread reprisal attacks on Roman Catholic families and schools. There is clear evidence from this time of brutality, murder and the burning of houses and pubs in Belfast and across the six counties of Ulster. At the same time similar atrocities were carried out against Protestants in the south. This evidence does raise the question whether, with the deep-seated hatred and religious bigotry, there was any realistic hope of an all-Ireland settlement. However much the politicians discussed, temporised and fudged, the reality lay in the murderous activities of Protestant gangs attacking Roman Catholics, and the IRA attacking Protestants, Loyalists and Orangemen. A belated but true comment came in the 1950s, in the Whitla Hall of Queens University Belfast, when Ireland's leaders were still anguishing over the situation. After the most distinguished Roman Catholic and Protestant speakers had stated their case, an undergraduate stood up and said 'In Ireland, if all the Protestants were atheists, and all the Roman Catholics were atheists, you might begin to live together like Christians.'

Early in 1922, with virtually two civil wars raging, a group of the IRA led by Rory O'Connor, which opposed the treaty, seized the Four Courts and other buildings in Dublin. Collins who previously had always been decisive, now gained a reputation for dithering and vacillation, but this arose from the real anguish he suffered at the thought of fighting against men who had been his comrades, and his desperate hope of preventing further civil war. As he campaigned for his cause all over the country – in Killarney, Sligo, Wexford and Dublin – his opponents began to use the type of guerrilla tactics, which he had taught them. They disrupted his meetings, blocked roads and railways bringing his supporters to meetings, and threatened his life. In May 1922, seeing a total calamity developing in Ireland, the two sides sought a truce and an end to violence. For a few weeks things improved, but then Rory O'Connor rejected the truce and violence escalated again. O'Connor's troops then tried to subvert the whole peace process by openly fighting the forces of the Provisional Government, and demanding that the British leave the country within 72 hours.

This wildly impractical call to arms by O'Connor and his faction of the IRA was backed up with a series of inflammatory speeches by de Valera, who called on the nation to fight, using phrases like 'wading through Irish blood' and 'over the dead bodies of their brothers.' Complex, passionate and violent negotiations continued. There was even a proposal for an electoral alliance between de Valera and Collins. Collins supported this far-fetched idea, still driven by his hope of avoiding further conflict, and mending the split between the army of the Provisional Government and O'Connor's IRA.

The agony of May 1922 focused particularly on Collins. As a senior member of the government, he had to devise a new constitution which would heal the wounds of civil war, and at the same time would have to be acceptable to Britain before it would confirm the treaty. Collins once again found himself in London negotiating with Churchill and Lloyd George. Churchill initially showed a warm respect for Collins, but, as discussions continued, he began to fear that the proposed new constitution would have elements that were unacceptable to Britain and would destroy the treaty. During these difficult days, the British criticised Collins for not dealing with O'Connor's forces still occupying the Four Courts, while Collins raised the vexed issue of sectarian attacks on Roman Catholic families in Belfast, an increasing number of whom were now refugees in the south.

The negotiations went on until the middle of June 1922 when the Irish election took place. Despite claims and counter-claims of vote rigging and intimidation, the election brought a strong majority in favour of Griffith and Collins and the other parties supporting the treaty. De Valera lost heavily, but still did not accept the democratic decision. The fierce tension was notched up further when Field Marshal Sir Henry Wilson, who had been involved with the B Specials and had backed the Black and Tans, was assassinated in London by two IRA men. This created another crisis, when it was assumed that O'Connor and the IRA occupying the Four Courts were involved in the assassination. Churchill increased the pressure by claiming that the occupation of the Four Courts was a grave violation of the treaty.

This pressure again fell on Collins, who in exasperation, uttered his well-known charge 'Churchill can do his own dirty work'. At the same time, he realised that there were still a formidable number of British troops in Dublin, and they might be ordered to subdue the Four Courts. Weighing up all these factors, the Provisional Government under Griffith and Collins issued an ultimatum on 28 June 1922 to the IRA in the Four Courts to surrender. They refused, and the army of the Provisional Government, under the command of Collins, and using guns borrowed from the British, bombarded the Four Courts, until, on 30 June, the occupants surrendered.

During the summer of 1922, Collins had done his best to avoid civil war between the rival pro- and anti-treaty factions of the IRA, but he had been drawn, almost inevitably, into the even more destructive civil war taking place in Ulster. Collins's view was that the IRA involvement in the north was necessary to protect the Roman Catholic population from the brutal excesses of gangs of Orangemen and even more from the depredations of the large number of B Specials. They had been enlisted and armed under the directions of Craig and Wilson, who had obtained vast supplies of arms and ammunition from the British government. It is now well-known that there were contingency plans to defend Ulster with massive force if the treaty failed and it came to open war. With the breakdown of law and order across much of Ireland, there was little hope of calm and reasoned solutions to its problems. In London, Lloyd George and Churchill's policy was being undermined by a right-wing Unionist Tory group, which claimed that the government was being too soft with Collins and the Irish.

In Dublin the Provisional Government remained deeply divided over the Treaty, while Collins was secretly involved in the IRA campaign. In Ulster, Craig's government appeared to condone the excesses of the B Specials. The horrifying lawlessness and mayhem across the whole country, and the impossibility of protecting the Roman Catholic population in the north, finally persuaded the Provisional Government to call off the campaign against Ulster on 21 August 1922.

In these last dreadful weeks of his life, Collins, as Commander in Chief of the Irish Army, was still trying to curb and to terminate the civil war between the two IRA factions. His close friends and colleagues were still being slaughtered, and Arthur Griffith, his friend and noble colleague, died from overwork on 12 August – the day when the two men who had shot Wilson were hanged. Still hoping to end the civil war, Collins left Dublin and, against all advice, went with only a small escort to West Cork, his own home territory, but now the base of O'Connor's faction. Careless as ever of his own safety, his convoy was ambushed and Collins was killed on 22 August.

The death of Collins was yet another tragedy for Ireland, for he had unsurpassed enthusiasm, ability, imagination and leadership – so sorely needed in the succeeding years. Although he had a vision of a prosperous and united Ireland, and had positive ideas to develop every aspect of the Irish economy, he must be remembered as the man who, by his brilliant guerrilla leadership and action, forced Britain, in a short space of time, to negotiate the treaty which established the two parts of Ireland which survive to this day.

In a brief span, and with no military training, Michael Collins had shown himself to be an outstanding guerrilla leader who, by practising sound guerrilla principles, had brought to the negotiating table one of the strongest powers of the day.

LAWRENCE AND GUERRILLA WAR

T. E. Lawrence's exploits in the Arab revolt, and his description of them in *The Seven Pillars of Wisdom*, gave rise to an enduring and controversial legend which has lasted eighty years. Books of commentary, biographies, films, TV programmes and law-suits have all prolonged the life of the myth. The change in social mores from 1918 to 1980, meant that much that was hardly mentionable in 1918 became headline news in 1980 and after. In the years immediately after 1918 Lawrence wrote and revised his great work – even losing one copy – and he discussed the script with many of his distinguished friends such as Bernard Shaw, Robert Graves and E. M. Forster. As a consequence, as the controversy developed, different versions were paraded, giving rise to the damaging charge that Lawrence was an habitual liar. The protagonists, of course, had their different motives. Sir Basil Liddell Hart, that doyen of military historians of the middle of the twentieth century, had supported Lawrence and called *The Seven Pillars of Wisdom* 'a masterly formulation of the theory of war'. Liddell Hart had admired Lawrence, and in the 1930s had written a number of books praising him, so when critics charged Lawrence with being a liar and a charlatan, Liddell Hart considered that as an assault on his own integrity. Along with Lawrence's friends and relations, he rallied to his defence.

Towards the end of the twentieth century, when his close friends and relatives had died, the controversy centred less on his military genius and more on the charge and countercharge about his homosexuality. This and his sado-masochistic activities seem well established and no longer shock. It is unfortunate that the prurient interest in this aspect of his life – which sells books and films – has masked his achievements as a guerrilla leader and as a significant thinker on the crucial issues of guerrilla war.

Lawrence was distantly related to Orde Wingate, the brilliant guerrilla leader of World War II, who created and led the Chindits in the Burma campaign. Wingate, the nephew of Sir Reginald Wingate, who had backed Lawrence's campaign from Cairo, also created a myth and suffered equally from harsh criticism. The two men shared in common their brilliance in thought and action in irregular war – something which has always antagonised the military establishment. Military critics levelled charges at both Lawrence and Wingate, that they used valuable military supplies blowing up railways, which could be quickly repaired, and their activities had no effect on the final outcome of the campaign. The age-old resentment of the regular army against the special forces, which appear to have glamour and panache, and unfairly gain the headlines for their exploits, focuses particularly on Lawrence and Wingate.

Wingate was a regular officer in the Royal Artillery who passed out of the RMA Woolwich but, in terms of preparation for military command, Lawrence's background was almost bizarre. Brought up in the snobbish atmosphere of Edwardian Oxford, he resented and was embarrassed by his illegitimacy. His powerful and outstanding intelligence won him a scholarship to Jesus College, Oxford. He was no routine undergraduate, and his reading encompassed wide fields of military history, including the ideas and theories of Marshal de Saxe, Napoleon, Clausewitz and Moltke. A shrewd tutor, Hogarth, encouraged Lawrence to travel in the Middle East, where he produced a work on Crusader castles, which helped him to gain First Class Honours. He then learnt Arabic and spent years studying the castles and battlefields of the Arabic world and of the Crusader campaigns. His success at Oxford enabled him to continue his studies in the Middle East, and he led a number of archaeological expeditions. He gained a reputation as an effective but sometimes foolhardy leader.

By 1914 he was well respected as an archaeologist and as a well-informed expert on Middle East affairs. He had travelled extensively along the Red Sea coast, visiting Jeddah, Al Wajh and other places, and, while fascinated by the hopes and aspirations of the Arabs, he had developed a hatred of the Turks, who dominated the whole area under a brutal and sadistic regime. To his surprise, in 1914, he was taken on by Captain Newcombe, to take part in what purported to be an archaeological trip to Sinai, but which was in fact a military reconnaissance. By the end of 1914, he was in Cairo working as a staff officer at GHQ. Lawrence, as a fluent Arabic-speaker and with a vast knowledge of the Middle East, soon became a significant figure at headquarters. In the early stages of the war, the Allies were afraid that the Turks, spurred on by the Germans, might attack and capture the Suez Canal in order to stop the transport of troops from India, Australia and New Zealand to the Western Front. In fact they mounted a minor attack in January 1915 but it was quickly repulsed, and their hopes of getting the Egyptian people to rise up against the British were never realised.

In a welter of conflicting personalities and rival interests in Cairo in 1915, the Arab experts, like the High Commissioner Sir Henry McMahon, Sir

Ronald Storrs and Sir Reginald Wingate, were generally ranged against the military establishment over strategic issues. The failure of the Gallipoli expedition, and the stalemate on the Western Front, made the authorities look again, and reconsider a plan to encourage the Arabs to rise up in revolt against the Turks. The plan faced considerable opposition. The French saw it as a possible threat to their post-war ambitions in Syria. The Indian government was already involved in Mesopotamia (modern Iraq). In addition, many Arab rulers might object as they, at that time, thought that Germany and Turkey might win the war. There was strong anti-French feeling among the staff at GHQ, and some even suspected a French attack on the Suez Canal after the war. Lawrence shared these views. He was therefore pleased when, because of the lack of enthusiasm among the military for an Arab uprising, a separate Arab Bureau was set up in Cairo, to oversee and encourage an Arab revolt.

Plans for the revolt centred on King Hussein, the Sharif of Mecca and head of the Hashemite family, together with his sons Abdullah and Faisal. On the British side, the High Commissioner, Sir Henry McMahon, undertook the discussions. In a series of letters, subsequently known as the Hussein–McMahon Agreement, McMahon, on behalf of the British government, promised to support the revolt, and offered Arab independence for those areas captured from the Turks – with certain specified exceptions. This agreement lay behind all of Lawrence's efforts to support the revolt, but, almost from the start, he had agonies of self-doubt. Throughout *The Seven Pillars of Wisdom* he agonised over the possibility – indeed the probability – that Britain might renege on its promises. Despite these doubts, Lawrence saw clearly that if the Arab revolt was to have any hope of success it would have to be backed by Britain.

During 1916, Lawrence, his mind teeming with ideas as usual, had put forward suggestions about the situation in Mesopotamia. There an Arab population was held down by the Turks, as they were in Arabia, and the first stirrings of an Arab uprising had taken place in Baghdad and Basra. Lawrence, although he was only a staff captain, was sent to Mesopotamia to find out if the Arabs were likely to revolt against the Turks. Because of massive incompetence, British and Indian troops were already besieged in Kut. There was no likelihood of an Arab uprising, and the army commanders treated Lawrence and his ideas with hostility and contempt. In assessing the situation in Baghdad and Basra, Lawrence made comments with significant undertones for 2003: 'Unfortunately, Britain was bursting with confidence in an easy and early victory' (*Seven Pillars of Wisdom*, p.59).

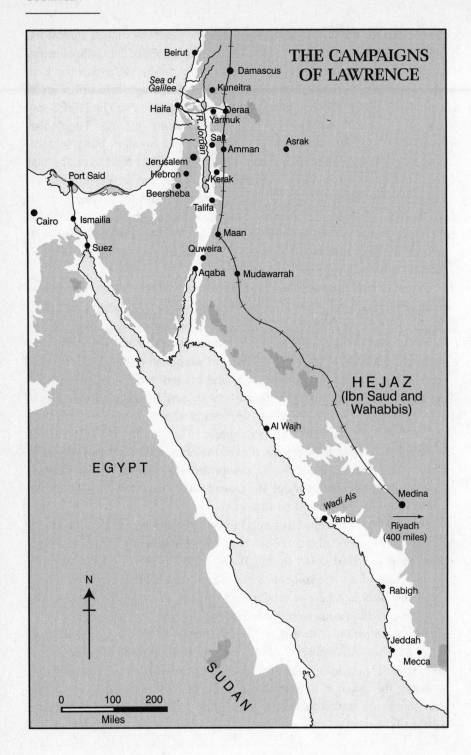

THE CAMPAIGNS
OF LAWRENCE

Beirut

Damascus

*Sea of
Galilee*

Kuneitra

Haifa

Deraa

Yarmuk

R. Jordan

Salt

Asrak

Amman

Jerusalem

Hebron

Kerak

Port Said

Beersheba

Cairo

Talifa

Ismailia

Maan

Suez

Quweira

Aqaba

Mudawarrah

HEJAZ
(Ibn Saud and
Wahabbis)

Al Wajh

EGYPT

Medina

Wadi Ais

Yanbu

Riyadh
(400 miles)

N

Rabigh

Jeddah

Mecca

SUDAN

0   100   200

Miles

He added that whilst the Arabs were prepared to oppose the Turks they were not ready to fight for yet another occupying power. Lawrence returned to Cairo having achieved nothing.

Soon after his return to Cairo, he found that at least two significant figures, McMahon and Storrs, were now more in favour of supporting an Arab revolt. The matter had been made more urgent, because Hussein and his sons had mounted an uprising against the Turks in Mecca and Jeddah, and they were in danger of defeat by Turkish forces based on the powerful garrison at Medina.

Throughout his time at GHQ, Lawrence had tended to keep away from the generally unruly and philistine expatriate society often dominated, as he saw it, by noisy Australians. To his relief he had been encouraged by Storrs and other senior figures to take part in lengthy discussions about all the current and future problems of the Middle East. His fluent Arabic and wide practical knowledge of Arabia had made him a respected figure in GHQ, and he was delighted when he had the chance to accompany Storrs on a visit to Jeddah to interview Hussein. This small incident illustrates some of the problems of finding the correct version of events in the Arab revolt. The official version states that Lawrence was sent to Jeddah to assess the situation, while Lawrence says he managed to wangle a trip with Storrs. In the dramatic events of the next two years, Lawrence often exaggerated his role, and his later, and more unkind, critics accused him of being a compulsive liar.

Lawrence was well informed about the complex situation faced by the leaders of the Arab revolt. They urgently needed military help to fight the Turks, but if a large British force – say a brigade – arrived in Jeddah, it would appear as an occupying power. It would also seriously offend the large majority of local Arabs, who would see it as an infidel invasion, so close to the holy cities of Mecca and Medina. Lawrence saw that his first priority must be to find a charismatic leader to head the revolt. In Jeddah, during discussions with King Hussein, he also met his son Abdullah. Lawrence summed up Abdullah as competent but completely lacking in those positive qualities of leadership which were necessary.

While Storrs continued his discussions in Jeddah, Hussein permitted Lawrence to travel north to meet his other son Faisal, who was with his troops near the port of Yanbu. From this point, Lawrence started his fascinating commentary on every aspect of the Arab revolt. In a constant, scholarly and colourful flow of language, he mixes history, politics, philosophy and religion, with vivid descriptions of the desert terrain, the vegetation, the weather, the people and the animals. He saw Bedouin society as a type of 'crazed communism', but in which they were served by Negro slaves. These people, sometimes descended from prisoners seized during the age-old Arabic East African slave trade, and sometimes people who had been brought on the Haj – the pilgrimage to Mecca – and sold, carried out the heavy work shunned by the locals. This tradition is still followed in Saudi society, using expatriates from the Third World.

Travelling to meet Faisal, Lawrence sailed by ship from Jeddah to Yanbu, and then inland by camel to Faisal's HQ. He was taken to Faisal's tent and introduced. Later he wrote 'I felt at first glance that this was the man I had come to Arabia to seek – the leader who would bring the Arab revolt to full glory' (*Seven Pillars of Wisdom*, p.91). Faisal asked Lawrence how he liked his HQ, and he replied, 'It is far from Damascus'. From that moment they had a close rapport. Faisal, tall, graceful and vigorous, had lived in Constantinople, had been a member of the Turkish parliament, and had served in the Turkish Army. Hussein made all his sons live and work in the desert with the Bedouin in order to harden them. Faisal's first clash with the Turks at Medina had been disastrous. The Turks had surrounded and captured a large group of Arab soldiers who were raped and then massacred. Lawrence soon saw that Faisal alone among his family had the qualities to control the quarrelling sheiks, who made up his force – about 8,000 men at that time. Hatred of the Turks alone bound them together.

As a result of their first clashes with the Turks the Arabs were terrified of Turkish artillery and they urgently requested that the British would provide them with artillery to hit back. Lawrence, having swiftly assessed the terrain through which the Hejas railway ran, with steep hills and narrow valleys, thought it was ideal for ambushing the Turks' lines of communication, and felt that artillery would only hamper the mobility of the type of guerrilla force he was envisaging. Lawrence left Faisal, and promised to try to have supplies sent to Yanbu. He rode back to Yanbu, 'the plain dancing in the unbearable heat'. Then, after crossing the Red Sea, he went to Khartoum to report to Sir Reginald Wingate, who was now effectively in charge of the British part of the Arab revolt.

In Khartoum, Wingate, who for years had hoped to see an Arab uprising against the Turks, was pleased to see Lawrence's hard-hitting report, which advocated assistance for the Arabs with technical advisers, some Arabic-speaking British officers, and supplies of explosives and machine guns. After his visit to Khartoum, Lawrence went down the Nile to Cairo where, at GHQ, he argued forcefully for the men and equipment. He was against a large British force, convinced that if a contingent of British troops arrived all Faisal's volunteers would vanish.

Lawrence had argued his case effectively, but he was genuinely amazed and appalled when he was appointed to go back to Yanbu and be the chief British liaison officer with Faisal. When Lawrence arrived back in Yanbu, Faisal had just been defeated again in a battle with regular Turkish forces. After a defeat, Faisal always listened patiently to comment and criticism, in order to keep up morale – and he added humour, that magnet of Arab goodwill.

During their earnest discussions, Faisal suggested that, in his new role, Lawrence should wear Arab dress; Lawrence was delighted and agreed at once. Military assistance did not arrive immediately, but in the meantime the Royal Navy gave decisive help. Two ships anchored off Jeddah and bombarded the Turkish lines. Then a naval seaplane carried out useful reconnaissance and dropped some bombs. In June 1916, the Turks withdrew and Hussein was able to occupy Jeddah and he recovered Mecca in July.

Lawrence now embarked on a campaign with Faisal which was to occupy him fully until the end of the war. He rapidly adapted to the numbing tedium of riding a camel for days at a time across the desert. He became accustomed to the daily meal of coffee and dates, and, when supplies were available, an evening meal of mutton and rice. His ascetic nature and his previous work in the desert, made it fairly easy for him to cope with the harsh regime of the nomadic Bedouin. He saw the Arabs as good friends in the struggle against the Turks, and he supported their requests for guns, armoured cars and aeroplanes. Thanks to his strong advocacy, all of these eventually arrived.

Almost from the start Lawrence suffered from deeply divided loyalties. The size of the British subsidy rapidly increased to £300,000 per month – much of it transported on camel back – and critics alleged that the Bedouin force would not fight unless they were paid in advance. Lawrence did not deny this, for it was all a part of a tradition to which they were accustomed. In contrast to Lawrence's favourable view of the Bedouin and their successful guerrilla activities, most British regulars regarded the Arab fighters with contempt, for their lack of discipline, their cowardice in face of Turkish troops, and their passion for looting.

The Royal Navy had helped Hussein to recapture Jeddah from the Turks and, in January 1917, they assisted a strong Arab force, led by Faisal and Lawrence, to capture Al Wajh, a small Red Sea port about 200 miles north of Yanbu. In this attack, Faisal showed considerable powers of leadership –

particularly in keeping his quarrelling group together. Strategically, this was a most important capture. Yanbu was very close to Medina, where the Hejaz railway terminated, and where there was a strong Turkish garrison. From Al Wajh, the Arab guerrillas would be able to range at will along the most vulnerable part of the railway, and from that base, easily reinforced by sea, would be able to make the next step forward to Akaba.

After the capture of Al Wajh, Lawrence returned to Yanbu, and then set out with an expedition against the railway. The expedition reached as far as Wadi Ais, where he became seriously ill with dysentery and a high fever. He lay hardly conscious for nearly ten days. During that time, he had to get up and settle a serious dispute, which would have led to a blood feud. A man had been murdered, and according to Arabic custom, it fell to Lawrence as the senior officer present, to shoot the murderer.

In *The Seven Pillars of Wisdom*, Lawrence describes how at the Wadi Ais, in between bouts of fever, he began to consider every aspect of guerrilla war and the Arab revolt in particular. He recalled in detail from his Oxford days, his admiration for Marshal de Saxe whose *Reveries on the Art of War* was published posthumously in 1757. This was an instant success, not because of the Frenchman's prowess as a commander in the field, but because of his radical and revolutionary views on military matters. De Saxe based his ideas on the Roman legion, and put forward ideas on armament, equipment and tactics. All his ideas aimed to increase mobility, the ability to manoeuvre, and, above all, to concentrate force and fire power. Years before Napoleon, de Saxe suggested that the art of war lay in the legs not the arms. De Saxe aimed to cut out slow-moving transport, and he foresaw the value of divisional transport to give a commander flexibility close to the battle. Lawrence had studied de Saxe's original and brilliant ideas, and he regretted that they had been overshadowed by Frederick the Great, who may have won battles, but lost sight of strategic purpose, and ruined his country. Lawrence, accepting the views of de Saxe, saw that Napoleon had started with sound principles about mobility, but later expected to win battles by his massive offensive power. In the end Napoleon's constant supply of manpower ran dry, and by then the lessons of economy of force, and the concentration of forces had been forgotten.

The Seven Pillars of Wisdom gives a most vivid impression of Lawrence's brilliant mind, which – especially during his prolonged bout of fever at Wadi Ais – ranged over every aspect of warfare, as well as ethics and sexuality. Until that time, his interest in military affairs had been mainly scholarly and theoretical but, suddenly and unexpectedly, he was plunged into the

Arab revolt and, to his amazement, he was given an almost free hand in organising the military side of the uprising. He then focused his attention – having taken part in relatively brief actions against the Turks – on the theory of guerrilla war, and its application to his campaign in the Hejaz. This combination of circumstances created his remarkable thesis on guerrilla war, which draws on Clausewitz, Napoleon and Saxe, alongside detailed thoughts about the situation there in the desert.

As early as 1914, when an Arab uprising had been considered, the official view had been that the Allies should hold the small port of Rabigh, which could be supplied and defended from the sea and held until a substantial British force could land and attack Medina. Any idea of help from the Bedouin had been discounted. In contrast, Lawrence proposed that the Bedouin, strengthened by a few British officers and some explosives experts, together with light machine guns, explosives and money, could make frequent attacks on the Hejaz railway to weaken and even threaten the position of the Turkish garrison in Medina. That was the base from which they held sway over southern Arabia and the Holy Places.

This argument was reinforced when Faisal moved his forces north and captured Al Wajh. Lawrence, in his semi-delirium, now developed it further by maintaining that, for the Bedouin, the desert provided the secure base so vital to all successful guerrilla activity. There they would be able to roam at will, relatively untouched by the Turks, who remained tied to the railway.

Lawrence's theory faced a serious hurdle in the assumption by contemporary military leaders, notably Foch, that guerrilla activity would always be secondary to regular forces and could not alone win a victory. This view had been supported by Clausewitz, who, earlier, had influenced Lawrence, and it had been backed up in modern times by the theory that all military activity must aim to destroy the enemy in a set battle.

Lawrence had to consider another factor – 'that the Arabs would not endure casualties'. While this remained true, he realised that even at this early stage, the Arab uprising had created a new military situation, because they controlled 99% of the Hejaz. The Turks merely controlled Medina and its tenuous rail link, which terminated in the town. From this point his mind raced ahead to another prospect. Why bother with Medina? By sabotaging the railway, his irregulars would make the Turkish position in Medina increasingly precarious. There was no point in risking casualties in an unnecessary assault on Medina, and anyway it was not the role of guerrillas to attack prepared defences. He then developed further arguments. Intelligence information showed that the Turks in Medina were already short of food and were having to eat their transport camels, so they were no longer a serious threat to Mecca, which lay 200 miles south of Medina. If the Arabs took Medina, they would capture many prisoners, who would have to be fed and guarded. So, he argued, much better to leave them half-starved in Medina at no cost to the Allies. He wrote: 'The Turks valued Medina, and wanted to keep it. Let them!'

Lawrence then considered what the Arabs were trying to achieve, and what was their relationship with the Turks. He surmised that their real aim was geographical – to remove the Turks from Arabic speaking lands – rather than, necessarily, killing them and suffering casualties too. For 'the Arabs were fighting for freedom, a pleasure only tasted by a man alive.'

From his sick bed and from the intricacies of the Arab revolt, Lawrence looked back to his Oxford studies of de Saxe, Clausewitz and even Sun Tzu. Saxe had argued that an able general could wage war all his life without being compelled to fight a battle, while Sun Tzu, with all his advice on strategy and tactics, had urged that the best solution was to win without fighting a battle. Such views had been rejected with contempt by Foch and other early-twentieth-century strategists, but Lawrence now began to apply some of the theory to the direct issues of the Arab position. They had been defeated when they concentrated to fight a battle against the Turks, but when they dispersed and took on their proper guerrilla role they immediately seized the initiative.

Lawrence then considered his own urgent problems, 'My personal duty was command, and I began to unravel and analyse it, both from the view of strategy ... which sees everything by the standard of the whole; and from the point of view called tactics, the means towards the strategic end, the steps of its staircase' (p.192). Considering how to attack the Turks, he suggested that armies were like plants, firmly rooted and immobile, but 'we might be a vapour, blowing where we liked. Our kingdoms lay in each man's mind, as we wanted nothing material to live on.'

He estimated that the Turks would need 600,000 men against a hostile Arab population. He mused:

'It therefore seemed the assets in this part of command were ours, and climate, railways, deserts and technical weapons could be attached to our interests, if we realised our raw materials and were apt with them. The Turk was stupid and would believe that rebellion was absolute ... To make war upon rebellion is messy and slow, like eating soup with a knife.'

Then, amid wild flights of fancy, he inserted a colourful epigram: 'Nine tenths of tactics are certain ... but the irrational tenth is like a kingfisher flashing across a pool, and that is the test of generals.' Assessing the separate importance of men and materials, he argued that for the Turks men were plentiful, but materials and equipment were scarce. Therefore it was more important to destroy railways, bridges and trains than to kill Turks. For the Arabs, men were more precious and they could not afford casualties, but materials were easier to obtain. 'Our war should be a war of detachment: we were to contain the enemy by the silent threat of a vast unknown desert, not disclosing ourselves till the moment of attack.' Lawrence applied this idea to his basic tactics, of attacking not Turkish units but empty stretches of rail, and, indeed of never engaging the enemy at all, and never giving the enemy a target at which to fire. Thus the Arab units would hardly ever be on the defensive. The corollary of this was accurate intelligence so that plans could be made with certainty, leaving no room for chance. 'We took more pains in this service than any other staff I knew', he would declare.

Dealing with psychological war, Lawrence affirmed the importance of the mood and morale of his men; the need to prepare their minds for battle; the need to assess the mind of the enemy soldiers, and, as well, the mind of the nation behind the troops, and of the hostile nation. He counted the printing press as 'the greatest weapon in the armoury of the modern commander.' His priority had to be to know what his supporters thought and their susceptibility to new ideas. Lawrence used these arguments to reinforce his view that they should not attempt to assault Medina, but leave the Turks there in large numbers so that the provision of food would confine them to the railways, with thousands of troops forced to defend it, while the Arabs controlled the other 99%. 'Our ideal was to keep his railway working, but only just, with the maximum of loss and discomfort to him.'

He continued, 'Our aim was to seek the enemy's weakest link, and bear only on that, till time made the mass of it fall.' The Arabs' largest resource was the tribesmen: 'Men quite unused to formal warfare, whose assets were movement, endurance, individual intelligence, knowledge of the country, and courage.' Lawrence planned to develop a highly-mobile, highly-equipped type of army, of the smallest possible size, and to use it across the widest area to force the Turks to deploy yet more troops to defend the railway. He believed they could be on equal terms with the Turks with just one fifth of their number. 'Our victory would lie not in battles but in occupying square miles of territory.' He ruefully looked to Napoleon, who said it was rare to find generals willing to fight battles. Lawrence added, 'The curse of this war was that so few could do anything else.'

He believed that the crucial element of his force were the Bedouin irregulars, and in Arabia, range of movement was more than force, and space was greater than the power of armies. Then, suddenly coming down to earth, he argued that the invention of bully beef profited them more than the invention of gunpowder. He concluded that his force had an unassailable base, and that an alien army of occupation could not control the country from fortified posts. The people were sympathetic to the rebels who had self-control, speed, endurance, and were independent of supply lines. 'We had won a province when we had taught the civilians in it to die for our idea of freedom; the presence or absence of the enemy was secondary.'

After the ten-day sojourn in his sick bed, which produced this remarkable thesis, Lawrence had to move about slowly – too weak to endure the normal camel rides. In considering how to put his plans into action, he reckoned that Murray the GOC in Cairo – shortly to be replaced by Allenby – would hardly understand the idea of the Arab movement, and Hussein in Jeddah was not supportive of Faisal's efforts. Lawrence, while still not fully fit, had to spend some time with Faisal's apathetic, idle and feckless brother Abdullah, who because of his father's agreement with McMahon, expected the British to do everything. Abdullah spent his days playing crude practical jokes with his hangers-on, and he stretched Lawrence's patience to the limit. He prompted Lawrence to give a most unflattering description of the Bedouin: 'Drunkards for coffee and milk, gluttons for stewed meat, shameless beggars of tobacco, and boasters of their sexual exploits.'

At this time, March 1917, Lawrence took part in a raid on a small railway station held by about 300 Turks. The raid illustrated the sort of problems with which he had to contend. He was awaiting 800 reinforcements so he posted troops to fire shots during the night to make the Turks jumpy. In the morning instead of 800, only 300 arrived, and he decided they were not strong enough to attempt to capture the station. So, instead, he decided to blow up the track in both directions. He was still on the edge of exhaustion, but he did watch while an ancient Krupp mountain gun scored a direct hit on the station. Then a train hurriedly left and was blown up by a mine. This should have been the signal for a machine gun group to attack the wrecked train, but they had gone off on their camels because they felt lonely.

As soon as he was fit enough, Lawrence went back to see Faisal in Al Wajh. He had already concentrated his forces there, and was slowly abandoning Yanbu and Rabigh. In Al Wajh, Lawrence met Auda, one of Faisal's bravest warriors, who had been married 28 times, wounded 13 times, and had a reputation for fearless courage. In discussion with Faisal, Lawrence developed his theory on the guerrilla element in their campaign. He claimed that guerrillas should not attack places, they should not defend a line, and they should always concentrate on the enemy's weakest link. The Arab war must be built on the Bedouin, whose assets were mobility across the desert, toughness, self-assurance and courage. 'With them, dispersal is strength', and, as de Saxe argued, they must strive to reach victory without fighting a battle. Lawrence explained to Faisal that he hoped to develop a highly-mobile, highly-equipped striking force of the smallest possible size, and to use it to attack all the way along the Medina railway. 'We must not take Medina. The Turks are harmless there. In prison they would cost us food and guards ... let the Turk keep the railway, but only just. His stupidity would be our ally.'

After lengthy discussions with Faisal at Al Wajh, Lawrence set off in May 1917 on what was to prove his most successful military exploit – the attack on Akaba. The expedition set off, well provided with dry flour for the journey, transport camels loaded with explosives and £20,000 in gold sovereigns to gain the as yet uncertain support of the sheiks around Akaba. On such a long journey, very careful planning was essential, and their route was always determined by the availability of water – as vital for the camels as for the men. For Lawrence, this was another painful and exhausting trip for his fever recurred and he had an outbreak of boils on his bottom, which made camel riding excruciating. He described day after day of painful travel through bleak hostile land, with burning winds. Then they had a halt in an area infested with venomous snakes, which killed several men, and depressed Lawrence, who 'had a shuddering horror of all reptiles'. Later their privations were eased when they entered the domain of a friendly sheik and, under the local custom of hospitality, they enjoyed two huge feasts of mutton and rice every day.

In justifying the expedition, Lawrence argued that Akaba was vital in order to extend the area of the Arab revolt as it would enable them to link up with the British and to give them control of Sinai: 'For the Arabs, Akaba meant plenty in food, guns, money and advisers.' He envisaged the Arab forces becoming the right wing of the British advance into Palestine and Syria.

During the long expedition to Akaba, Lawrence began to have disturbing doubts about the honesty of British promises and his Arab colleagues quizzed him about this. In 1917, there were strong rumours, clearly leaked from official sources, that Britain and France had made a secret agreement. In fact, the Sykes/Picot Agreement had been made as early as 1915, and it proposed that, after the war, France would have a mandate over Syria, and Britain over Palestine and Jordan. In *The Seven Pillars of Wisdom* (p.275), Lawrence states, 'I had no previous or inner knowledge of the McMahon pledges or the Sykes/Picot agreement.' Yet there is written evidence that when the issue was discussed in Cairo in 1915, it prompted an anti-French outburst among the British staff, and Lawrence was part of that. Perhaps he needed to quieten his conscience for he stated, 'If we win the war, the promises to the Arabs were dead paper. Had I been an honourable adviser, I would have sent my men home, and not let them risk their lives for such stuff.' In practice, he was carried along by the momentum of the revolt and its successes, and he decided that because of his invidious position, he would ensure that the Arab revolt would succeed and would force the powers to keep their word. This did weigh heavily on his conscience throughout the war and during the peace conference afterwards.

At the start of the Akaba operation, Lawrence led a fairly powerful group – about 700 men – northwards in order to attack and destroy the railway near Maan. To reach Maan, they traversed broken hilly country, ideal for their guerrilla tactics. In some places the Turks had blown up the wells, and they found empty boxes labelled 'Nobel gelignite.' At this early stage of the trip, Lawrence arranged for one of his British officers, Newcombe, to plant a document showing details of a completely different route, and they discovered later that this had completely fooled the Turks, whom Lawrence always regarded as very stupid. During their march they saw a small Turkish patrol and his men were eager to attack, because it would have brought honour and booty, but he was just able to prevent this by arguing that nothing must endanger the prize of Akaba. Later they did cut off a small railway station and captured a flock of sheep, which provided everyone with a feast of mutton.

Early in July 1917, Lawrence faced a more serious clash. Against a larger Turkish force he marshalled his men on a reverse slope position, to protect them from the Turkish guns, and then he led a wild camel charge against the enemy positions. In the charge he was thrown from his camel and was knocked unconscious. In spite of this, the charge succeeded, and the Turks were defeated, losing 300 killed. The Turks had molested and raped many local women, and the Arabs took their revenge on their many prisoners. After this victory, their momentum carried them confidently forward to

Akaba. There, the approach of Lawrence, his promise to spare the lives of prisoners, and the threat of a naval bombardment encouraged the Turks to surrender the town, which they did on 6 July 1917.

The capture of Akaba was the greatest victory so far for the Arab revolt but when Lawrence arrived in the port there were no supplies, no food and no arms. He therefore set off on a hectic ride across the desert to Suez. He covered 150 miles in 49 hours, but upon arriving in Suez he had serious problems convincing the Military Police who he was. In spite of this short delay, he rapidly reached the base commander, and as soon as possible HMS *Dufferin* was loaded with food, ammunition and money, and sent off to Akaba. It arrived on 13 July 1917, exactly one week after the capture. Lawrence reported to GHQ, and Allenby – freshly arrived from the Western Front – interviewed him. After some initial reserve, he promised to do all he could to help. The Royal Navy, which had played a decisive role in taking control of the ports along the Red Sea, now helped again. They sent a four-funnelled ship to Akaba, and hugely impressed the Arabs, who always judged a ship by the number of funnels. Lawrence flew in a plane up country to see Faisal, and so 'we crossed comfortably at 60 miles an hour, hills learned toilsomely on camel back'.

Lawrence's capture of Akaba was a tremendous achievement, and Sir Reginald Wingate recommended him for the VC – in fact he was awarded the CB. His victory made him a hero in Cairo, where he stayed briefly before he had to rush off to confer with Faisal and Hussein. With them, he argued strongly that Al Wajh should now be closed and Faisal's forces moved north to Akaba, which could be their base for the advance on Allenby's right flank.

As the revolt moved north into what was loosely called Syria, Lawrence, in a significant chapter of his book, described the different peoples and problems and drew on his wide knowledge of the Bedouin, Arab, Druse, Turk, Sunni, Shia, Christian and Jew – often intertwined and riven by blood feuds. He described Jerusalem as 'a squalid town, which every Semitic race had made holy ... and some Jews now looked to it for the political future of their race'.

Even while he was in Akaba, Lawrence still pondered over the proper role of his irregular forces. He argued that, as the British controlled the sea, so they controlled the desert, and their tactics should be tip and run using the smallest force in the quickest time at the farthest place. All this using the camel, 'that prodigious piece of nature'. A camel carrying half a bag of flour made a man independent for six weeks or 1,000 miles. A camel could move

250 miles between watering; could in an emergency carry two men; or if a patrol faced starvation it provided 200 pounds of meat.

Before the next campaign started, Lawrence sent urgent demands for Lewis guns and explosives. Allenby backed him and was generous with supplies except field guns. Lawrence, knowing the Arabs' fear of Turkish artillery, commented, 'One long-range gun outweighs 99 short.'

He considered that irregular war demanded special qualities of character such as initiative, endurance and enthusiasm; it was far more exhausting than service in the comfortable imitative obedience of an ordered army. 'If two men are together, one is wasted. Our ideal is a series of combats, our ranks a happy alliance of agile commanders-in-chief.' Their situation was different, because an Arab could go home at any time without penalty – his only contract was honour.

Lawrence next had to plan the detail of the campaign towards Maan and Mudawarra, and against the railway between them. In Maan the Turks had 6,000 troops and a German adviser, Falkenhayn, and Lawrence had learnt through intelligence that they were planning to recapture Akaba. He therefore used aircraft to bomb and strafe Maan, and he kept them jumpy by constant attacks on the railway and the disruption of their supplies. He also used a new type of mine specially adapted to blowing up railways. To start the campaign, the expedition moved off towards Guweira in hilly country half way between Maan and Akaba. Two British and Australian sergeants accompanied the group, and because they had not ridden camels before, it moved slowly. Hot sweet tea with rice and meat was provided at the halts. Once again serious disputes developed between men of different tribes, and on one occasion Lawrence had to rush back to Akaba to fetch Faisal to adjudicate. From Guweira, they moved towards their objective, the railway in the area of Mudawarra. Here they were occasionally attacked by Turkish aeroplanes from Maan airfield, and they had several skirmishes with Turkish patrols.

After reaching their target, Lawrence laid explosives on a large railway bridge, and the whole group withdrew to hills overlooking the spot. They watched intently as a train with two engines and twelve carriages slowly puffed towards the bridge. He gave the signal and there was a huge explosion. At this point in *The Seven Pillars of Wisdom* Lawrence explained at length that the main purpose of Bedouin raids, hallowed by custom and tradition, was the capture of booty. When the whole group saw the wrecked train and carriages, they surged forward completely out of control in a frenzy of greed and destruction. He wrote, 'The Arabs had gone raving mad, and were rushing about, bare headed and half naked, screaming and looting to their absolute fill.' Then a group of Austrians appealed to Lawrence to get a doctor for a wounded man, and he went off to get help. While he was away, a dispute broke out between the prisoners and his bodyguard, one of whom was shot. Then the infuriated Arabs turned on the prisoners and killed nearly all of them, before Lawrence returned. He was deeply disturbed by this incident, but it illustrated the volatile nature of the troops he was leading. Finally, after sabotaging the railway several times, and after more clashes with the Turks, the expedition, weighed down with loot, returned to Akaba, 'entering with glory, laden with precious things and boasting that the trains were at our mercy'.

From Akaba, he planned many operations against the railway, and he led some himself. The fighting patrols usually consisted of about 100 men, and they always took pack camels to bring back the loot. He highlighted his problems in a colourful description of another raid. 'In the six-day raid, there came to a head and were settled twelve cases of assault, four camel liftings, one marriage, two thefts, a divorce, fourteen feuds, two evil eyes and a bewitchment.' While he described these problems with half-amused detachment, his conscience still burdened him, and he confessed that 'the fraudulence of my business stung me ... I was raising the Arabs on false pretences'.

Effective training courses taught others to lay mines and handle explosives, and soon strong teams had established domination of most parts of the Hejaz railway, and had destroyed over 20 locomotives. There was rarely any shortage of volunteers for an activity which promised so much booty. Then Allenby called Lawrence to GHQ in Cairo. Their interview – less cordial than the one before, shortly after Allenby had arrived – highlighted the perennial suspicion between regular armies and guerrillas. Allenby asked 'what our railway efforts meant, or rather, if they meant anything beyond the melodramatic advertisement they gave to Faisal's cause?'. Thus challenged, Lawrence explained his policy of allowing the line to Medina to operate under great difficulty, so that there would not be vast numbers of prisoners to look after. He also impressed Allenby with the intelligence network he had established, which stretched as far as Amman and Deraa.

Allenby was clearly convinced by Lawrence's argument, and continued to give his support to the revolt, but Lawrence was still torn by his conflicting loyalties, and his doubts over the integrity of the British government. He had intended to make an attack on Deraa, but this was refused for strategic reasons.

Instead, in October 1917, he undertook a lengthy and ultimately unsuccessful project to destroy the railway from Deraa to Haifa where it went
through the Yarmuk Gorge. His group travelled fairly quickly towards
Asrak, and were able to hear Allenby's artillery from further west. When
the group were approaching the gorge, one Arab leader, Abd el Kader –
about whose loyalty they had been warned – defected to the Turks and
betrayed the group. In spite of this, Lawrence pressed on closer to the
bridge over the gorge, but then a careless movement alerted the guards,
and the whole expedition had to run for their lives. They made another raid
but that, too, failed and then they returned to Azrak.

Lawrence decided to stay in Azrak for the winter and made a ruined
castle habitable; although there was nothing they could do could keep out
the heavy rain and the bitter cold. Having established a relatively secure
base, many visitors arrived, including merchants from as far away as
Damascus. They brought sesame, caramel, apricot paste, nuts, spices,
sheep-skin rugs and Persian carpets. Lawrence welcomed visitors as they
enabled him to build up support and to spread the message of the revolt.
As the winter closed in, they were able to shut the gate of the fort at dusk,
and make a great brushwood fire in the courtyard, where they sat around
drinking coffee and telling tales of heroism.

While they were at Asrak, Lawrence made a decision which, while
unimportant militarily, was to have a profound effect on his future reputation. In mid-November 1917, he decided to go with a few companions to
make a recce for a future guerrilla attack in Deraa. They entered the town
easily enough, and noted details of the railway station, German ammunition
dumps and the aerodrome. Then, while wandering closer to the centre,
Lawrence was grabbed by Turkish soldiers, separated from his companions
and taken to the Bey. He was held for a day, and then at night was taken to
a detached house and taken upstairs to a bedroom, where there was a large
officer. He dismissed the guards and attempted violently to seduce
Lawrence. Then he promised favours and 'would even pay me wages if I
would love him'. Lawrence rejected his advances, and the sentries were
called. They took him away, tortured him with a bayonet between his ribs,
and then held him down and whipped him until he lost consciousness.

This description in the 1935 edition of the *Seven Pillars* – the first
public edition – covers the incident with vivid and harrowing descriptions
of his brutal torture and whipping, but it does not say he was sodomised.
It does conclude with the words 'that night the citadel of my integrity had
been irrevocably lost' (p.447). Lawrence later gave different versions of

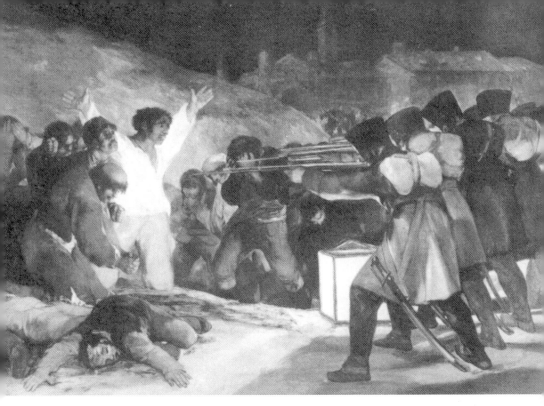

Above: During the Peninsular War the French took fierce vengeance on Spanish guerrillas. Goya illustrated many of the horrors.

Right:
Giuseppe Garibaldi (1807–1882), Italian patriot and leader of the Risorgimento who developed his skills in the South American wars.

Above: A Boer Commando – each man had to report with his rifle
and a bandolier of ammunition. These were the men who were led by Botha,
Smuts, De Wet and Reitz.

Right: Michael Collins (1890–1922),
Irish patriot and C-in-C of the Irish Free State Army,
who developed a new style of guerrilla war.

Right and below:
Lawrence of Arabia –
Thomas Edward
Lawrence
(1888–1935), soldier
and writer. He was
brilliant both as a
theorist of guerrilla
war and as a leader
in action.

Right: Mao Zedong
(1893–1976), the
revolutionary guerrilla
leader who became
head of state.

Josip Broz Tito (1892–1980) – **right:** the guerrilla leader on a German 'wanted' poster; **below:** the statesman.

награда од 100.000 рајхсмарака у злату!

100.000 Рајхсмарака у злату добиће онај који доведе жива или мртва комунистичког вођу Тита.

Овај злочинац бацио је земљу у највећу несрећу. Као бољшевички агент, овај скврнавитељ цркава, лопов и друмски разбојник хтео је да организује у земљи совјетску републику, а к томе је уобразио да је он позван да „ослободи" народ. За остварење тога циља он се спрема у шпанском грађанском рату и у Совјетској Унији, где је упознао све теро-

мир сељака и грађанина и баци[ла] земљу у неописиву беду и невољ[у]. Порушене цркве и спаљена села тр[а]гови су којима је он прошао.

Стога је овај опасн[и] бандит у земљи уцењен[а] са 100.000 Рајхсмарака злату.

Онај који докаже да је ово[г] злочинца учинио безопасним или г[а] преда најближој немачкој власти н[е] само што ће добити награду о[д] 100.000 Рајхсмарака у злату, него [ће] тим извршити и једно национал[но] дело јер ће ослободити народ отаџбину од бича бољшевичког к[р]вавог терора.

Врховни Заповедник немачких трупа у Србији.

Right: Orde Wingate (1903–1944), unorthodox soldier of deep religious faith, whose brilliant ideas founded the Chindits.

Right: Paddy Blair Mayne, a pre-war Irish rugby international and British Lion, joined the SAS under David Stirling and won four DSOs. This is his statue in New-townards, County Down, Ireland.

Left: Ernesto 'Che' Guevara (1928–1967), charismatic Latin American revolutionary.

Below: A propaganda poster of Osama Bin Laden found in an Al-Qaeda classroom in Eastern Afghanistan.

مُجاهد اسلام
أُسامہ بن لادن

نُور خدا ہے کفر کی حرکت پہ خندہ زن
پُھونکوں سے یہ چراغ بُجھایا نہ جائے گا

this incident to different friends. Many of his critics and several biographers seem to focus deliberately on the prurient aspect of the whole affair. To back up their claims they cite details of his known homosexual interests from Oxford onwards, for instance his dedication of *The Seven Pillars of Wisdom* to an Arab boy with the words 'I loved you', and his post-war homosexual and sado-masochistic activities. More than one biography claims confidently that he was repeatedly sodomised by the staff of the Bey. Whatever the truth of the matter – and his critics cannot know for certain – it is irrelevant to any consideration of his prowess as a guerrilla leader.

Early in December 1917, he was called to Allenby's HQ, now near Gaza. Lawrence was there when news arrived of the fall of Jerusalem, and Allenby invited him to go to the city. Togged out as a British army major, he entered Jerusalem. For him 'it was the supreme moment of the war'.

After this, in a brief period of leisure, he recorded his views about the best type of man and the best type of camel for the guerrilla sorties he made into the desert. He trained both man and beast to go for long periods uncomplainingly without food or water, and then to eat and drink heavily to sustain another period of privation. Arab men were eager to serve under Lawrence, because they rode his camels – not their own – and they were proud to be seen as his bodyguard.

He and his men continued to suffer from the intense cold during the winter, but in January 1918, they had a break from their rather dismal routine. Setting out from Kerak, Lawrence led a party of about 70 men mounted on horses and attacked a Turkish naval port on the southern shore of the Dead Sea, destroying all their boats and taking 70 prisoners. This success lifted their morale briefly but they soon had to return to the wet and the cold.

While Lawrence had to sustain all the pressures of high command, he also had to cope – often in appalling physical conditions – with the daily irritation and frustrations of controlling his quarrelsome and inadequate men. After one unsuccessful raid on Mudawarra he complained bitterly of the constant difficulty of co-operation between regulars and irregulars. Then disaster struck. While he had been away, he had had to leave a large sum in gold sovereigns, £30,000, in the charge of Faisal's weak and incompetent brother Zeid. When Lawrence returned, he found that Zeid had given it all away. He felt totally mortified by this disaster, and, with his mercurial temperament at its lowest point, he rode to Allenby's HQ near Beersheba, and begged to give up his independent command.

At the HQ he learnt that General Smuts had come from the war cabinet, whose members desperately wanted an advance and a victory over the Turks to offset the stalemate on the Western front. Allenby, in his turn, needed the forces of Faisal and Lawrence to secure his eastern flank and, even more, to turn the Turkish defences. So, Lawrence commented, 'I must take up again my mantle of fraud.' He then demanded that if his 4,000 troops were to attack and capture Maan, he would need more field guns and machine guns and 700 baggage camels. Allenby agreed and also proposed that while the Arabs attacked Maan, regular forces would advance across the River Jordan, north of the Dead Sea, and attack the railway south of Amman.

Ultimately, these plans did not materialise because Allenby had to divert some of his forces to the Western Front, and when he did advance towards Amman his forces were driven back by the Turks, and there was even a possibility that they would recapture Jerusalem. At the same time, Lawrence planned to cut the railway north of Maan, to attack Mudawarra with an armoured car patrol, and to further isolate Medina. In his book he often interspersed his personal thoughts and ideas with high level strategy and local tactics, and after outlining his military plans, in an almost off-hand paragraph, he described how he went into Amman dressed as a woman and then was importuned by Turkish soldiers before narrowly escaping. Other versions of this incident state that, along with two colleagues, he was approached by some prostitutes and they took the women's clothes before going into the town. This incident does illustrate his rather odd views on sex, and it seems strange that he should do this so soon after his experience at Deraa. In another comment at this time he thought that love, companionship and friendship were impossible between a man and a woman.

After a period of boredom, he was suddenly involved in a fierce fight with an aggressive Turkish patrol. In this, one of his closest friends among the bodyguard was seriously wounded, just when the Turks counter-attacked. There was no hope of rescuing him, and since it was known that the Turks took wounded prisoners and burnt them alive, Lawrence shot him. This was the Arab custom. The incident illustrates the perennial problem of wounded men in a guerrilla group on the move and pursued by the enemy. It was seen again in the first Chindit expedition in Burma, when any seriously wounded man had to be left behind, with a grenade or a round in the barrel.

In April 1918, Faisal and Lawrence led the long awaited attack on Maan. Several columns of armoured cars, Rolls-Royce tenders, and Bedouin camel patrols approached the town and very rapidly overcame the opposition. Then there was unstoppable chaos as the Bedouin rampaged over all the loot. Further south, the Turks still held Mudawarra, but the railway was permanently closed.

By 1918 British power had gradually built up and the Royal Air Force was able, almost at will, to bomb the railway anywhere between Damascus and Maan. Allenby also received reinforcements from India and Mesopotamia. Then Lawrence had to take on another responsibility, when King Hussein in Jeddah, in an attitude of pique and vindictiveness towards Faisal, refused to allow a large contingent of their regular troops in Jeddah to transfer north to help in the campaign. Lawrence went to Jeddah to try to persuade the King, but he retreated to Mecca, where infidels were not allowed.

For Lawrence these were tedious and frustrating times, and he was still plagued by serious doubts about the role he was playing. He longed for 'the moody skies of England'. And then, on a short plane trip, he hoped to crash and die. He constantly asked himself if he had offered up his life for a cause in which he could no longer believe, and he agonised over his acquiescence in the Arab fraud, 'hence the wobbling of my will'.

His morale improved when, in August 1918, there was a well-planned attack on Mudawarra. Accurate artillery fire, effective bombing by the RAF, and well-sited fire from concealed Lewis guns prepared the way for a dawn attack. By 7.00am the town was taken.

During 1918, the murkier depths of Middle Eastern diplomacy and chicanery were unravelled. Details of the Sykes/Picot Agreement, with the arrangements for French and British mandates over Syria, Palestine and Jordan, were definitely confirmed when Lenin grasped power in Russia and published them. Faisal, for his part, contacted Mustapha Kemal, who was seen as the leader of the nationalist anti-German element in the Turkish forces. Then further confirmation came to Lawrence and the Arabs of the total duplicity of Britain, when the British government published the Balfour Declaration which viewed with favour the establishment in Palestine of a national home for the Jewish people.

In August 1918 yet another significant factor emerged into the imbroglio. A powerful Arabian sheik, Ibn Saud, at the head of the Wahabis – then considered an unimportant minority of fanatical Muslim zealots – clashed with King Hussein's troops at the Khurma oasis and defeated them. Lawrence was almost contemptuous of the Wahabis, and believed he could have easily defeated them if he had been given a few tanks by Britain. These were absolutely crucial moments in the Middle East. How different the history of the Middle East and of the world might have been if Lawrence with a few squadrons of tanks had defeated Ibn Saud and if the British had kept their promises for independent Arab control over territory won from the Turks.

Also in August 1918 King Hussein caused another foolish and unnecessary crisis, which Lawrence finally solved by marginally adjusting a cipher message. After that, the long awaited attack on Deraa began, with aircraft, armoured cars, the Camel Corps and the Bedouin irregulars. The joint attack aimed to destroy the three railways leading out of Deraa – the ones north to Damascus, south to Maan and Medina, and west to Haifa. Lawrence commented on the sensuous luxury of riding in the Rolls-Royce over the same ground that previously he had covered with 20 hours a day on camel back. Yet, as the forces built up, he could not throw off his misgivings and depression. He wrote 'I was tired to death of the Arabs ... my nerve was broken', but now he saw that his false position might soon be over. Deraa was defended by Turks and Germans and, although the preliminary attacks started around 17 September, confused fighting continued for two more weeks. Lawrence was pleased to be given the task of destroying the railway going westwards to Haifa, since his previous attack at the Yarmuk Gorge had failed. This time he led his group to a small station, which unexpectedly yielded vast booty and the relatively easy destruction of both the railway and the telegraph. When the looters finally staggered off, the station buildings were liberally doused with petrol and incinerated. The flames attracted visitors from miles around, and the leaders of Deraa offered their town to the guerrillas, but Lawrence realised that serious fighting still lay ahead before Deraa could be captured. Now he had field guns, more than 30 machine guns and plenty of explosives, and he was able to encircle Deraa and blow up the railway when he chose. While the confused fighting continued around Deraa, he had to go to Allenby's HQ, where he heard the news of victories for the British, and the capture of Haifa and Nablus. After that success, Allenby planned to drive across the Jordan to Amman, and to send Chauvel's Australian forces northwards past the Sea of Galilee to Kuneitra. Linked to these movements, when Deraa was taken, Faisal and Lawrence would drive north and join up for the final assault on Damascus.

There was again some tension between the regulars and irregulars, but by the end of September Deraa had fallen, and Lawrence felt that his Bedouin had acquitted themselves well. He was full of praise for Allenby 'who could use infantry, cavalry, artillery, Air Force, Navy, armoured cars, deception and irregulars each in its best fashion.'

In the final part of *The Seven Pillars* Lawrence described how he arrived in Damascus and was the key figure in settling disputes and quarrels between Arab chiefs before either Faisal or Allenby arrived. He stressed that the tried and trusted leaders of the Arab revolt were quickly able to take over the civil administration from Arab colleagues who had served under the Turks. They restored electricity, water and sanitation, re-opened the hospitals and reorganised the distribution of food. When Allenby reached Damascus, he approved of what Lawrence had done. Then Faisal's train arrived and he was escorted to the town hall by enthusiastic crowds. Lawrence introduced Allenby and Faisal.

This description has been seriously challenged by the majority of biographies of Lawrence. In many he was shown to be on the edge of a nervous breakdown, unable to control the Bedouin, who indulged in an orgy of rape, murder and destruction, including the murder of Turkish prisoners in hospital. He was also shown to be at loggerheads with nearly all the regular commanders, including Allenby.

In the years after 1918, Lawrence enjoyed considerable fame as, with Faisal, he strove unsuccessfully to obtain justice for the Arab cause at the Versailles Conference. To a country sickened by the carnage of war, in which few leaders emerged as heroes, Lawrence was seen as a romantic knight-errant, with colour, daring and panache. Books and films assisted in the creation of the myth, which has centred on his sexuality, his bizarre behaviour during the 1920s and until his dramatic death in a motor cycle accident in 1935. The legend and the myth still continue, but they have added little either to the detail or the understanding of Lawrence's role as an outstanding thinker on the great issues of guerrilla war, and as a brave and successful guerrilla leader.

MAO THE GUERRILLA LEADER

Mao Zedong was brought up in the early years of the twentieth century in Hunan province – over 600 miles west of Shanghai. He was the son of a brutal father, a reasonably successful peasant farmer, was given little education and had no formal military training. Yet, from these humble beginnings, he became the classic guerrilla leader who achieved power by military means and became head of state. He grew into a man of restless energy and ruthless self-confidence, who was prepared to use fear and violence to achieve his aims, and is universally remembered with awe – either revered or execrated.

Born in 1893, Mao attended school until 1907, when he was thirteen. His father encouraged his study of figures so that he could leave school and help with the farm accounts. Mao had more rapport with his mother, a Buddhist, who had a deep compassion for all human beings. Out of six siblings, only Mao and two brothers survived.

At the end of the nineteenth century, China was going through a period of chaos and anarchy. Tyrannical warlords held sway and foreign powers treated China with contempt. Japan took Taiwan, planned expansion in Manchuria, and easily defeated the Chinese Army and Navy. In 1900, rebel Chinese forces seized Beijing (Peking) and massacred many foreigners. Foreign powers, notably Britain, France and Germany, carried out reprisals and then grasped concessions along the east coast of China. Modern developments in industry, science and business spread slowly, but made little impact in Hunan.

Mao, having few educational advantages, none the less read widely and was strongly influenced by books which warned of the dangers to China from foreign intrusions if it did not adapt and modernise. He admired the ancient Chinese heroes and enjoyed tales of heroic resistance to foreign enemies. By the age of seventeen he had left his father's farm and, with the help of two tutors, was studying the impact of Japan in Taiwan, Korea and Manchuria, of the French in Indochina and the British in Burma and Hong Kong. A serious famine, which affected Hunan, awoke Mao to the realities of peasant suffering, to the brutal injustice of many landlords, and their repression of any protest. He was able to enrol in a college with a radical reputation, and there is evidence of him reading about Wellington, Napoleon and Washington, as well as western philosophers, including Rousseau.

In 1911, Mao was living in Changsha, the capital of Hunan, during the last chaotic months of the Qing dynasty. Revolutionary ideas abounded, encouraged by the energetic Sun Yat Sen. That year the authorities suppressed a serious uprising in Canton and executed 70 of the leaders. In 1912, the Qing leaders finally abdicated, and Sun Yat Sen established a short-lived republic. During these chaotic events, when there were many student uprisings, and many radical and socialist newspapers were published, Mao remained cautious. He even enrolled in the army, which had gone over to the rebels. He found the army stultifying, and once again became a student, studying politics, economics and social problems. After the demise of the Qing rulers, an election took place in 1912, in which Sun Yat Sen won most seats, but the warlords drove him into exile and misruled China for another 14 years.

In 1913, Mao enrolled in a college back in Changsha, and spent five years of study under inspiring teachers who demanded high standards in writing, in poetry and in the study of ancient Chinese classics. It is believed that while he was studying here he first read *The Art of War* by Sun Tzu. He developed an intense interest in the organisation of society, and in western commentaries about this issue. Developing his own ideas, he was critical of the isolation and the frailty of scholars, and he became the leader of a group of students who spent days of vigorous walking and swimming – which became a lifelong passion – and long nights of discussion.

As the First World War ended, Mao moved to Beijing, where one of his former tutors had become an influential professor. Mao was excited by the new ideas sweeping over China at that time, but having only a menial job in the Beijing University library, he felt he was only on the fringe of events, and he felt slighted by the attitude of most of the professors and students. News of the Bolshevik revolution caused great excitement and gave another boost to the Marxist debate. Before the end of 1918 he returned to Changsha because his mother was ill and he obtained a post as a history teacher, but he kept abreast of radical ideas by editing a left-wing magazine. Soon, the local warlord closed it down, but when he was driven out in 1920, Mao obtained another post as head of a primary school. Soon afterwards, both his parents died and, with a small legacy, Mao was able to start the Cultural Book Society. He also edited another magazine, and his ideas focused on independence and improvement for Hunan province, rather than the wider problem of the sloth and corruption across the whole of China.

Communist ideas, supported by the reformed Cominform (set up by Lenin in 1919), spread fairly rapidly in the more advanced cities along the eastern seaboard. In Hunan Mao remained fairly isolated, but he enjoyed

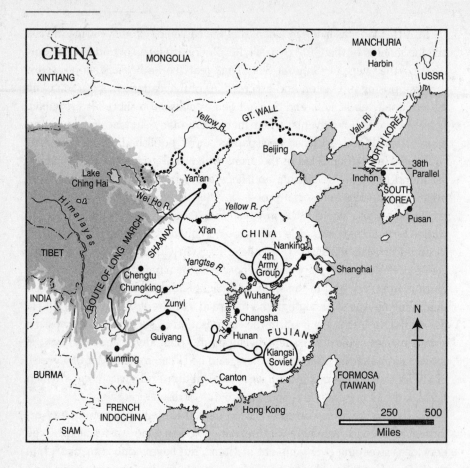

considerable success in organising the Cultural Book Society and this gave him useful financial independence. In 1920, the Chinese Communist Manifesto was published. Virtually a copy of Marx's original, it called for the overthrow of capitalism, the dictatorship of the proletariat, and the common ownership of the means of production. In the following year Mao attended the first Communist Party Congress in Shanghai, but the Chinese delegates clashed with an overbearing Russian agent and nothing was achieved.

Back in Changsha, Mao used his fierce energy in organising a mass literacy campaign and a self-study university. He used both of these to recruit communist supporters and his hard work spread his influence among many workers' organisations in Hunan. During the early 1920s, the Chinese communists kept up an uneasy alliance with the Kuomintang, the political organisation under Sun Yat Sen, and for a time Mao held a fairly senior position with the organisation in Shanghai.

He resigned all his positions in 1925, and returned to his home village in Hunan in order to carry out intensive research into the effectiveness of communist policies on peasant life. Throughout his life, he was renowned for the thorough and detailed reports he made on different aspects of communist policies, and this, on peasant life, was one of the most significant. It formed the basis of his philosophy of rural-based peasant revolution. At the same time, as a member of both organisations, he became increasingly critical of the link between the Communist Party and the Kuomintang, which, he felt, was biased towards the merchants and the military. Sun Yat Sen died in 1925 and Chiang Kai-Shek (subsequently Chiang) took over the leadership of the Kuomintang, aiming to overthrow the local warlords and re-unite the country. In spite of his suspicions, Mao initially supported this policy, and in Hunan he organised peasant forces in support of the successful Kuomintang campaign against the landlords who were driven out.

In 1927, Mao produced the first of his major reports about different aspects of communist policy. His report included the seizure of land by the peasants in the areas controlled by the communists; descriptions of landlords being humiliated in the villages; and women being freed from tyrannical husbands. Mao was now recognised as a senior figure in the Chinese Communist Party, and their expert on rural affairs. This proved to be a crucial year for both Mao and for the Communist Party. In the spring, Chiang and his allies among the warlords around Shanghai turned on the communists and killed thousands. Their organisation in the city was wiped out. Soon afterwards Chiang ordered the Kuomintang forces to overrun Hunan, and Mao, with just a handful of supporters, was driven to a very remote area.

This period of suffering and reverse prompted Mao to start thinking through his overall policy, which would ultimately bring him to power. In the autumn of 1927, he was involved with the Harvest Uprising in Hunan, when the peasants resisted the grain collectors of the Kuomintang. From these experiences, Mao envisaged a widespread revolutionary process based on peasant power, which would gradually encircle towns and cities from rural base areas. This became a critical factor in much of Mao's thought. He believed that all guerrilla units needed a rural base area, which, in his earthy way, he likened to someone's buttocks which enabled them to sit down and rest, instead of having to stand up or run all the time. It was at this time that he made the statement that 'political power is obtained from the barrel of a gun', but, significantly, added: 'Politicians must control the gun.'

The year 1927 saw the start of Mao's wandering in the wilderness – a period of anguish, suffering and death. He had already formulated his ideas on rural bases, and he strongly disagreed with official party policy, which was still influenced by Russian advisers. As his group moved about, he felt dangerously isolated, he thought his supporters were ill-disciplined and the masses cold and aloof. Mao had several small victories over Kuomintang forces but, in contrast, some larger communist units suffered serious defeats when they attempted to capture larger towns.

In the limited areas under his control, Mao carried out drastic land reforms, confiscating all land, and giving it directly to the peasants. This policy often created temporary local shortages, and he therefore started his campaign of guerrilla attacks, usually to obtain food, weapons and ammunition. This land policy was not universally popular, and when he moved to a different area he modified it in order to gain more general support.

While he was on the run from the Kuomintang and the warlords, he had been separated from his wife and family in Changsha. Then he heard that the warlords had captured Changsha and had shot his wife. He had, in fact, already met He Zizhen who became his lover and, over the following years, bore him five children. The Kuomintang had driven the main communist forces to a remote part of Fujian, nearly on the coast south east of Hunan, and here Mao had several bouts of sickness from tuberculosis and malaria. He was also seriously at odds with the communist hierarchy, and at times was virtually their prisoner.

By 1934 the Kuomintang were harassing the communists so severely that they decided to abandon the area near the coast. This was the start of the Long March, when tens of thousands of people moved about the country. Amid indescribable suffering, death and chaos they initially moved westwards almost to the Tibetan border. The Kuomintang troops attacked their defenceless masses with artillery and aircraft, causing horrendous casualties, but still they kept going. Battle casualties, sickness, desertion and death substantially reduced their numbers. It was impossible to organise food supplies for such numbers in the grim, cold, hostile landscape they traversed, and malnutrition and starvation added to the casualty lists. From the Tibetan border the mass of people moved slowly north, often milling about, uncertain of their direction, through desperate cold and storms, and often attacked by local tribesmen. By the autumn of 1935, after months and months of appalling suffering, when it was a struggle just to survive, Mao and He Zizhen – now pregnant again – with a tragically reduced number of followers, reached the north of Shaanxi province, near the Great Wall. Here, near Yan'an, in an arid, desolate and almost treeless area, they set up a base, living in caves which the local peasants had made in the soft local rock.

Having obtained a bleak but fairly secure base at Yan'an, Mao was able to take stock of his situation. On a personal level he heard through the communist authorities that his two sons from his first marriage had survived in Shanghai, and they soon came to Yan'an. By 1936, the Japanese had made deep incursions into China from their northern puppet state of Manchukuo, and also in the Yangtse valley. The Kuomintang were still trying to eliminate the hard-pressed communist forces and at the same time to fight the Japanese. In this situation Mao slowly came to the conclusion that instead of fighting each other they should unite in order to fight the Japanese.

In December 1936 he had a remarkable opportunity. Chiang had come to Xian, the capital of Shaanxi in order finally to wipe out Mao's base. Illustrating the continuing power of the warlords, an influential local leader, General Zhang, who had been wooed by both sides, now kidnapped Chiang and demanded a united front against the Japanese. Mao, despite his isolation at Yan'an, and his precarious situation, still held senior and important positions in the communist hierarchy. He took a prominent part in discussions with the party headquarters, with General Zhang and even with Moscow. Mao backed a proposal, which suggested a ceasefire between the communists and the Kuomintang, in order to give top priority to uniting against the Japanese intruders. The wily and evasive Chiang made enough promises to obtain his release, but his support for a united front against the Japanese remained lukewarm. Mao hoped that General Zhang and other warlords would use their military strength, to join up with both the communists and the Kuomintang to fight the Japanese, but this rarely occurred. While the support of Chiang was equivocal, Mao used the situation to strengthen his appeal to the whole of China to give support to the communists in the national struggle against Japan. His argument was sound, but in Yan'an he was far removed from the main Japanese armies, and the heaviest fighting still took place between the Japanese and the Kuomintang forces along the Yangtse river and around Shanghai. Then, in December 1937, the Japanese perpetrated the Rape of Nanking – which to this day shocks the civilised world – and they also inflicted a series of defeats on Chiang and the Kuomintang as the Chinese retreated towards Chungking.

Communist opposition to the Japanese had not been entirely eliminated, and several of the surviving soviets across central China waged an underground guerrilla war against the Japanese occupation forces. Despite this, and other opposition, the Japanese established a number of effective puppet regimes, to collect taxes and to fight the communists. For those Chinese who wished to take a more active role in fighting the Japanese, some went to Yunnan near the border with Burma, some to the Kuomintang centre west of Changsha at Chungking (Chongqing) and some to Mao's centre at Yan'an.

As the military situation stabilised, Mao in Yan'an came under increasing pressure and criticism from other communist leaders, and was often blamed for many of the past disasters which had led to the death or imprisonment of tens of thousands of Chinese people. Younger members who had been to Moscow for training often supported this criticism. Mao therefore concentrated on the writings of Marx and Lenin and the application of communist theory. With his powerful energy, determination and persistence, he now undertook to adapt the ideas of Marx and Lenin to the Chinese situation, where the majority of the people were peasants and not the industrial proletariat. A brilliant young Chinese scholar called Chen, who had been trained in both Moscow and Beijing, and who became Mao's secretary and confidant, now assisted him in this monumental task.

In his writings at this time, Mao stressed the importance of the Chinese Red Army, but repeated that the Party must command the gun, and the gun must never be allowed to command the Party. The Red Army had played a significant part in supporting a policy of loyalty, discipline, self-sacrifice and in gaining mass backing for the Party. Mao was prominent in emphasising the need for the army to be thoroughly indoctrinated, because there were always those who might betray the cause and there was always the danger of soldiers deserting.

When he was starting his great ideological task, he faced serious practical problems. He wanted his base in Yan'an to be a model communist society, but the difficulties were enormous. The whole area was poverty stricken and the marauding Japanese forces, along with the doubtful support or hidden opposition of the Kuomintang, increased its problems. It became very difficult to give recruits effective indoctrination and military training.

His substantial writings on military issues were based both on his harrowing experiences of the Long March, and also on his plans for the war against Japan. There are many published editions of these works, but the most significant for a study of guerrilla war are *Basic Tactics* and *Guerrilla War*. They will be considered in that order.

Mao compiled the book *Basic Tactics* from lectures he gave to communist recruits at Yan'an, and he intended them to be basic. He emphasised that for a guerrilla fighter any weapon will suffice – a kitchen knife, an axe or even a stone. Through all his lectures, he stressed the importance of strict discipline at all times, especially on the march and at halts, and the need to be ready to disperse if a fight was unsuccessful. Ambush was an essential tactic for all guerrilla activity, and could be used defensively if a unit was being pursued, or offensively, when very careful preparation was needed.

While Mao was producing these lectures, Japanese forces controlled much of China, and he gave advice on how to counter enemy occupation. When facing an enemy advance, guerrilla forces must empty the countryside, by hiding, moving or destroying everything – food, stores, weapons and grain. Women and children should be left behind in the villages, as a possible source of intelligence and information. Mao drew very extensively on the writings of Sun Tzu, though he does not always acknowledge this openly. For example *Basic Tactics* includes the following:

When the enemy retreats, we advance
When he halts, we harass him
Make him uneasy day and night
Exterminate a weak enemy
To gain territory is no cause for joy,
To lose territory is no cause for sorrow
The only crucial thing is to destroy the enemy
Always use surprise, always be secret
Develop a resolute spirit

These precepts were taken almost exactly from Sun Tzu.

Such general ideas were interspersed with very specific rules. The task of a guerrilla unit is to destroy roads, railways, telephone and telegraph wires, supply depots, stores and equipment; to capture couriers; to organise aggressive cavalry and infantry patrols. Units must have a political director to control training on political issues, as well as an engineer to destroy installations, and a nurse to help the wounded. Units must always guard against desertion.

Mao gave clear instructions about spies, and the need for accurate reports on the size and strength of enemy units. He believed that a good and reliable informer should be well paid.

141

He reverted frequently to the ambush – 'the habitual tactic of the guerrilla'. He issued guidelines on the ambush of transport which, in the early days, was essential because the top priority was the capture of food, weapons and ammunition, rather than the defeat of the enemy.

In Mao's general advice on training, political issues seem, if anything, more important than military. The good government of communists must be stressed in contrast to the ravages of the enemy. The political aim is to raise the masses, and encourage them to accept communist leadership, therefore you must emphasise national consciousness and patriotism.

He strongly advocated a code known as 'The Three Rules and Eight Remarks':

Rules
All actions are subject to command
Do not steal from the people
Be neither selfish nor unjust

Remarks
Replace the door when you leave the house
Roll up the bedding where you have slept
Be courteous
Be honest in your transactions
Return what you borrow
Replace what you break
Do not bathe in the presence of women
Do not without authority search those you arrest

The constant repetition of rules was accompanied by encouragement to discuss and analyse either victory or defeat, and achieve maximum publicity after victory. Instructions even included advice on telling jokes – 'not too obscene'.

Basic Tactics, which Mao outlined after his years of fighting against the Kuomintang and during the Long March, gave sound advice specifically about guerrilla fighting. His more mature thesis *Guerrilla War*, published in 1937, was of wider relevance and applied particularly to the planned struggle against the Japanese occupation of China. The preamble focused on this: guerrilla war is valid when a weaker country is overrun by a stronger, but guerrilla units should develop and join up with regular forces in order to win a national revolutionary war. Guerrilla war is not an independent form of war, but a part of total war of the oppressed against the oppressor. It cannot succeed alone. Guerrilla war must be conducted as a part of national policy, and the political role must always have priority.

Mao carefully listed the essential steps for the conduct of successful guerrilla war:

Arousing and organising the people
Achieving internal unification politically
Establishing bases
Equipping forces
Recovering national strength
Destroying the enemy's national strength
Regaining lost territory

He again stressed that all units must have both political and military leadership. Leaders must be resolute, loyal, sincere and robust, well-educated in revolutionary technique, and able to instil discipline. Without a political goal, guerrilla war, which depends on the sympathy, assistance and co-operation of the people, will fail. He faced critics who maintained that guerrilla war was for vagabonds and bandits, but argued that while some groups contained those elements, a good guerrilla unit will use their skills but discipline and educate the bandits.

In a crucial paragraph on guerrilla tactics, he virtually quotes directly from Sun Tzu:

'In guerrilla warfare, select the tactic of seeming to come from the east and attacking from the west; avoid the solid, attack the hollow; attack, withdraw, deliver a lightning blow, seek a lightning decision. When guerrillas engage a stronger enemy, they withdraw when he advances; harass him when he stops; strike him when he is weary; pursue him when he withdraws. In guerrilla strategy, the enemy's rear, flanks and other vulnerable spots are his vital points, and there he must be harassed, attacked, dispersed, exhausted and annihilated.'

Mao listed examples of successful guerrilla war, including the Red Guerrillas in the Russian Revolution, the struggle of the Abyssinians against the Italian occupiers – the Italian invasion was in November 1935 – and the guerrilla attacks against the Japanese in Manchuria. All these were examples where the guerrillas had mass support. He quoted Clausewitz – supporting the theory that guerrillas alone cannot win a war, but he added that without guerrilla warfare the Japanese could not be defeated. 'Every period must have a new theory of war,' he declared. Guerrilla war is different from normal war, because of constant movement and activity, because units vary from a few men to thousands, and because there is no direct command control.

Mao defines the responsibility of guerrillas to exterminate small forces of the enemy, to harass and weaken larger units, to attack lines of communication and supply, to establish rural bases in the rear of the enemy lines, to force the enemy to disperse his troops, and to co-ordinate with the regular forces. Guerrilla units must be 'like innumerable gnats', which ultimately exhaust the enemy.

Having given examples of guerrilla activity supported by the mass of the people, he gave others to show that guerrillas had to be ancillary to regular forces, and he quotes particularly the co-operation between the Cossacks and the regular Russian armies in their attacks on the French armies during Napoleon's retreat from Moscow. In contrast, he mentions the Boxer Rebellion of 1899, when there were many guerrilla attacks against foreign interlopers in China, but these were not linked to regular forces and were less successful. He next gives examples from the guerrilla attacks on the Japanese between 1931 and 1933, which were not co-ordinated with regulars, but more importantly, did not have the necessary political leadership and guidance.

He posed the question 'can victory be attained by guerrilla operations?'. Then he assessed the wider factors in the Japanese situation. Japan had the advantage of technology and industrial power, but its forces were widely spread, and it did not have enough men to hold down the whole of China. Therefore guerrilla attacks on Japanese lines of communication are crucial but they must be united with the strength of the armies. This was written at the start of the uneasy alliance with the Kuomintang against the Japanese, so Mao played down the communist ideology and, instead, stressed that there must be a united front against the common enemy.

In considering the ideal make-up of guerrilla groups, Mao stated 'guerrilla hostilities are the university of war'. Units could form from regular forces, from local militia, from enemy deserters, or even from bandits, but to succeed they must have the support of the mass of the people.

He stressed that the control and organisation of guerrilla groups was vital, and in any given area they must come under political and military commanders. They in turn should divide the area into smaller units, and appoint a committee to decide on guerrilla attacks. If there is sufficient support, smaller units could build up into brigades or divisions. The smallest viable unit would be about ten men armed with some rifles or any available weapons and, where possible, units should receive supplies from the central government.

Guerrilla units should be backed up by anti-Japanese defence units, whose role was to obtain information, arrest traitors, prevent enemy propaganda, take tea and rice to the fighters, and act as stretcher bearers – 'deceive, hinder and harass the enemy'. When a unit is strong enough it should establish a secure supply base, but initially the enemy should be the main source of supply for weapons and ammunition. Later an armoury is needed for the repair of weapons, the production of ammunition and of bombs for demolition. The largest units will have telephone and radio communication, medical facilities, and a small propaganda department with basic printing facilities. He stressed that 'military action is a method to attain a political goal'. Having covered almost every eventuality, he did add, with a flicker of honesty and humour, that 'we must be good at running away because we do it so often'.

In summing up, Mao affirmed that because China was such a vast country a protracted war was inevitable, and the basis of success was to arm the people, to organise self-defence units, to train guerrilla bands, to encourage political awareness, and to increase martial ardour.

The uneasy alliance with the Kuomintang against the Japanese was difficult to enforce, and in some areas their local rivalry took precedence over any offensive against the invader. Mao was still isolated in Yan'an, and far removed from the most serious fighting, which was undertaken by Chiang's forces. The Japanese appeared gradually to slow their advance and to consolidate their positions in China, until, in December 1941, the world understood why.

The Japanese attack on Pearl Harbor brought no immediate change to Mao's situation, although he was occasionally approached by American agents interested in encouraging the opposition to Japan. During these years, he immeasurably strengthened his personal position, by his energy and determined persistence, backed up by the whole apparatus of communist propaganda, which stretched from Yan'an as far as occupied Shanghai. At the same time, while his real power increased and he gained in confidence, he became more arrogant, more critical of any intellectual opposition, more dogmatic, and more crude and vulgar – as if he wanted to emphasise his peasant origins. These were ominous signs with grave significance for the future.

The Japanese attack on Pearl Harbor and on the European possessions in the Far East brought the US and Britain into the war, which China, in lonely isolation, had been waging against Japan since the early 1930s. The Japanese had driven Chiang and the Kuomintang far to the west, and Chiang's capital – having as he said 'exchanged space for time' – was at Chungking. This brought him substantial advantages.

After the British were bundled out of Burma in the initial Japanese attack in 1942, while the British regrouped and prepared to counterattack, the Americans poured vast resources into backing up Chiang's forces in north Burma. The American commander, 'Vinegar Joe' Stilwell, was given command of several of Chiang's divisions operating from the northern outpost of Fort Hertz. His aim was to drive south from there and open the old Burma Road up to Kunming so that military supplies could be sent up to support Chiang's campaign against the Japanese. Before the road could be opened, the Americans mounted a remarkable campaign to airlift supplies on a massive scale, over 'The Hump' to Kunming, in order to help Chiang. While the Americans devoted men, aircraft and millions of dollars' worth of supplies to encourage Chiang, he, with total duplicity, did his best to avoid battles with the Japanese, and, instead, stockpiled most of the American equipment. He hoped that America and Britain would defeat Japan, and when the war was over, he would be able to use all the military resources provided by the Americans to defeat Mao and the communists. Stilwell quickly saw through Chiang's scheme, and, perhaps justifiably, referred to Chiang either as 'the rattlesnake' or the 'bloody little peanut'. Mao enjoyed no such outside strategic advantages, but with the communist propaganda apparatus behind his policy of gaining the backing of the people, he laid the foundations of much future success.

Because of Mao's tireless work, by August 1945, when the atom bomb finished the war, the communists controlled an area with a population of over 100,000,000 people, and both the Kuomintang and the communists were ready to take advantage of any Japanese withdrawal.

After Hiroshima – 6 August 1945 – Chiang, using his substantial American armoury, advanced eastwards from Chungking towards Canton, and then northwards towards Shanghai. Mao had more advantages in the north. Russia declared war on Japan two days after Hiroshima, and rapidly overran Japanese occupied territory. The Russian forces readily handed over huge arsenals of military *matériel* to the Chinese communist armies, and they often drove out the Japanese and then handed over the area to their new Chinese allies. In Manchuria, the Russians transported over 100,000 Chinese troops to occupy a large area of the country, previously held by the Japanese.

In spite of these deep-seated rivalries, both America and Russia encouraged the idea of a coalition government for China. In September 1945 Mao went to Chungking to discuss the possibility of a national army and the long-term future. Even during these talks both sides were secretly planning to double-cross the other.

Mao planned a big expansion from his strong base in Manchuria, to take over rural areas, to gain peasant support, and to encourage mass enrolment. Only moderate land reform was introduced, in order not to alienate too many of the landowners. There was a conscious policy to attract people away from the Kuomintang, but even in Manchuria it did well and captured some areas from the communists. By 1946 the fragile alliance was seen as a sham, and communist propaganda began to attack the Kuomintang and the Americans equally, and used every incident to inflame the situation. In north China, action on land reform became increasingly violent, and thousands of landlords were murdered.

The uneasy posturing continued until September 1947 when, from Yan'an, Mao announced a clear policy which was a virtual declaration of war on the Kuomintang. He called on communists to launch a nationwide offensive; to move out of their bases and, in each area captured, to form new bases and to give top priority to destroying the enemy and seizing weapons. Then, reverting to the Sun Tzu style, he advised fight no battle unprepared, fight no battle you are not sure of winning, be relentless and give the enemy no chance to recover.

This policy proved very successful and the Kuomintang was driven out of the whole of Manchuria in one year. In January 1949 Mao's forces captured Beijing. As the Kuomintang authority collapsed, the chaos and corruption of their rule was revealed and the people turned violently against them. The capture of Nanking, Changsha and Shanghai soon followed, and, on 1 October 1949, at the Great Tiananmen Gate in Beijing, Mao announced the formation of the People's Republic of China.

In December 1949, Mao, with a substantial delegation, went to visit Moscow. He had inherited a country almost completely destroyed and in chaos. It had suffered nearly fifty years of fighting under the warlords, the destructive rule of the Kuomintang and Japanese occupation. There was no country-wide administration or currency, inflation raged out of control, transport, especially the railways, had been destroyed – often by communist guerrillas – and millions of people had been displaced. Many schools and universities had been destroyed. Faced with such a critical situation, Mao varied his policies and included bourgeois elements, in order to gain the support of professionals, intellectuals and the business community.

During the bitter years of struggle before 1949, Mao had little time or inclination to consider foreign policy, but now he had to face intractable problems. In Mongolia, in Tibet and in some of the vast areas of Central Asia, demands for independence were growing. The British had returned to Hong Kong, and the French to Indochina, while the defeated forces of the Kuomintang under Chiang now occupied Taiwan. In spite of his massive deception of the US during the war the Americans now strongly assisted Chiang's defence, and backed his claim to represent China at the newly established United Nations. All these problems had to be discussed with Stalin.

In spite of Stalin's immense prestige after his victorious leadership of the Soviet Union in the overthrow of Nazi Germany, this prolonged meeting between the leadership of the two countries was not conducted in a warm, co-operative atmosphere. Stalin was suspicious of Mao's claim to interpret Marxist doctrine, and there were other areas of tension if not of dispute. Mao stressed that China needed years of peace to restore the country and especially the economy, and he sought Stalin's opinion on the likelihood of war, because he had to decide on whether to develop China's industries along the eastern coast or in the interior. Stalin had concluded a treaty with Chiang in 1945, and they decided to let this stand, though Stalin agreed to withdraw from Port Arthur and to hand over the Manchurian railways to China when requested. China did obtain a loan of 300,000,000 dollars but Stalin refused to assist in any attempted re-conquest of Taiwan.

Mao then returned to Beijing to tackle the mammoth task of Chinese reconstruction. The reconstruction had to work in parallel with the implementation of radical communist policies. In rural areas, land reform and land redistribution had top priority, while in the towns and cities industrial development and the state control of the means of production came first. At the same time, central and regional administration had to be set up, and the majority of schools and universities rebuilt.

Mao constantly stressed the significance of party propaganda, whether at national level or in a small rural group, and this lay behind his decision to replace many of the ancient and exquisite cultural treasures in the walled city of Beijing by modern industrial development and by the establishment of Tiananmen Square for massive party rallies.

Soon after his trip to Moscow, Mao had to divert his attention from the daunting task of reconstruction to the less welcome issue of Korea. His lack of experience in this field caused him to make several serious blunders. The former Japanese colony of Korea had, in 1945, under pressure from the USSR and the USA, been divided by the 38th parallel. Kim Il Sung, backed by Stalin, established a communist state in the north, while the south, under American influence, became a democracy. In 1950, it was rumoured that Stalin had agreed to an attack by North Korea, and this posed a serious dilemma for Mao. In Beijing, there was lengthy and anguished debate about whether to support Kim Il Sung. Military leaders demanded Soviet equipment and air support before China took part. Others argued that the war would destroy the more important progress on national reconstruction. In the end, Mao took the decision that China had to help a communist neighbour and to secure its frontiers, and he sent back thousands of Korean soldiers who were serving in the Chinese forces.

The military showdown came after a prolonged effort by the United Nations to re-unify the whole of Korea, but this had been resisted by both north and south, each hoping eventually to take control of the peninsula. The attack by North Korean armies on 25 June 1950 – when most of the South Koreans and their American advisers were away for the weekend – achieved complete surprise.

Stalin had encouraged Mao to take part in the Korean campaign but, both directly and indirectly, he failed to support him. Mao had calculated that South Korea could be overrun before there was any reaction from the USA or the outside world, but because the Soviet Union was boycotting the UN at that time, and was not present to use its veto in the Security Council, the US rapidly gained support for a UN force to oppose the invasion. General MacArthur, the American hero of the Pacific War, took command of five UN divisions. These were weak and not fully trained, and were rapidly pushed back, until they finally stood firm on a perimeter around Pusan in the extreme south. The only effective retaliation by the UN during this period of defeat came with a successful amphibious landing at Inchon on the west coast, where a fairly strong base was established.

Mao had 40 divisions in the Chinese 4th Army Group, located just north of the Yalu River, which divided China from Korea, but he had not yet committed them. He was still undecided when, in September 1950, UN troops, who had been substantially reinforced, broke out of the Pusan perimeter and drove back the North Korean forces, advancing as rapidly as they had previously retreated. They soon reached the Inchon base and advanced as far as the 38th parallel. Then MacArthur raised the grave issue of whether he should stop there.

This created a world wide crisis. Mao, through Chou en Lai, the Chinese prime minister, warned that if American troops (a significant phrase) crossed the 38th parallel, the Chinese would act accordingly. Britain and the US disagreed strongly over this issue. Britain, extremely apprehensive about Stalin's possible aggression in Europe, felt that Chinese involvement should be avoided at all costs. Eventually, the Security Council, under US pressure, decided to invade North Korea, in order to unite the whole peninsula as a democratic – i.e., western – republic.

Mao was not bluffing. As the South Korean and UN forces advanced across the dividing line, General P'eng advanced with 130,000 Chinese troops, pretending to be volunteers, so that China could at least appear neutral. By the same token, Stalin reneged on his promise of air cover for the Chinese volunteers so that he, too, could keep up his pretence of neutrality. Despite these setbacks General P'eng adapted rapidly. He used well-tried guerrilla tactics, moving his troops at night, and making swift advances. He achieved surprise, fought largely at night, and then, keeping to guerrilla principles, withdrew with captured weapons and ammunition.

MacArthur replied to the Chinese advance with 12 divisions, but P'eng had 30 divisions and handled them effectively. He drove the UN forces back over the 38th parallel, until, about 100 miles south of that, a fairly stable line was established. The more static type of warfare caused heavy casualties among the Chinese, and in January 1951, in an unusually severe winter, because they had neither suitable clothes nor equipment, they lost thousands of men to cold, starvation and frostbite. The UN forces slowly moved north once again to the 38th parallel. In spite of his appalling losses, P'eng attacked again in the spring of 1951, but powerful UN air attacks halted his advance, and he was unable to keep up his momentum. There ensued a type of static trench warfare, while bitter divisions prolonged and complicated the peace negotiations – e.g. Mao was outraged when some Chinese prisoners wanted to be repatriated to Taiwan, and the UN tried unsuccessfully to achieve a quick victory by air bombardment. Eventually, the spiralling costs of the continuing conflict forced both sides to make a new effort, and, in July 1953, an armistice was agreed. One ironic result of the Korean War was that Truman taught MacArthur Mao's adage that the Party must control the gun.

The war damaged Mao both personally and professionally – he had what is believed to have been a nervous breakdown, he lost his son in the fighting, and the expense and huge loss of life, with casualties estimated at nearly one million, seriously set back the progress of reconstruction. His guerrilla instincts did not serve him well in conducting a major war at the top level, and he was further harmed by the duplicity of his supposed ally Stalin. Finally, he was humiliated by the UN seat for China being allocated to Chiang in Taiwan. Ironically, fifty years later, with the Korean problems still unsolved, the situation still threatens the stability of the Far East.

In spite of his preoccupation with the war, Mao launched the reconstruction plan in 1950, with land reform given the top priority. Carried out vigorously over the next three years, it is estimated that nearly half of the cultivated land in China was redistributed and a million landlords executed. Land redistribution was the first part of a fundamental reorganisation of Chinese society. Under the overall plan, the state imposed compulsory purchase of grain from the peasants, in order to provide cheap food for the industrial workers in the cities, who were provided with accommodation, together with free medical care and free education.

In the rural areas, peasants were graded into rich, medium and poor, and frequently the rich peasant lost everything including his life. Clearly, the rich peasants were the ablest and most competent farmers in their villages, and soon the production of grain began to decline. The land reforms also included the establishment of peasant co-operatives, and while in the towns it was intended that the workers would be part of the system for life, so, in the villages the peasants would be more or less tied to their village.

The end of the Korean War in 1953 brought dramatic changes for Mao. Stalin died in that year, making Mao the most formidable figure in the communist world. By this time, most of the industry and agriculture in China were under state control, and Mao was ready for the next step. In 1957 he went to Moscow – his last trip abroad – and Khrushchev came to Beijing, but their tense relationship, which started with Khrushchev's denunciation of Stalin and, by implication, Mao as well, did not improve. In considering his new policies Mao distanced himself from the Russian models.

The clash with Russia lay at the back of his thinking when, in 1957, he launched the Great Leap Forward. He saw this almost in the guerrilla terms of human will, enthusiasm and tenacity and he was highly critical of managers, experts and intellectuals. He aimed to carry out a major assault on China's pitifully backward economy, and to do this by using China's plentiful supply of labour. At the same time, he made another famous

speech 'The Hundred Flowers in the Garden', which encouraged intellectuals to speak out. He was horrified when a wave of criticism swept the
country, and swiftly took strong measures to silence the critics.

The Great Leap Forward made an immediate impact in the rural areas,
when the recently established co-operatives were now dragooned into
20,000 vast communes, where all the land was owned by the state, people
were fed from communal kitchens and the state provided education and
medical care. While the commune system was being set up, Mao launched
a large number of large-scale but senseless projects, which achieved little,
but took thousands of labourers away from the urgent task of growing food.
At this time, the most popular economic theory, in both east and west,
proposed that for a backward country to develop, it needed industry, and
industry needed steel. Economists argued that industrial potential and
achievement should be measured in steel production. This idea lay behind
Mao's decision that a part of the Great Leap Forward, would be to
encourage peasants to produce steel in backyard furnaces. This once again
took labour away from food production, and nearly all the steel produced
by the peasants was absolutely useless.

There is little doubt that before the end of his life, Mao was virtually
insane, and 1958 could be the year when his decline started. He made a
speech extolling the marvellous achievements of the rural communes,
and he envisaged China producing so much food that no one would
have to pay for it and the huge surplus could be sent to feed the poor of
the world. This magnificent bounty would also extend to textiles, and
then everyone would be clothed by the state. Within a couple of years of
this speech, the Great Leap Forward had produced a famine in China,
one of the great disasters of the country's history. It killed more people
even than Stalin's policy of collectivisation in Russia. In some areas, half
of the population starved to death, and the total estimate of deaths from
the famine exceeds 30 million people. In spite of the countrywide catas-
trophes, the rural policies continued. At one point during the famine,
Mao blamed it on the sparrows, and encouraged everyone to kill all the
sparrows. In spite of starvation in the countryside, the state – like the
British government during the Irish famine – took grain away from the
villages for export.

By 1961, even Mao and the top hierarchy were aware of the magnitude
of the disaster, and slowly things began to change. Peasants who had gone
to the towns were sent back to their villages. Communal living was abandoned, and the cultivation of private plots was encouraged. Deep and bitter

divisions emerged between Mao's group and his increasingly severe critics. Mao himself became more and more cut off from reality, as he travelled from one luxury guesthouse to another, in his private train escorted by comely young women who provided sexual favours.

Having come close to destroying his country with the Great Leap Forward, Mao now again used his simplistic guerrilla views to decide his foreign policy. His almost complete ignorance of the outside world – he never left China except for two brief visits to Moscow – led him into major blunders. From the days of the Korean War, he saw American imperialism as wholly evil and implacably hostile to China, and he believed the very existence of China was at stake. He believed that his ideas of revolution could be applied to Asia, Africa and Latin America, where he expected the masses to rise up with revolutionary fervour. This whole policy included the basic assumption from his early days of guerrilla struggle, that the rural masses would rise up and encircle the cities. He even believed that the European working classes would rise up in response to his clarion call.

As his grip on reality weakened, Mao was still going to perpetrate one more disaster – the Great Proletarian Cultural Revolution – launched in November 1965. This great movement was sparked off, it is believed, by an opera performed in Beijing in which the hero dared to challenge the Emperor. In his paranoid state, Mao saw this as a thinly-veiled attack on him, and became more and more distrustful of his Party colleagues and of intellectuals. In this situation he turned to young people and encouraged them to attack their teachers, and children their parents. Groups of Red Guards sprang up all over China, and in August 1966 Mao reviewed a million Red Guards in Tiananmen Square. He saw this movement as an opportunity to eliminate some of his enemies, and to reassert his leadership. To support his claim that he was fit and well and could deal with his enemies, he took his celebrated swim in the Yangtse. Meanwhile the Red Guards spread mayhem and destruction across the whole country. Jung Chang, in her brilliant book The Wild Swans, vividly describes these ghastly days. Another commentator wrote, 'it is Mao gone mad, but it is Mao just the same.' Just to make sure his message got across, over 700,000,000 copies of Mao's Little Red Book were published to spread the cult of the Great Helmsman.

The chaos created by the Red Guards threatened everyone. Even Chou en Lai and Den Xiaoping, seen as sane moderates during this period of madness, came under attack. Ironically, Mao's last wife, Jiang Qing, originally considered just a bimbo, became a powerful operator during these last confused days and was a ruthless member of the Gang of Four. Mao continued to travel about the country, becoming more paranoid about security. In 1971, he became suspicious of Lin Biao, who had supported Mao throughout all his struggles, from his guerrilla days, and had considerable influence with the army. Later that year, Lin Biao and all his family were killed in a plane crash – almost certainly by deliberate sabotage.

The Cultural Revolution created serious problems between China and Russia, with frequent incidents along their northern border. This was the main reason why Mao made the final effort to impress his people. Partly to counterbalance Russia, but also to prove himself on the world stage, he invited President Nixon to Beijing – both principals having their own domestic reasons for this bizarre meeting. During Nixon's visit, Mao was too ill to stand up unaided, and he deteriorated further until his death in 1976.

Towards the end of his life Mao made grievous mistakes, which cost millions of lives, but in spite of his ultimate madness he is the man who, starting as a guerrilla leader, eventually brought unity to China and had the power and the ideology to change society. While he made appalling errors, he did bring vast improvements to millions of Chinese people and he never forgot the guerrilla principles which brought him to power.

TITO: FROM GUERRILLA
TO WORLD STATESMAN

Like several men who made their mark during World War II, Hitler and Mao among them, Josip Broz – subsequently called by his later nickname of Tito – had a hard time as a child, with a drunken father and a more sympathetic mother. His parents, father a Croat and mother a Slovenian Roman Catholic, illustrated some of the problems he would later have to face.

Tito left school at the age of twelve in 1904 and was apprenticed as a mechanic. In 1910, he visited Zagreb and was amazed at the city's prosperity and elegance, then, venturing further afield, he found work with the car firm Daimler near Vienna. He was called up into the Austrian Army and soon became a sergeant major. When war came, after the assassination of the Austrian Archduke Franz Ferdinand in Sarajevo by the Serb Gavrilo Princip, Tito served in the mountains of eastern Hungary, and often led fighting patrols against the Russians. In 1915, in a clash with a Russian unit, he was wounded and taken off to Russia as a prisoner of war. The prison conditions were not too severe, and he was able to learn Russian and travel about. A friend helped him to reach Petrograd, and there, gripped by the excitement of the times, he joined the Bolsheviks. He was in Omsk when the White Russians captured it, then he joined a band of nomadic horsemen, married Polka, a beautiful Russian woman and returned to Petrograd. Having witnessed the foundation of the Soviet state he became a dedicated communist, determined to spread the revolutionary ideals.

In 1920, with Polka now pregnant, he returned to the newly formed Yugoslavia – the south Slav state. Historic ethnic rivalries between Serbs, Croats, Slovenes and Bosnians, and deep religious divisions between Orthodox, Muslim and Roman Catholic, still smouldered. The Serb King Alexander ruled from the Serb city of Belgrade. This gave the Serbs a certain arrogance. In 1920, in the first election in Yugoslavia, the communists won over 50 seats; Tito joined the Yugoslav Communist Party and became a staunch supporter of Soviet influence. His experience of the revolution in Russia gave him great clout, and he rose quickly in the metalworkers' union. In the 1920s there were many strikes because of high unemployment and this resulted in the Communist Party being outlawed. Tito soon discovered that there were endless bitter arguments in the party and very little was achieved.

He gained steady promotion in the Party and worked for a time in a shipyard on the Adriatic coast of Croatia until, having organised a strike, which gained better wages, he was sacked. He then returned to Zagreb in 1926. Now an aggressive campaigner for the Communist Party, he was imprisoned. He demanded a trial, and then appealed so that he was released until his appeal could be heard. The party remained hopelessly divided, but, after another crisis, Tito became secretary and used his strong influence to end factional strife.

Ethnic divisions and the demand for a separate Croat state nearly caused the break up of Yugoslavia during the 1920s. Tito was considered a dangerous agitator and was again caught by the police. In court he denounced the bourgeois regime and he was imprisoned for five years. As in Russia, the conditions were not too severe, and he was able to read widely; his mechanical skills helped him to obtain various useful jobs, and he even established a communist cell in the prison.

In 1934, just when Tito was expecting his release, the Croat underground movement, the Ustase, carried out their most daring action. King Alexander was on an official visit to France and, just as he was landing at Marseilles they assassinated him. King Peter, aged 11, succeeded to the throne with his cousin Paul as Regent. Italy, Hungary and other greedy neighbours viewed with relish the possible break-up of Yugoslavia.

After the assassination, security became much tighter and Tito, for his own safety, was sent to the exiled communist HQ near Vienna, but then he was sent back under cover to Zagreb, to organise the party. He was able to build up a new organisation with able younger men, who followed his lead and tried to eliminate the ethnic divisions. The Serb regime in Belgrade was becoming increasingly unpopular because of corruption and injustice, and a wide cross-section of people began to turn to the communists as the best alternative, and because they were the only country-wide political party. Tito had done good work in organising communist activities, but as the threat of the security forces increased, and because he was so well known, it was decided that he should be sent to Moscow.

In Moscow, during 1935, he worked in the Comintern HQ, at a time when Russia had joined the League of Nations, and had modified some of its revolutionary aims. Here he led a lonely life, because his wife had divorced him, but he read widely, including Clausewitz and other military experts. While he was in Moscow, he observed the change in Soviet foreign policy, which began to soft-pedal its anti-bourgeois stance and to stress the anti-fascist drive. Tito still held his passionate belief in the communist cause, but now he was slightly disillusioned and began to notice Stalin's arrogance and his contempt for minor countries like Yugoslavia. Tito returned to Yugoslavia in 1936, to be the second in command of the party, but there were still acrimonious divisions and much of the party organisation had been destroyed.

After he returned home, Tito had to arrange the Yugoslav support for the left-wing groups in the Spanish Civil War. As the fascist forces advanced, with increasing help from Hitler and Mussolini, the communists felt that they could not just stand aside. By the end of 1936, the Soviet Union sent substantial help to the International Brigades, which were able to save Madrid from Franco's attack. Despite this success, the left-wing forces were deeply divided, and the communists, while attacking Franco, also fought against the Anarchists and Trotskyites. Tito's organisation sent more than 1,500 volunteers to Spain and they suffered very heavy losses in killed and wounded. Many ended up in concentration camps. Tito himself spent considerable time in Paris helping his volunteers, but he was always in danger and always on the run. He felt disillusioned when Stalin, seeing that he could not match the forces sent by Hitler and Mussolini, cynically pulled out.

In 1937, the year of the great purges by Stalin, Tito was summoned to Moscow. Many party leaders summoned in this way had just disappeared, but Tito was to be promoted. He became Secretary General of the Yugoslav Communist Party. The HQ had been in exile in Vienna, but Tito, in spite of the added danger, moved it back to Zagreb, saying, 'even if you risk your life, it is better to be in the country with the people.'

Tito, who had charisma and total faith in his cause, was determined to unite the party under his control, and he created a strong team of able young men, under firm discipline. He had to travel widely, and always in secret, in order to extend communist activities across the whole country and he used a number of aliases. He often appeared as an engineer, working for the ministry of forestry and mines. Like Michael Collins, he was always well dressed, and he travelled first class. Many people were disgusted by the corruption of the Serb government, and Tito found it fairly easy to set up cadres of sound and reliable supporters – even in the armed forces. Early in 1939, he visited Moscow, where he felt he was in real danger from the ruthless brutality of Stalin's regime. Back in Europe, he was still on the run, and to return home he went by sea to Le Havre, then to Paris, Vienna, and, finally, by boat to Yugoslavia. The war was getting closer. Hitler had already taken Austria and Czechoslovakia, and in April 1939 Mussolini invaded Albania.

During the fateful summer of 1939, Stalin was considering an alliance with Britain, but he calculated that if war then came he would bear the brunt of it. In contrast, an alliance with Germany could give him expansion into Poland and a buffer against the west. Therefore, for cynical self-interest and to the consternation of his anti-fascist supporters throughout the world, he agreed the Nazi-Soviet pact on 23 August 1939. War came a week later, and with Hitler he carved up the unfortunate Poland, which Britain and France could do little to help. With the ominous presence of the Nazis looming over Yugoslavia, Tito faced serious dilemmas. He again travelled to Moscow in December 1939 to discuss these problems, but received little help. Still travelling incognito and with another false passport, he returned via Istanbul.

Soon afterwards, he called a conference in Zagreb for the Yugoslav Communist Party to discuss the dramatic events that had taken place. Throughout the conference he emphasised that Yugoslavia must stay neutral in what was an imperialist war between Britain, France and Germany. At the same time, after the swift collapse of France and the Scandinavian countries, the question arose whether Germany now had designs on the Balkans, where Hungary and Bulgaria were under intense Axis pressure. Within Yugoslavia the pre-war tensions had only worsened. The right-wing Ustase were still working for a separate Croatia and now had Italian support. Serb-Croat rivalry remained bitter.

Hitler had, in fact, decided to attack and destroy Yugoslavia, to create a semi-independent Croatia, to occupy Serbia, and to put Montenegro under Italian control. Early in 1941 he put the Regent Paul under intense pressure to join the Axis, and when he gave in a popular outcry overthrew the government. Hitler, with most of Europe at his feet, was outraged and ordered the immediate destruction of Yugoslavia. On 6 April 1941, the Luftwaffe bombed Belgrade and, by 17 April, German forces, assisted by Italian, Hungarian and Bulgarian troops, had defeated the Yugoslav Army and driven the king and government into exile. Hitler announced the creation of an independent Croatia, and installed a fascist puppet, Pavelic. He, with ominous significance for the future, started to clear Croatia of Serbs, Jews and gypsies. He gave the Ustase free rein. Further south, Italy took over Montenegro and Dalmatia and added them to Albania, which had been occupied in 1939. Throughout the country, the Axis hunted down known communist leaders – particularly Tito. The situation changed dramatically when, on 22 June 1941, Hitler launched Barbarossa, the massive attack on the Soviet Union. This appeared to take the Soviets by surprise and destroyed over 1,000 aircraft on the first day. Moscow appealed for help to fight 'the German and Italian fascist bandits'. Tito issued a call to arms to support 'our socialist fatherland'.

The attack on Russia was the signal for Tito to start guerrilla war and to organise his partisan detachments across the country, all based on the communist cells he had so carefully built up. Initial raids often aimed to capture weapons, because some groups had taken to the hills and forests armed only with axes and cudgels.

Tito soon called a conference of partisan leaders in Belgrade and this gave him the opportunity to outline his policy. From the start his consistent aim was to take over the country. He insisted that partisan groups must have a political controller, that partisan attacks must be co-ordinated and that their purpose must be to destroy the existing administration and take control. Tito stayed in Belgrade to oversee the uprising in Serbia, but sent trusted colleagues to take over activities in Bosnia, Herzegovina and Slovenia. Although Tito became a brilliant military leader, his political aim and political control were clear from the start.

Tito's sound work in setting up communist cells across the country soon paid off, although in Belgrade the police worked with the Germans and killed a number of partisan leaders. This caused fury among Tito's followers, and prompted aggressive attacks on ammunition dumps and armouries, and the ambush and derailment of trains. In August 1941 Tito signalled to Moscow that partisan activity in Serbia was virtually a national uprising and asked urgently for help, but he received none. The partisans were encouraged when they intercepted a German report which said it was impossible to do anything with the Serbs, because they were tough, their system was excellent, and they were the perfect secret organisation.

As the uprising spread, so did the activities of the Germans in Belgrade. Therefore, at the end of August, Tito left Belgrade and established his political and military partisan HQ in hill country south west of Belgrade. Partisan activity increased all the time, and soon villages and small towns had been taken over, and the Germans were beleaguered in the cities and big towns. The occupying forces of both the Germans and Italians had severe difficulties in guarding their lines of communication, particularly in the mountainous west of the country. Here the steep cliffs, the deep forest and narrow valleys were ideal for ambushes by the partisans. The hardy people of the hills and mountains – whether Serb, Croat or Bosnian – had a tradition of resistance going back generations and they gave positive support to the partisans, even though they suffered savage reprisals from the fascist occupiers. Tito, now operating across the country, called his movement the National Liberation Partisan Detachments, which were armed units of the people. With shrewd political sense, he stressed the anti-fascist front rather than the communist message, but he made it clear that he wished to destroy the old pre-war corrupt bourgeois system.

In the early months of the occupation, the well-established Serb underground movement, the Cetniks, under Mihailovic, also opposed the enemy but they supported the exiled king and looked to the restoration of the monarchy and the Roman Catholic Church. Mihailovic frequently failed to act against the enemy in order to avoid reprisals.

After the initial blitzkrieg by the Axis, the main fighting units had moved on, leaving poor and weak garrison troops. These very soon had great difficulties even defending themselves against constant attacks. Both partisans and Cetniks – sometimes together – captured large supplies of weapons and ammunition, and before the end of 1941 much of Serbia was free of German control. A meeting was arranged between Tito and Mihailovic, who appeared in an ostentatious uniform and with an arrogant attitude. He advised caution in order to avoid reprisals, and forecast that the partisans would soon be wiped out. Tito saw that there would be little co-operation with the Cetniks.

In the autumn of 1941, Tito was in a strong enough position to call a conference of partisan leaders. The conference set up a command HQ in each area, all under the authority of Tito's HQ, which had now moved again to Uzice, close to the mountains and seventy miles south west of Belgrade. This small market town proved invaluable to the partisans, and when they captured it they found millions of dinars in a bank vault, and there was a small arms factory in the suburbs. They established a National Liberation Council to administer the area, set up a People's Court, and published a regular newspaper.

In October 1941 Tito had another meeting with Mihailovic but they disagreed fundamentally and, before the end of the year, after a few more attempts to co-operate, the partisans and Cetniks were fighting each other rather than the Germans. The German occupation forces, alarmed at the scale of partisan activity, sent in more divisions and stepped up their reprisals. They destroyed towns and villages, and massacred men, women and children – in one instance 5,000 people in revenge for a partisan attack. These savage reprisals failed to cow the people, and drove more and more men to join the partisans. Next, the Germans launched an attack with tanks, artillery and air support against Uzice and Tito was nearly captured, but he escaped further into the mountains. As a part of that attack, the Germans overran a field hospital with over 60 seriously wounded men and merely drove their tanks over them until they were all dead. Under such intense German pressure, the Cetniks started to co-operate with the enemy – laying up deep bitterness for the future. But Tito, even in desperate straits, looked forward. From the remnants of his troops, he established an elite unit called the Proletarian Brigade as the nucleus of a future People's Army, aiming to achieve the control of the country by the Yugoslav Communist Party. A brigadier and a political commissar commanded each Proletarian Brigade and together they aimed to raise military, political and ideological standards.

For some time to come, Tito laboured under the disadvantage that, because of the link between the exiled king and Mihailovic, British support went to the Cetniks, even when there was clear proof that they were co-operating with the Germans. This anomaly took many months to rectify.

At the same time, the Croat leader, Pavelic, created further division. In an early example of ethnic cleansing, he set out with the Ustase to rid Croatia of Serb people and Orthodox believers. Carrying out unspeakable atrocities, they desecrated Orthodox churches and massacred women and children. In one instance, when 700 women and girls refused forcible conversion to the Roman Catholic Church, they were thrown over a cliff. Even the German and Italian troops were sickened and horrified at their excesses. Pavelic's appalling policy drove thousands of Serbs, and even Croats, into the hills to join the partisans. These were welcomed by Tito, but then the Germans and Italians combined to make another attack in order to kill Tito and destroy the partisans. Once again, Tito, almost surrounded, managed to lead his brigade through the encircling enemy lines to the safety of the higher mountains further south. The Axis attack petered out, and Tito still held a substantial area south of Sarajevo.

During the winter of 1941–42, Tito, hard pressed in a remote mountain stronghold, had to take stock of his position. He had suffered very heavy losses among his old and loyal friends, and the Axis forces were still pursuing him, but even in this situation, because so many volunteers were joining his movement, he was able to set up four more partisan brigades. Then, in another incident, indicative of future problems, Montenegro, which had a proud warrior tradition, and which in the past had never succumbed to the Turks, rose in revolt against the Italian occupation. The revolt nearly succeeded, but it was poorly co-ordinated, and, during the severe winter, the Italians sent in large reinforcements and with massive air support they recaptured most of the territory they had lost. The rebels lost the support of the people when they proposed an extreme form of communism and planned to join the Soviet Union. Tito remained critical of these unwise moves.

By the middle of 1942 Cetnik and Ustase groups in Montenegro and Bosnia were often co-operating with the Germans and Italians against the partisans and putting out anti-communist propaganda. During this time Tito received no help from Mosow, which, like the western Allies, had been taken in by Mihailovic. It was doubly galling for Tito, when Moscow criticised him and told him to contact the exiled Yugoslav government in London. During July 1942, when the partisans were out of supplies and nearly starving, Tito decided to go on the attack. The partisans surrounded a village on the railway from Sarajevo to the Adriatic coast, and Tito led a battalion attack, which overwhelmed the Axis defence. They took the station and then a train came in fully loaded with tons of food and supplies, and even a truck full of dynamite. The partisans then blew up a bridge and a tunnel, sent the train over a cliff, and went off with as much loot as they could transport. They followed this success with several more, in spite of severe reprisals.

By August 1942, the partisans were strong enough to capture Livno, a pleasant market town 40 miles west of Sarajevo. These were great successes, but at a heavy cost among the more experienced fighters, and both the Germans and the Ustase carried out reprisals. Tito kept his forces moving so that the enemy never had a firm target, and he found that the reprisal policy of the enemy was providing him with many recruits. The partisans were now operating fairly freely in the mountainous area of Herzegovina to the north of Livno. The terrain, with thick forests and deep, steep-sided valleys, was ideal as a guerrilla base. By September, Tito had established his HQ in a small town where he was able to receive reports from partisan units across the country, including the Dalmatian coast and the area around Dubrovnik. Most told the same story, of partisan successes, but also heavy losses, which were made up by recruits infuriated by the brutality of the Germans and the Ustase.

Ambush – that key tactic of guerrillas – kept the different units well supplied. On the railway from Zagreb to Belgrade over 70 trains had been looted and destroyed. Across the whole country, the partisans, in spite of reprisals, were seizing and keeping the initiative. Tito had sent experienced leaders to take control of operations in the larger towns, like Zagreb, Belgrade and Banja Luka. This policy was now well established and working effectively. The large number of volunteers increased the need for weapons, but despite urgent appeals, Russia sent nothing, and kept its ties with the exiled monarchy in London, which continued to favour Mihailovic. Tito protested as strongly as possible, and informed Moscow bluntly that the Cetniks were openly co-operating with the Axis. He was again rebuffed.

The partisans, using sound guerrilla tactics – particularly the ambush of trains and enemy convoys – were now well provided with weapons, ammunition and food. Tito, who had always looked to the time when the communists might control the country, now began to set up a more formal control of the different partisan groups. His personal prestige remained unassailable, and with no serious opposition from different ethnic groups, he established military divisions and even corps, in order to emphasise the Army of

National Liberation. In angry signals to Moscow, Tito gave clear evidence of partisan successes and of Cetnik collaboration with the Germans, but still his view was rejected. Russia was even considering sending a military mission to Mihailovic.

By the end of 1942, Tito had moved his HQ to the small town of Bihac, on the border of Bosnia and Croatia, and here he held another conference of partisan delegates. He stressed the need to fight for liberation, and to play down sectional or ideological differences, and emphasised the essential unity of all the people of Yugoslavia regardless of race or religion. At about the same time, Hitler had summoned the Croat leader Pavelic and gave him a severe dressing down. Hitler had expected Croatia to destroy the communist guerrillas and then supply materials and troops to help in the Russian campaign. Instead, large numbers of German troops were needed to prop up his wretched regime. Hitler therefore announced that the Axis would make a final attack to destroy the partisans. In January 1943, seven German and Italian divisions with tanks, artillery and air support, and assisted by Cetniks and the Ustase, moved rapidly to surround Tito's HQ. Tito had four divisions – though they were not as large as the enemy divisions. He had warning of the proposed attack, and planned to leave one division to delay the Axis advance, while he led the majority towards the south, aiming to break through the weaker Italian lines and reach the relative security of the mountains of Montenegro. At the same time, partisan units were ordered to make all-out attacks on roads, railways and supply dumps, and to ambush convoys moving towards the battle. Tito, in moving his main base, held absolutely to guerrilla principles, and he again emphasised that this was the time to prepare for offensive action.

The move to the south, with thousands of sick and wounded, and with women and children, caused great suffering. Many died of cold, starvation or typhus, while the Axis attackers kept up the pressure. Tito again appealed urgently to Moscow, and again received nothing but platitudinous good wishes. His main force reached the area of Mostar, but this brought little respite from the enemy attacks. Then, prompted by Hitler himself, two more German divisions advanced towards Tito's southern redoubt. The Cetniks were now openly co-operating with the Axis forces on a big scale, but still Moscow did not believe it.

By March 1943, Tito and his forces faced almost certain defeat. With their slow moving baggage train caring for the sick and wounded, they had been cornered and surrounded. They had to get thousands of people across a narrow plank bridge over a river, while the area was pounded by artillery and bombing – but still they kept moving. They held on, in spite of the over-whelming force of the enemy, and received a glimmer of hope when many of the Cetniks on the Italian front, disgusted at what the Axis were doing, decided to change sides. Hitler had warned Mussolini about the treach-erous nature of Mihailovic and the Cetniks but, now more than ever, Hitler was determined to destroy Tito. He had massed over 100,000 troops against the partisans, outnumbering them by five to one.

Hitler had been forced to admit defeat at Stalingrad in February 1943 and, by May 1943, the Axis had finally been driven out of North Africa. The Allies were now poised to attack Europe's southern shore. Hitler, in a frenzy, felt that surely he could win a victory against the despicable partisans. He ordered all partisans and everyone who helped them to be shot, and all food and all supplies of every description to be destroyed or removed from the area where the partisans were again cornered. More German fighting divisions were sent to southern Montenegro – moving in for the kill.

The Germans used five divisions to surround Tito's battered remnant in a remote mountain fastness about fifty miles north-west of Dubrovnik. Here peaks rose to four thousand feet, and precipitous gullies dropped down to fast running rivers. Whichever way the partisans moved, the Germans seemed able to block their progress. Their tragic ordeal had continued since early March, when at the beginning of June, with the Axis attackers advancing ever closer, a partisan reconaissance patrol found a short stretch of river, which was not held by the Germans, and from which a hidden path led up a steep hill and through the mountains. On 7 June, Tito had to make the momentous decision to bury or destroy all their artillery and heavy weapons. Horses and mules were killed and some were eaten. An advanced guard crossed the river, then the wounded were brought over, while two experienced divisions covered the rear of the whole force. Even this success brought little relief because they were still surrounded by Axis forces and they had lost their main firepower. The Germans repeated the order that every partisan should be killed. The partisans continued their grim march, assaulted by constant air attacks against which they now had no defence. Eventually, after six days of constant and devastating attacks by the German forces, during which Tito was wounded, a partisan unit forced a way through the German line. After another day of close fighting, the partisans reached an area of thick forest where the Germans did not pursue them. Djilas, Tito's loyal comrade from the earliest days, had commanded the rearguard, which suffered horrendous casualties and also witnessed the massacre of the wounded men whom the Germans had captured. Djilas reached Tito's HQ in the forest more than a week later. German reports on this battle confirm that their forces were fought to a standstill and when the partisans reached the forest there were no reserves at all to follow up. The partisans lost 8,000 killed. At the end of June 1943, in spite of the loss of a large number of experienced fighters, and most of his effective fire power, Tito, showing amazing qualities of leadership, decided that once again the partisans must go on the offensive and spread the communist revolt to other parts of the country.

After the last harrowing weeks, when the Germans came so close to wiping out Tito and the whole force of partisans, outside events at last began to benefit the partisan cause. Throughout the war, this had been dogged by the view of both Moscow and London, that Mihailovic and the Cetniks were the main opposition to the Axis invaders. Even when there was incontrovertible proof that the Cetniks were not only co-operating with the Axis, but were in the forefront of attacks on the partisans, London and Moscow were slow to change their minds. Now things changed.

During the summer of 1943 the Allies had driven the last of the Axis forces out of North Africa, had rapidly overrun Sicily, and then launched massive attacks on the Italian mainland. Powerful German units were allowed to escape from Sicily across the Straits of Messina to Italy, and consequently the Allies faced a long grim fight up the length of the peninsula. This immediately focused more interest on Tito and possible operations along the Dalmatian coast. The announcement of Italian surrender on 8 September came as a complete surprise, but gave Tito a great opportunity. He took swift action, which illustrated the effective power wielded by the partisans. They occupied much of the Dalmatian coast, from Istria in the north, to Dubrovnik and beyond, as well as many of the islands, one of which, Vis, was to become Tito's HQ. More importantly, the partisans were able to take over the weapons, ammunition and supplies of ten Italian divisions. This makes the interesting point that Tito and the partisans occupied considerably more Axis divisions than the twelve which took part in the battle of El Alamein.

Tito's successful situation arose from his clear policy of turning the partisan revolt into a movement of national liberation which he controlled and disciplined. When an area was taken over, a just civil administration was quickly established under party control. This always contrasted dramatically with the corrupt brutality of the German occupiers and their Cetnik and Ustase collaborators. From the start, Tito had also aimed to build the partisan groups into a national army, which would have the support of the whole people. He had suffered enough from the deep ethnic divisions of the country, and he had a shrewd and far-sighted aim that, under the tight discipline of a national army, those divisions could at least be kept in check.

When Tito looked back over the months of fighting, he was able from his own direct experience to give his views on guerrilla war. These came not from some respected training manual but were hammered out in the harsh reality of war. His most particular personal view concerned morale, and stressed that whenever there was a defeat, a new attack must be planned immediately so that an offensive attitude is maintained. He even managed to do this after the terrible hammering his partisans had endured during the final German assault. He always tried to avoid pitched battles and to fight and move at night. So many of the partisan commanders were Tito's old friends, and this strengthened his determination that wounded must be rescued at all costs. He believed that, for the sake of morale, it must be known that a wounded man would be rescued, even if it cost other lives to achieve this. This is why he was personally so upset when, in the final battle, the Germans overran a large convoy of wounded and massacred them. Tito ensured that he, and other senior commanders, were always in the thick of the fighting and he believed that this stopped the men cursing the top brass who were safely behind the lines – as happened in most other fighting formations. By 1943, Tito had a team of experienced, able and dedicated leaders, personally devoted to him, who understood and practised the essential political message, which accompanied military command. Finally, it gave him great satisfaction that his favourable situation in September 1943 had been achieved with no help whatsoever from the USSR.

Tito's situation was about to change dramatically. The British agent Brigadier Fitzroy Maclean parachuted in to link up with the partisans. At last the true situation was reported, and because of Maclean's high level links, the partisan issue was discussed at the Teheran Conference, with Churchill showing considerable personal interest. Fitzroy Maclean remained deeply involved with Tito, and later wrote two admirable books, *Disputed Barricade* and *Eastern Approaches* (London, 1957). Positive help for the partisans soon followed, but there remained very complicated issues for the British government, which was still committed to supporting the Royal Yugoslav government in exile in London. Naturally, King Peter protested strongly against giving help to the communist partisans, whom he saw as a possible threat to his kingdom after the Germans were defeated. Before long there was again very clear evidence that Mihailovic was co-operating with the Germans against the partisans.

It is easy to imagine the anger and frustration Tito felt when, even after he was receiving British support, he still had nothing from Russia, which was even considering sending a mission to Mihailovic. In October 1943, Tito therefore sent a strong policy statement to a conference of the Foreign Ministers of the US, the USSR and Britain claiming to speak for the National Liberation Army, and the Anti-Fascist Council. In his signal he stated that the king would not be allowed to return because for two years he had supported the traitor Mihailovic; the king's return could mean civil war; the majority of the people of Yugoslavia wanted a democratic republic based on the National Liberation Council. To Tito's chagrin, the issue of Yugoslavia was not on the agenda, and his signal was not answered.

Having been ignored by the Foreign Ministers' Conference, Tito called a meeting of the Anti-Fascist Council in November. The council eagerly supported Tito's proposal that they should form a National Committee of Liberation with constitutional powers. He further proposed that the Royal Government in exile was totally discredited, and King Peter would be refused entry until the people had decided what type of government they wanted. This too was agreed, and Tito assumed the title of Prime Minister and Minister of Defence. While the British and Americans did not demur, Stalin, apparently, was furious at Tito taking such an independent line.

In June 1943, Tito had barely escaped with his life from the final German onslaught on his guerrilla forces. Then, within a few weeks, Churchill and the Allies were supporting him, and he was virtually prime minister, but his guerrilla skills were still required because Germany still occupied a large part of Yugoslavia. After the June débâcle, he had carefully dispersed his forces across the country in order to spread the revolt, but also to ensure that the Germans could not inflict a single decisive defeat. This had weakened his own striking force but, fairly rapidly, large numbers of men were coming forward to join the partisans, and he was able to arm these with captured Italian weapons. The Germans still deployed powerful military forces, including some divisions from the Russian front, but now they were hard pressed to keep their units supplied. This was because of constant partisan attacks on their lines of communication and the ambush of their convoys. Vicious reprisals by the Germans had little effect.

With the increasing danger of Allied landings from the Adriatic, the Germans could not afford to leave the partisans in control of the Dalmatian coast. Using more divisions, which were urgently needed on the Russian front, they counterattacked the partisans and recaptured much of the coast and most of the islands, except for Vis, which was reinforced by the Royal Navy and garrisoned by a commando brigade. The partisans held strong positions in the wild country west of Sarajevo, and the Germans, with troops trained in winter and mountain warfare, launched another offensive. They were unable to pin down the partisans who kept to their sound guerrilla tactics of rapid dispersal. Although they were better equipped with Italian weapons, the partisans suffered severely from a prolonged campaign through the severe winter of 1943–44.

Tito was now operating at a high level and negotiating with the Allies about anti-Axis strategy, but he was still the guerrilla commander and he gave top priority to co-ordinating the tactics of his partisan groups. When the enemy attacked in the Sarajevo area, Tito ordered partisans to attack their lines of communication across the whole country and they made a large scale attack on Banja Luka in northern Bosnia. They actually captured the town and briefly held it, but German reinforcements were too strong, and once again Tito and his HQ were on the run, pursued by the enemy.

In *Disputed Barricade* (p.250), Fitzroy Maclean vividly describes how, as Churchill's envoy, he met Tito and presented him with a signed photograph of Churchill and a friendly letter at this critical juncture. The letter contained two significant policy decisions. The British government would send no more help to Mihailovic and they would not try to dictate the future government of Yugoslavia.

In contrast to this warm, friendly and enthusiastic response from one of the top leaders of the capitalist west, the long-awaited arrival of a delegation from Moscow – the Mecca and Jerusalem of faithful communists – was from the start dogged by almost Gilbertian difficulties. The Russians refused to come in by parachute, so the partisans cleared a runway of snow, then it snowed more heavily and it was cleared again; then, the Germans, noticing the extra activity, captured the runway. Finally, the delegation arrived by glider, with supplies of vodka and caviar, but few weapons. They were not an impressive looking group and, from the start, they were niggling, critical and condescending. There were no lavatories, and they demanded that one was built immediately. It became clear that the Russians expected to take over the partisans whereas Tito merely wanted a reliable supply of weapons and equipment. The British and American air forces regularly dropped supplies to the partisans, and supported them with tactical and strategic bombing, while, week after week the Russians shamefacedly had to say they could not supply anything at the moment. In these guerrilla days lay the seeds of one of the great post-war political denouements when Tito, as President of Yugoslavia, rejected the control of the Soviet Union.

While Churchill – later a formidable Cold War warrior – appeared laid-back about the possibility of Tito and the communist movement taking over in Yugoslavia, the Americans were more apprehensive and kept up their links with Mihailovic (see *Tito of Yugoslavia* by K. Zilliacus, London, 1952). During this time, Tito's overt communism, and the blatant display of Red Star badges, worried Stalin, who thought it would offend Britain and America unnecessarily. In fact, they took little notice.

In 1944, Djilas, Tito's closest colleague and friend, spent several months in Moscow. He established a good rapport with Stalin, who congratulated the partisans on their achievements, but he did not publicly recognise Tito's National Committee as the legitimate government of Yugoslavia – which had been the main purpose of Djilas's visit.

Tito's land HQ, now located at Drva in the mountains about 50 miles south east of Banja Luka, had rapidly grown in size. It now had both British and Soviet missions, and heavy signals equipment for communicating with all the partisan units. German reconnaissance and intelligence had clearly identified this and, in May 1944 – realizing that Tito himself was the key to the success of the partisans – the Germans attacked his HQ with parachute troops backed up by armour and infantry. The attack nearly succeeded, but Tito managed to escape through the mountains – on the run once again. The Germans massacred every man, woman and child in Drva.

Tito had escaped the initial airborne attack, but the Germans massed their troops in the area, determined finally to catch him. The size of his HQ now made him increasingly vulnerable to German air and ground attack, and made it difficult for him to control the nationwide network of guerrilla units. Therefore, after many more days on the run, Tito agreed to be flown out to safety. The RAF had considerable experience of rescue missions and Tito with members of the British and Soviet missions were taken out by Dakota and safely delivered to the island of Vis. Because of Allied air and sea power, Vis was relatively safe from German attack, and it had already been built up into a powerful base from which air, sea and commando raids were launched against Axis forces on neighbouring islands and on the mainland. From Vis, frequent sorties were made to support and supply the partisans.

Tito's presence on Vis, closely supported by powerful Allied forces, again brought into focus the question of British support for the Cetniks under Mihailovic. There is no doubt that Mihailovic consistently duped and misled his British mission, and hid from them his collaboration with the Nazis and his attacks on the partisans. He profited from the presence in London of the exiled king and official government, through which all major policy issues had to be directed. His chicanery was now uncovered and, in May 1944, the British government informed him that he would receive no more support, though the Americans did maintain a link.

The final decision not to support the Cetniks had far reaching strategic consequences. The British had assumed correctly that the Cetnik's greatest strength lay in the flatter open country around Belgrade, but now the partisans moved in with substantial Allied support. Those partisans who had been left behind when Tito and the main body had been driven out to the more secure bases in the mountains of Bosnia and Montenegro, had enjoyed scant success. Now, with the open backing of the Allies, and with the Cetniks proved to be traitors, volunteers flocked to the partisans, who because of their new sources of supply, were able to arm them effectively.

The Allies were delighted to have partisan help, particularly in Belgrade and eastern Serbia, which covered the main supply routes for the Nazi armies further south and in Greece. Mihailovic had consistently failed to disrupt the substantial road and rail traffic on this route, and the partisans rapidly showed what could be achieved by clearly directed ambush and sabotage.

Tito had always emphasised the significant political aim of the guerrilla movement, and he realised that his hopes of gaining political control after the defeat of the Germans would depend substantially on the level of support he could achieve in Serbia. Therefore, in August 1944, having increased guerrilla activity across the province, he moved his main formations, amounting to over twelve divisions, into Serbia to back up a drive on Belgrade. At the same time, Tito was kept up to date with the latest Allied intelligence, and he knew of the terrific Russian advances, the Allied advance to the Rhine, and the Allied progress through Italy, which had now reached as far north as San Marino.

A likely German defeat raised urgent political questions – the most urgent for Tito being the future of Yugoslavia and the role of King Peter, still nominally backed by the Allies. The first move came when a Dr Subasic – known to be a conciliator – was brought to see Tito, who from his powerful position, felt he could afford to be magnanimous. Tito agreed to the formation of a provisional government under Subasic, made up of partisans and exiles, with the role of the king to be decided after the war. The provisional government would call on everyone to support the partisans, and at last the king publicly repudiated Mihailovic.

In August 1944, Tito visited the Allied HQ in Italy, and was, rightly, accorded the respect due to the Commander of a National Army. There is an interesting contrast between the warm and cordial relations Tito always had with the British, who did all they could to help and supply the partisans, and the generally tense and miserable relations with the Soviet delegations. During Tito's visit to Italy, Churchill, in a typical gesture, came to see him on the Isle of Capri. Churchill offered all possible help for the partisans in their continuing fight with the Germans. On the political issues in the future, he argued strongly in favour of a constitutional monarchy, and of conciliation between Serbs and Croats. He made it clear that Britain did not intend to supply arms for a civil war.

As recently as the spring of 1944, Tito escaped from German paratroops, who had been ordered to shoot on sight, by climbing up a secret passage out of a cave at the back of his HQ, and then was on the run with a guerrilla band. Yet, in August 1944, he was meeting Churchill and in September – not being entirely honest with his British protectors – he slipped away to visit Moscow to discuss the role of the partisans and the Red Army, which was at that time drawing close to the Yugoslav border. Stalin, surrounded by his acolytes, gave Tito an enthusiastic welcome but the atmosphere did not remain cordial.

Tito was proud to visit Moscow as the leader of his country, and he did want Soviet help in the final campaign to capture Belgrade, but he made it clear to Stalin that, if Soviet forces were involved, they would come under his command and would not remain after Belgrade was occupied. Stalin, accustomed to obsequious agreement from his subordinates, was taken aback by such forthright views, but he did agree to send Soviet forces from Romania into Yugoslavia for the assault on Belgrade. In October 1944, after a prolonged battle, in which the Germans lost nearly 20,000 killed, wounded or captured, the city was taken. Tito reviewed his troops and congratulated them on a magnificent victory. After the fall of Belgrade much of the country was cleared of Germans, but they tried to keep open a road and rail route going north through Zagreb so that their remaining men could escape. Tito encouraged his partisan units to keep up their guerrilla attacks and ambushes on these fairly vulnerable targets.

Even in the earliest guerrilla days, Tito had stressed the significance of the political role of the partisans, and the importance of good relations with the people. The stern discipline and firm central control of partisan activity by Tito himself had built up a sound administrative machine. After Belgrade was captured, although the city had been largely destroyed by the recent fighting, and by previous Allied air raids, the position of Tito and the communists was unassailable. It was not too difficult to adapt their military control system to civil administration.

As the Germans withdrew, the future of the country became the top priority. Subasic – still the representative of King Peter – was in Belgrade for some time, and was involved in long and tortuous negotiations with Tito and London and Moscow. Although the monarchy had been discredited by its association with Mihailovic and the Cetniks, and by their collaboration with the Nazis, it was far from certain that the Yugoslav people would welcome a communist dictatorship. Tito had worried whether Britain might try to back the return of the monarchy – indeed Churchill had asked him this – but early in 1945, much to his relief, it was announced in the House of Commons, that if King Peter did not agree with the constitutional proposals, then they would proceed without him. After some further niggling discussion, agreement was finally reached. Tito was recognised as head of a government, which included several former royal supporters, but in which, real power lay with Tito and the communist party.

Tito's recognition came early in 1945, but large Nazi forces were still fighting a desperate rearguard action as they tried to get back to Germany. Estimates of numbers in this campaign tended to be erratic, but Tito controlled four armies, with perhaps 200,000 men, and they exacted savage vengeance on the retreating Germans, as well as those collaborators who surrendered.

The euphoric days of victory in the spring of 1945, when Tito enjoyed the admiration and support of both Stalin and Churchill, were not to last and the harsher realities of peace soon intruded. In Italy, Field Marshal Alexander, directing the Allied drive north, ordered his troops into Trieste, the Adriatic port vital to the Allies' continuing advance. When the British troops reached Trieste, they found Tito's partisans already occupying part of the city – the population made up of both Yugoslavs and Italians. In a tense and bad tempered stand-off between two previously cordial allies – indicative of what was to follow in the Cold War – Tito, who was not supported by Stalin, was forced to compromise. While Yugoslavia kept Istria, Trieste remained under Allied control. This arrangement was confirmed officially in 1947, and, finally Trieste was returned to Italy in 1954.

When Soviet troops advanced into Germany, remembering all the horrors of the Nazi attack and occupation of their country, there were cases of brutality, rape and destruction. Antony Beevor in *Berlin – The Downfall 1945* (London, 2002) has vividly described the depredations carried out by Soviet troops on the women of Berlin. Perhaps the Soviet divisions diverted to assist the partisans in the assault on Belgrade had not been instructed that Yugoslavia was not enemy territory. The behaviour of Soviet troops towards the women of Yugoslavia – even those who had fought as partisans – enraged many Yugoslavs. This tension, especially over the cases of rape, was but one factor behind the rapidly deteriorating relationship between Tito's new government of Yugoslavia and the Soviet Union.

The Soviet delegation were, from the start, tactless and insensitive. They rejected and resented any comment about their behaviour; they assumed they would have control over the administration of the country; they tried to make the partisans into units of the Red Army, and they even stated that Yugoslavia would soon become a part of the Soviet Union.

In November 1945, after a democratic election – in fact totally dominated by the Communist Party – a new constituent assembly was created. It abolished the monarchy and established a Federal Republic. The six federated states; Serbia, Croatia, Slovenia, Bosnia, Macedonia and Montenegro, had limited powers for local affairs, while federal powers were deliberately strengthened in order to eliminate ethnic divisions. From the start of the war, Tito had purposely followed a similar policy in building up partisan units as the nucleus of a regular army, so that ethnic divisions could be controlled or removed by military discipline and by the comradeship engendered by wartime campaigns.

How often during the immediate post-war years, must Tito have looked back nostalgically to his relatively uncomplicated role of leading the partisan movement! Quite soon after the clash with Britain over Trieste, he was drawn into the similar and equally serious problem of Greece. During the war the Greek communist guerrillas had been less effective than Tito's, and when the Germans withdrew, British troops occupied the country, after a brief skirmish with the guerrillas. Elections were held in 1946 and, by September 1946, King George was back on his throne. This was the signal for an immediate communist uprising in Greek Macedonia – the birthplace of Alexander the Great. As the communists took over most of Macedonia, they relied increasingly on arms and supplies from Yugoslavia; meanwhile the UN were powerless to assist the Greek monarchy because of the Soviet veto in the Security Council.

While the Greek crisis was building up, Tito had another serious clash with the USA, which illustrated to the world the harsh realities of the Cold

War. During 1946, US planes had frequently flown over Yugoslav territory and Washington had just ignored the protests from Belgrade. This new issue of the invasion of airspace – still a critical matter for Saudi Arabia in the Iraq clash of 2003 – triggered a world crisis. The Yugoslavs shot down a US plane, and the US administration was outraged and took the matter to the UN. The world appeared on the brink of war. Advised by Stalin to calm things, Tito climbed down, but international tension had been notched up another rung.

At home, as soon as the Germans left, the partisan command machinery was ready to take over all the organs of state. They quickly implemented a programme of nationalising all industry and commerce in a centralised system controlled from Belgrade. This proved fairly straightforward compared to the next step – establishing communist policy on land reform. In the 1930s, Stalin admitted killing 5,000,000 peasants in his attempt to enforce his land policy – that most catastrophic of all Marx's ideas. In the 1960s Mao Zedong, pursuing a similar policy, caused the biggest famine in human history. Tito, slightly more pragmatic, still faced major problems with the Balkan peasants. First, his government took over the largest estates, and this was no problem. Then it limited personal land holding to 60 acres – again no problem. Finally, it imposed the compulsory purchase of 80% of peasants' produce at an artificially low price in order to feed the industrial workers in the towns. This caused massive opposition among the peasants, many of whom just stopped growing commercial crops and merely grew enough for themselves, creating a serious shortage.

The difficulties caused by the land reforms stretched across the whole country but the next crisis Tito faced centred mostly on Croatia. Almost as soon as the partisans took over Croatia at the end of 1944, they quickly settled old scores. The predominantly Roman Catholic Croats had supported the Ustase, and many, including some priests, had been drawn into fighting against the partisans, and collaborating with the Germans. Tito, a convinced atheist, was unlikely to compromise with a church which had collaborated with the Nazis against him. He was also conscious – like Henry VIII before him – of the great wealth of the church and its vast land holding – estimated at 150,000 acres. The clash resulted in a show trial of a Roman Catholic archbishop, which for weeks had world-wide publicity and which highlighted the universal issues between the Roman Catholic Church and the communist state. In October 1946, the court sentenced the archbishop to a long term of imprisonment and Tito again featured as the hard man in the forefront of the Cold War.

As a result of these events, the west was beginning to see Tito as the front man for the increasingly bellicose attitude of the Soviet Union and its allies. That situation was shortly to change. The west, which had revered Stalin and the Soviet Union as magnificent allies in the fight against fascism, were slow to realise that the real aim of Stalin and all dedicated communists was the overthrow of capitalism throughout the world. Parallel to this was Stalin's own policy that all communist states – and particularly those in eastern Europe and the Balkans – should come under his direct control.

Tito, who had spent much of the 1930s in Moscow, considered himself the loyal archetypal communist. While several post-war difficulties were being dealt with, he laid the foundations, with sound communist ideals, of a Five Year Plan to industrialise the country. He faced daunting problems. The towns, the factories, the railways and the roads had all been devastated by the war. There was a dire shortage of factories and machines, and an equally severe shortage of industrial skills among the people. Russia appeared more eager to take control of major parts of the Yugoslav economy than to provide disinterested help. As the Cold War increased in intensity, it became increasingly difficult for Tito to obtain technical or industrial help from his erstwhile allies in the west.

By 1947, by which time Tito had established good relations with most of the Balkan countries, and had discussed with other leaders the possibility of a Balkan federation, Stalin decided that his satellites, as he saw them, should be brought to heel. He therefore established the Cominform, but Tito, alert to what was happening, refused to attend the meeting. Early in 1948, Stalin, who was infuriated by Tito's independent stance, summoned him and Dimitrov of Bulgaria to Moscow. Tito refused to go. Stalin then put the maximum pressure on Yugoslavia. A Yugoslav delegation in Moscow was insulted and humiliated. Then all Soviet advisers were withdrawn because, it was claimed, they faced hostile attitudes, and all Soviet help was stopped. Tito received a letter with ominous phrases about Trotsky and disloyalty. In April 1948, Tito received almost total backing from the Central Committee in Belgrade for his rejection of the Soviet demands. Stalin then stepped up the pressure on all the other Balkan countries, and in June 1948, the obsequious Cominform members duly threw out Yugoslavia. In a final dig, the Soviet Union appealed to all loyal communists to rise up and throw out their misguided leaders, but the people remained steadfastly loyal.

Because the world's media now focused on Tito, Stalin did not dare to have him assassinated, but, having tried everything else to remove what he saw as a grave danger to the communist cause, he imposed a total economic blockade. This was particularly damaging, because the whole slant of the Yugoslav economy had been towards Russia, in terms of technical help, supplies and markets. Stalin now abruptly cut off all links and leant on the subservient Balkan countries to follow his lead. Tito was now dangerously isolated from both east and west. He wondered how long the people would tolerate the privation and suffering which this caused, but when he tentatively approached the west, the reaction was more favourable than he expected. To his surprise, he found it was possible to establish trade and other exchanges, and, later, reconstruction loans and grants, and military support. The west now had its own interest in maintaining his independence – so much for political morality.

In his period of total isolation, Tito knew that Stalin was contemplating military invasion and he had the grim thought that, in the face of the overwhelming might of the Red Army, he might have to take to the hills again with his partisans. This did not happen. Tito's situation improved slightly when, in 1950, the west gave a robust response through the UN to the communist invasion of South Korea. This was made possible because, at the time, Stalin was boycotting the Security Council and could not use his veto. This response gave heart to Tito and to those in the west, who feared the inexorable advance of Soviet and communist power and aggrandisement across the world. Slowly and at first discreetly, Tito started to obtain western weapons and supplies to re-equip his forces in the face of the continuing Soviet threat. By the mid-1950s, he felt that his courage and tenacity had paid off, because the Trieste crisis had been settled with a compromise, he had established good relations with Greece and Turkey, and on an official visit to Britain, he had been warmly welcomed by Churchill and Field Marshal Alexander – with whom he had first clashed at Trieste – and he even had lunch at Buckingham Palace.

While the international situation improved Tito faced serious problems at home. The Five Year Plan was abandoned in favour of a more pragmatic approach, the policy of central state control was reversed, and the disastrous compulsory purchase of all agricultural produce was given up. His most threatening problem came, surprisingly, from one of his oldest and most loyal comrades, Djilas. The highly intelligent Djilas focused his formidable attention on the future development of the state, and the route to democracy. At first, Tito did not discourage a stream of radical and critical articles from Djilas, but in the end they created a crisis. Djilas was called before the Central Committee, and after a long and anguished debate in which Djilas gained considerable support, he was expelled from the party and, effectively, ruined. Tito's firm leadership and resolve held sway.

No part of the communist world remained unaffected by the death of Stalin in 1953, but the succeeding uncertainty held further danger for Tito. At first Khrushchev, in an inept and clumsy manoeuvre, tried to gain support for an aggressive policy towards the west. Tito demurred. Further uncertainty emerged after Khrushchev's dramatic denunciation of Stalin in 1956, but despite blandishments from Moscow, and upheavals in Poland, Tito held firmly to his policy.

Tito had one more role to play in world affairs. During 1956, with the Suez crisis, and with Russian tanks rolling into Hungary – against which he protested strongly – he had entertained Nehru and Nasser in Belgrade. This was the start of what became the Non-Aligned Group – countries which were independent of either the capitalist west under the USA or the communist east under the USSR. This group were shortly joined by Kwame Nkrumah, who had led his country, Ghana, to independence in 1957 – one of the first independent African countries. The following year, Nkrumah, enjoying the limelight, made a passionate appeal to the US Senate to help the Non-Aligned Group. He also added another dimension, supported by Tito and Nehru, to keep the Cold War out of Africa. Tito welcomed Nkrumah's rather brash enthusiasm, in contrast to the patrician and condescending attitude of Nehru and, in 1961, Tito visited Ghana. He offered industrial help and established a good rapport with Nkrumah. Then Nkrumah, after a visit to Kennedy in Washington, and a prolonged visit to Moscow and Beijing – illustrating the super powers' interest in Africa – attended the very important Non-Aligned Conference in Belgrade in August 1961. The conference passed a significant resolution – to establish a moral third force to balance East and West, and to oppose imperialism and colonialism in any guise.

By the 1960s, Tito was at last secure, a respected world figure, who kept alive the ideals of the Non-Aligned Group, and who used his influence towards moderation in international affairs. He tried, without much success, to reduce the tensions centred on the Vietnam war, and he flew to Prague to support the Czech people in the crisis of 1968 – a revered peacemaker.

Tito died, after a long illness, in 1980. Not long before he died, he spoke to Sue Ryder, the intrepid English woman who set up the Sue Ryder Homes to care for disabled people from eastern Europe. He spoke movingly of his country, and said 'Sue, my dear, when I die, all this will fall apart'. That proved to be tragically true.

Tributes to his greatness came from all over the world, except from those eastern European countries still under the heel of the USSR. Margaret Thatcher spoke of a staunch ally in peace and war, Indira Gandhi spoke of his inspiring work with her father Nehru, and Chancellor Schmidt spoke of his willpower and his support for the world community of nations. President Jimmy Carter called Tito 'a towering figure on the world stage'. Tito loved the trappings of power, the luxury, the yachts, the clothes, the drink, the women, but his people forgave any excesses, and deeply mourned his passing.

Tito should be considered the greatest guerrilla leader, who rose to absolute power, but made none of the catastrophic mistakes which besmirched the reputation of Mao Zedong. Tito proved himself in the disastrous conditions of guerrilla war after the Nazi invasion of 1941. Then, purposely and deliberately, he built up the power of the partisans in order to overcome the dangerous ethnic divisions of the country. Next, he transformed the partisans into a regular army, where military discipline could curb those same divisions. As head of state he used all the skills, determination and willpower he had learnt from his guerrilla fighting to support and protect Yugoslavia against all the unscrupulous and vicious attacks Stalin could unleash against him. Was Tito's brave stand against Stalin perhaps the first step in the revolutionary changes which followed in eastern Europe and led to the break up of the USSR?

Yet another measure of Tito's greatness is the horror of what followed his demise, when Serbs, Croats, Bosnians and Montenegrins all indulged in savage civil war, and created a new and horrendous phrase 'ethnic cleansing'. Entering a new century, the International Criminal Tribunal at the Hague is attempting to bring to justice people like Milosovic, Mladic and Karadzic. They are charged with crimes against humanity, including the massacre at Srebrenica, and they remind the world of the greatness of Tito, who for 45 years saved his country from its murderous divisions.

GUERRILLA FIGHTERS: WORLD WAR II

Brigadier Michael Calvert, DSO and bar, whose career in the Commandos, the Australian Commandos, the Chindits and the SAS encapsulates much of the guerrilla activity in World War II, had personal contact with many of the brave and distinguished soldiers who served in the different units of the Special Forces.

The German blitzkrieg in 1940, which rapidly overran most of western Europe, created a situation – as the Romans and Napoleon had done – ripe for the development of guerrilla activity. Churchill recognized this when, as one of his earlier acts as prime minister in May 1940, he encouraged the creation of the Commandos so that they could threaten every part of the coastline of Hitler's fortress Europe from Norway to Spain.

By 1939, Calvert had already proved himself as an outstanding and highly professional officer in the Royal Engineers. Posted to the International Settlement in Shanghai in 1938 he took every opportunity to study the tactics of the Japanese army as it approached Nanking. By careful observation, he noticed that the Japanese had developed the use of landing craft. Excited by the significance of his discovery, he sent a report to the War Office, but it was not even acknowledged. On one occasion, when he had been found close to some Japanese units, he was captured and put in the guardroom. He was extremely worried because he had heard that the Japanese usually stripped you down to your underpants, and he was wearing pants with the Rising Sun on the bottom. When his guards got drunk celebrating the fall of Nanking, he managed to bluff his way out.

In the early months of the so-called Phoney War there were few opportunities for action against the enemy, but one did occur when the army called for volunteers to fight for Finland against the Russians. The volunteers, who were given training in skiing, included many men who were eager to fight and were not content just to do their bit in a normal unit. They were enrolled in the so-called 5th Battalion of the Scots Guards, but the brave resistance of the Finns was overcome before any help could be sent. This group included Bill and David Stirling and others who were to make their names in the Long Range Desert Group, the SAS and the Chindits.

Meanwhile, Calvert had been recognised as an explosives expert and he took part in the British expedition to Norway in the spring of 1940. His role there was to blow up railways, roads and bridges on the routes down to the west coast, in order to delay the German forces pursuing the retreating British. He took part in several dangerous escapades, including an unsuccessful attempt to bring down a Stuka dive-bomber, by exploding a naval depth charge. The remnants of the British units arrived back in Britain just when Churchill became prime minister.

Calvert, his expertise with explosives now clearly recognised, became an instructor at Lochailort, the first Commando training centre in the west of Scotland. Here he met up with several old friends from the 5th Scots Guards battalion. Many men of ability and powerful personality, who rebelled against the out-of-date instruction and mind-numbing tedium of many regular training units, had assembled at Lochailort. Among these was David Stirling. He had the arrogance and self-confidence of a well-to-do young man, whom the Roman Catholic public school, Ampleforth, had not entirely disciplined, and who, during a short time at Cambridge, spent too many hours at Newmarket or in London at White's Club. During his early months of training at the Guards' depot at Pirbright, he was described as 'incorrigible but great fun', and he was renowned for objecting to rules or activities he thought stupid. He left with a very poor reputation. The concept of the Commandos appealed to men like Stirling, and they responded eagerly to the tough and challenging regime (see *David Stirling* by Alan Hoe, London, 1992).

The early intake at Lochailort Commando Centre contained a number of men attracted by the glamour and the chance of action against the enemy, but it also contained men who were to give serious thought to the issues of guerrilla war and who were to initiate and develop new concepts. Freddie Spencer Chapman – fieldcraft expert – and Mike Calvert – explosives expert – were the outstanding instructors and were tremendously encouraged by the enthusiasm and by the calibre of the trainee Commandos. Then, to his dismay, Calvert was posted away to the Military Intelligence Department at the War Office. He wondered what this involved. He was about to see guerrilla war from a different angle.

He was sent with the writer and traveller Peter Fleming to organise auxiliary units which were to stay behind and carry out sabotage if Germany occupied southern England. During the summer of 1940, Calvert travelled across Kent and Sussex, preparing explosive charges and booby traps on roads, bridges and railways, and in large country houses that might be used as German headquarters. The pair also picked out leaders, usually from the farming community, and gave them basic training in sabotage technique.

By October 1940 invasion appeared unlikely, and Fleming was sent off to Greece to what was to become the SOE, whilst Calvert, with Spencer Chapman, was sent by sea to Australia to set up a Commando training school. Calvert paid tribute to Spencer Chapman's skill at fieldcraft, and Spencer Chapman, in *The Jungle is Neutral*, described Calvert's infectious enthusiasm in teaching his men how to blow up everything from battleships to brigadiers. The new Australian Commando units were called Independent Companies and, as the Japanese threat increased, the Australian government gave them strong support. Later re-named Commando Squadrons, they acquitted themselves well in New Guinea, Bougainville and Timor.

While Calvert made his way, indirectly, to Burma many of the staff and students from Lochailort had been transferred to the Middle East under the name Layforce – after Robert Laycock, their inspirational commander. In February 1941, Layforce, made up of 7, 8 and 11 Commandos, started their operations along the North African coast, but these were not a success. Stirling, in 8 Commando, felt deeply frustrated because it appeared that all the training to produce a superb force was wasted and they were lying idle. Then he had an accident in parachute training, which seriously injured his back, and he also had a painful injury to his eye. He was even suspected of a self-inflicted wound.

From this nadir of both his morale and his career he decided to act decisively. He had studied the map of North Africa, and remarked on the Great Sand Sea, which backed the narrow coastal strip. The relatively unsuccessful Commando raids, with about 200 men landed by destroyers near well-defended ports, had always met fierce and effective opposition. Then Stirling had the brilliant idea of using the huge and largely unmapped Great Sand Sea to attack enemy positions from the desert not from the sea. Small groups would be dropped into the desert, where they could lie up and then make surprise attacks with guns, bombs and explosives against unsuspecting enemy airfields. He put his idea to Jock Lewes, a Commando friend, who was critical. Having accepted some of Lewes's criticisms and suggestions, Stirling then worked hard to produce a short memo, which he was determined to deliver to General Ritchie, the Deputy Chief of the General Staff in Cairo. When the memo was ready Stirling, still hardly mobile and in great pain from his injured back, approached the GHQ perimeter. He used various subterfuges to gain access to the HQ and had an unpleasant brush with an apoplectic major who remembered him from Pirbright. Eventually, with remarkable luck, he reached General Ritchie, and he read the memo.

At that time Ritchie and Auchinleck, who had just arrived in Cairo as Commander in Chief, were under great pressure from Churchill to take action against Rommel.

In July 1941, Stirling was called back to see Auchinleck and Ritchie, who welcomed the idea of effective diversionary attacks on German positions. They hoped these could take place before November when another offensive was planned. As a result of the meeting Stirling was promoted to captain and given authority to recruit sixty men. The new unit was given the title Special Air Service. After the lack of success of the initial Commando raids, many Layforce members were not fully occupied. Stirling looked to them, and further back to the Scots Guards ski battalion as the main source of volunteers for the SAS.

The authorities allocated them a basic camp in the Canal Zone, and they raided another camp belonging to a unit away on exercise and made themselves a comfortable home. Stirling was pleased with the quality, experience and calibre of his initial volunteers, and then he was told of an officer who was in a military prison awaiting trial for hitting his commanding officer. The victim was Geoffrey Keyes, a regular colonel from the Scots Greys, who was shortly to win a posthumous VC for his action in a raid on Rommel's HQ. The disgraced officer was Paddy Blair Mayne, who was to become one of the really great characters of the SAS, and who would win four DSOs before the war was over. A graduate of Trinity College, Dublin, and a renowned Irish rugby international, he was a man of volcanic temperament, and liable to uncontrollable bursts of violence. Blair Mayne was initially suspicious of Stirling, as a snooty public school type, but they both overcame their early reservations, and Mayne became one of the strongest leaders in Stirling's teams.

Under great difficulties, and with little outside help, Stirling and Lewes drew up a tough and demanding training programme, under severe discipline, which included parachute training in which two men were killed. The main SAS targets would be German and Italian airfields along the North African coast, and they had an encouraging start when they succeeded in a practice attack on the RAF station at Heliopolis and merely stuck labels on the aircraft where they would have placed bombs.

Thus Stirling's own idea, which completely reversed the accepted policy of Commando raids from the sea, had been accepted by Auchinleck and Ritchie. In November 1941 the first SAS unit was ready for action. Then, when the first operation was due to start, Stirling faced a crisis because there was a seriously adverse weather report for the landing area. He was under intense pressure, since he knew there was a number of the staff at GHQ, who would have been pleased if the whole scheme were cancelled. He therefore decided to go ahead. The raid was not a success, and out of 62 men who started 40 were killed, injured or captured. Fortunately, the SAS was given another chance. They gained the support of the Long Range Desert Group – LRDG – a small and well-tried unit, which had been operating behind enemy lines in the desert since 1940. Captain David Lloyd Owen, of the Queen's Royal Regiment, who was to have a distinguished career in Special Forces, witnessed the problems faced by the SAS and offered to help.

In spite of the casualties and the necessary reorganisation, the SAS were ready for their next operation in December 1941. This would be against the Axis airfields at Sirte, Agheila and Agedabia. This time the four teams were delivered safely to their rendezvous by the highly experienced LRDG. The raiding groups, led by Stirling, Mayne, Lewes and Fraser, achieved almost total surprise and destroyed 61 enemy aircraft. Sadly, Lewes, who had done so much to establish the expertise and high professional standards of the SAS, was killed in the raid. The success of this raid secured the future of the SAS, and vindicated Stirling's initial idea and his determination to establish a new type of clandestine war – quite an achievement for a disgruntled lieutenant facing a possible court martial.

During 1942, the SAS under David Stirling enjoyed a series of successes. Helped by the LRDG, which delivered them accurately to their rendezvous, they attacked airfields, petrol dumps, ammunition dumps and supply convoys along the narrow coastal belt. They made a substantial impact on the Axis airforces, and in July 1942 alone they destroyed over 100 Axis aircraft. Their achievements stemmed from large numbers of small raids. But higher-level planners soon intervened and when the SAS were used in a joint operation with Commandos against Tobruk and Benghazi, it went disastrously wrong.

After the battle of El Alamein the SAS reverted to the type of operation at which they excelled. As the Axis forces retreated the unit attacked their lines of communication, stretching right back to Tunis and caused mayhem and destruction in airfields, ammunition dumps and supply depots. The year 1943 brought dramatic changes. David's brother, Bill Stirling, was despatched to set up a second SAS Regiment and David was captured in January 1943. His place was taken by Blair Mayne but there were a number of unnecessary problems because David Stirling had run the unit without informing colleagues of the whole picture. Although David Stirling was in

Colditz, to him must go the credit for conceiving the role of the SAS, leading its first tentative steps and establishing what would become one of the finest Special Force units in the world.

When the Allies drove the Axis forces out of North Africa, the SAS, along with the Special Boat Squadron, made successful attacks on targets in Sicily and Italy. The LRDG continued with its key role of observing and collecting intelligence and, as the Allies advanced through Italy, it operated effectively with the Special Boat Squadron in the Adriatic and among the Greek islands.

In November 1943 1 SAS returned to Britain for retraining. The SAS, while holding to the traditions established in the desert, now retrained for a slightly different role in the Allied advance across France after the Normandy landings of June 1944. There were serious discussions and deep divisions over the role that the SAS should play in the new situation – so deep that Bill Stirling resigned his command. But, in the end, it was agreed that the SAS were to operate in conjunction with the advancing American, Canadian and British forces, but also to link up with and co-operate with the various French, Dutch and Belgian resistance movements. Lieutenant Colonel Blair Mayne led the SAS units after they landed near Dijon on 8 August 1944. Mayne was a sufficiently powerful and colourful personality to mould the SAS and to develop its legendary reputation. He provided daring leadership, ruthless and brutal retribution, astonishing bravery, and wild high-jinks. When he received the second bar to his DSO the citation referred to his fine leadership and example and his utter disregard of danger. Eisenhower personally commended the award. The other side of Mayne's character was illustrated when, after one of his escapades, he drove through Le Mans – already occupied by the Americans – firing in the air from his jeep, for which he was personally reprimanded by General Patton.

Mayne continued his boisterous and unorthodox leadership of the SAS as the Allies advanced across the Rhine and into Germany. He was commended by General 'Boy' Browning, who commanded the Airborne forces. Mayne was to be involved in another incident, which admirably illustrates his bravery, and highlights another aspect of the dynamic leadership of the SAS. On 9 April 1945 the Allied advance was held up near Oldenburg; the leading unit suffered serious casualties and its commander was killed. Mayne drove forward under heavy fire, entered two houses from which the firing was coming, and killed the occupants. He next drove off another section of Germans. Then, while still under fire, he caught sight of wounded men lying exposed to enemy fire. He drove his jeep to them, and, with his colossal strength, lifted the wounded men on to his jeep and drove them back to safety. He was recommended for the VC, but received instead a fourth DSO. Normally, and Mayne was anything but normal, colonels are considered too senior to receive the MC – hence the fourth DSO. The same problem faced another superlatively brave leader, Mike Calvert, who was awarded two DSOs, but not the MC.

In considering the rationale behind new types of guerrilla war, the SAS, which became, perhaps, the greatest of the modern special forces, started from the most modest and unlikely base. The motivation of David Stirling, who was himself facing a possible court martial, was, primarily, the relative failure of the early Commando raids along the North African coast. He realised that there were a large number of highly trained Commandos, whom he knew and with whom he had trained, who were not being used effectively to attack and destroy the Germans. In conceiving the idea of the SAS, Stirling grasped the fundamental rule of guerrilla war, that there must be a secure base for guerrilla groups – in this case not the mountains, not the jungle or the forests, but the desert.

When Stirling and the Commandos of Layforce were posted to the Middle East, Calvert and Spencer Chapman were already actively occupied in establishing the Commando Training School at Wilson's Promontory in Victoria – the southern tip of Australia. As the Japanese threat in the south Pacific increased, the training school was moved to Queensland, where the training could take place in jungle conditions. Although Calvert only stayed a short time at Wilson's Promontory, life-long feelings of loyalty and respect between him and the Australian Commandos remained.

As at Lochailort, Calvert was dismayed when he received another War Office posting – on this occasion to be Chief Instructor at the Bush Warfare School at Maymyo in Burma – a pleasant town similar to the hill stations in India. The unit he joined, although containing the title Commando in order to confuse the enemy, produced not commandos for the British forces, but demolition experts who were sent up the old Burma Road to train and assist Chiang Kai-Shek's forces in southern China. Early in 1940, when Calvert had been in a desk job in London, he had said, 'I want to fight,' yet here he was in October 1941 in yet another training unit and the war seemed far away. This was soon to change dramatically.

The Japanese attacked Burma in 1942 and rapidly defeated the 17th Indian Division, which had been trained for desert warfare, and the Burma Division, whose role was little more than internal security. These unfortunate troops paid the price of the almost complete failure to prepare the defence of Burma.

Calvert, like Stirling and Mayne, had a wild mischievous streak to which war gave full vent. When the Japanese approached Maymyo, Calvert did not join the retreat but, instead, commandeered a river steamer, filled it with stores and explosives and, with a few of his staff, set out down the river intending to cause as much mayhem and damage to the advancing Japanese as possible. The trip was a great success, but, instead of being congratulated for his spirited action, he was reprimanded for taking the boat without permission. In an evil mood he returned to his office to find a rather scruffy full colonel sitting in his chair. 'Excuse me,' he said, 'that is my chair.' Thus Calvert met Wingate.

Calvert had considerable experience of guerrilla-type operations, in Norway, at Lochailort, in the Kent and Sussex defences, at the Australian Commando School and the Bush Warfare School. Later he described his meeting with Wingate: 'Clearly he knew all that I knew about unconventional warfare and a lot more, he was streets ahead of anyone, including the Lochailort boys ... something of the driving inspiration inside Orde Wingate transferred itself to me' (see *Mad Mike*). Wingate was to have been in charge of all irregular operations against the Japanese but like all the British units they were defeated by the speed of the Japanese advance. Both Wingate and Calvert survived the horrors of the retreat from Burma and in August 1942 Wingate summoned Calvert to GHQ in Delhi.

Wingate, that most cerebral of all the wartime guerrilla leaders, had applied his formidable intelligence to the issues of guerrilla war since serving in Palestine in 1938. An able regular officer – he was commissioned into the Royal Artillery from RMA Woolwich in 1923 – he made himself unpopular in Palestine with most of the British military authorities by becoming a passionate Zionist and by establishing the Special Night Squads. These taught the Jewish settlers to defend themselves and the oil pipeline from the attacks of Arab infiltrators. Next, early in 1941, he had the opportunity of leading Gideon Force, a guerrilla style unit, in the campaign to restore Haile Selassie to his Kingdom in Ethiopia – again making dangerous enemies among the military establishment. Wingate had always enjoyed the support of Wavell, who now supported him once again.

When Wingate arrived in India early in 1942, Wavell had appointed him, as a full colonel, to oversee operations behind the Japanese lines. This was when he met Calvert at Maymyo, but both were swept away with the retreat from Burma. Wavell still supported Wingate, and encouraged his theory of

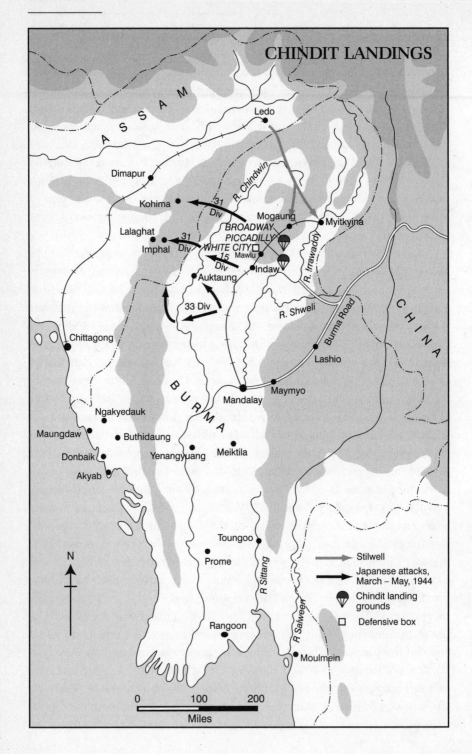

CHINDIT LANDINGS

A S S A M

Ledo

Dimapur

R. Chindwin

Kohima

31 Div

Mogaung

Myitkyina

Lalaghat

31 Div

BROADWAY
PICCADILLY
WHITE CITY Mawlu

Imphal

15 Div

Indaw

Auktaung

R. Irrawaddy

33 Div

R. Shweli

C H I N A

Chittagong

B U R M A

Burma Road

Lashio

Ngakyedauk

Mandalay

Maymyo

Maungdaw

Buthidaung

Donbaik

Yenangyuang

Meiktila

Akyab

N

Toungoo

Prome

R. Sittang

→ Stilwell

→ Japanese attacks,
March – May, 1944

Chindit landing
grounds

☐ Defensive box

Rangoon

R. Salween

Moulmein

0   100   200
Miles

Long Range Penetration, which he presented to a conference at GHQ in Delhi. Wingate's brilliance – or, as Churchill put it, genius – was to work out his theory in exact detail, to train men to the highest pitch of fitness and understanding and then to lead them against the enemy.

Wingate's idea of Long Range Penetration – LRP – was to establish a large body of troops – up to brigade strength – behind the enemy lines, and supply them by air. Their role would be to destroy roads, bridges, railways, ammunition stores and convoys in order to disrupt the supply and logistics for front line Japanese divisions. Essential to the concept of LRP was control of the air, an efficient supply system and, most crucial of all, an effective signals system, so that accurate detail of exact locations – with map references – would be radioed to HQ for the supply drops. Wingate himself wrote the training directives, and his passionate belief and attention to detail shine through what is usually the turgid prose of training manuals. He wrote, 'Hit the enemy at vital spots; always take the offensive view; attack with surprise; concentrate to strike and disperse for security; leave wide scope for commanders to adapt or exploit success.'

By August 1942, despite petty and often vindictive opposition from many of the staff at GHQ, Wingate was already putting his ideas into practice. He had taken over a camp at Gwalior in the Central Provinces and here 77 Brigade started its training. This unit was made up of the 15th King's Liverpool Regiment, 3/2 Gurkha Rifles, the 2nd Battalion Burma Rifles and 142 Commando. Under a very tough and demanding training regime, many men went sick, but Wingate persisted and gradually his force reached his exacting standards. He organised the Brigade into eight Columns. Each Column would operate independently behind the Japanese lines, with its own mule transport, controlled by radio signals and supplied entirely by air.

Early in 1943, the brigade moved by rail to the great supply base at Dimapur, and then marched the remaining 100 miles to Imphal, the HQ of the 4th Corps. Wingate had misunderstood the name of the lions – cinthe – which stood at the entrance to Burmese temples, and he dubbed his unit the Chindits. Wavell's strategy at the time was for 4th Corps to advance down towards the Chindwin, for Stilwell and his Chinese divisions to advance from the north, for Chiang Kai-Shek to advance westwards down the Burma Road and for the Chindits to move in behind the Japanese lines to disrupt their transport and supplies while these three major attacks took place. This was a sound plan, but when the Chindits reached Imphal none of the attacking forces were ready or prepared to move. Wingate, with the sympathetic support of Wavell, had to decide whether to proceed with the operation, although this would mean that the Japanese, instead of facing three major attacks, could focus all their forces on destroying the Chindits. Under this grave disadvantage, Wingate decided to go ahead, determined to prove his theory against the hostile attitude of the military establishment. The Columns under Wingate, Calvert, Fergusson, Gilkes, Scott and others began to infiltrate the jungle on 12 February 1943.

The Chindit Columns faced many teething problems but they fairly soon settled down into the routine of movement, signals to HQ and the supply drop. Calvert was the most aggressive and successful Column Commander and defeated a Japanese force in a fierce battle at Nankan. He won his first DSO on his 30th birthday. He further enhanced his reputation for effective demolition and macabre booby traps.

To lead a column of troops behind the enemy lines was the most severe test of leadership and, naturally, some were proved inadequate. The majority fulfilled their role and often, after stiff fire fights with the Japanese, patrols went on to demolish railways and bridges and to destroy Japanese convoys and supply trains. The railway at Bonchaung Gorge – an engineering masterpiece built before the war by the British – was demolished by Fergusson's Column. Soon afterwards he had to make the difficult decision to leave badly wounded men behind, as his Column fled from his more powerful pursuers. After some weeks Wingate took the difficult decision – for which he was viciously criticised by his opponents, but in which he was supported by all his Column Commanders who were on the spot – for all the Columns to cross the Irrawaddy and move east. This decision, based on inaccurate information about the favourable terrain east of the river, caused severe difficulties and privations to the Chindits, exacerbated by all the Japanese units now engaged in hunting them down. Shortly after this, Corps. HQ ordered Wingate to return to base. Then, after further anguished discussions with the Column Commanders, he made the decision for the Columns to separate and move independently to get back to the British lines. Some went north towards Fort Hertz; one group went east and after severe privations reached the forces of Chiang Kai-Shek, from where they hitched a lift with an American plane returning over the Hump. The majority returned by different routes to Imphal.

Assessment of the first Chindit campaign has been almost as controversial as Wingate himself. He was abrasive, and often appeared to offend people unnecessarily and he gave ammunition to his critics, who maintained that the whole operation was a waste of men and resources. On the other hand, Mutaguchi, the crude and brutal Japanese commander, confirmed that the Chindits had completely disrupted his plans for the 1943 campaign. They had also taught him the vital lesson that it was possible for troops to travel on an east–west axis in Burma – a tactic he used the following year.

When he got back, Wingate, who had lost nearly 1,000 men out of 3,000, wondered if he might be court martialled, but then, on 20 May 1943, he gave a press conference and stressed the achievements of the Chindits. The media, hungry for some good news from Burma after a series of often gutless defeats, latched on to the story of the Chindits. Louis Allen, the doyen of historians of the war in Burma, wrote in his book, *Burma: the Longest War* (p.101) that Wingate's first expedition 'had panache, it had glamour, it had cheek, it had everything the successive Arakan failures lacked'. In contrast, the official *History* written by Wingate's arch enemy, Kirby, stated: 'The operation had no strategic value.'

Then, while recovering from the ordeal and visiting the sick and wounded Chindits, Wingate, to his surprise, was called to Downing Street to see Churchill. In a succession of amazing events (see *Wingate and the Chindits*, p.102) Churchill took Wingate and his wife to the Quebec Conference with Roosevelt and the American Chiefs of Staff. Rarely had the issues of guerrilla war been considered at such a high level. Wingate, not over-awed by the occasion, confidently proposed the extension and enlargement of Long Range Penetration to three brigades, to operate and support Allied forces in the three main areas – Imphal, Fort Hertz and the Burma Road. Wingate's remarkable achievement – particularly in gaining the support of General George Marshall and General 'Hap' Arnold – resulted in generous American backing 'for this Limey who actually wants to fight the Japanese'. The Americans' wider aim was to open up the Burma Road and to provide arms and equipment for sixty Chinese divisions under Chiang Kai-Shek so that he would drive the Japanese out of southern China. The Americans also hoped to obtain forward air bases for the bombing of Japan.

Wingate, promoted to major general, was allocated six brigades and, most significantly, given the American Air Commando with several hundred aircraft to fly the Chindits to their dropping zones and to supply them during the operation. Wingate returned to Delhi in an exultant mood to be met by almost total and vindictive opposition. To create his Chindit brigades, a tried and experienced British division – the 70th – had to be broken up, and the military establishment has never forgiven Wingate for this. Auchinleck, who had just replaced Wavell, who became Viceroy of India, protested strongly against the Quebec decision, and this attitude was reflected down to the lowest level. Wingate, although he was now a major general, was told there was no office available and he would have to work in the corridor of GHQ.

The high level and substantive backing for the Chindits enabled Wingate to develop a new aspect of guerrilla war – linked again to massive air support. His new idea, culled from his deep knowledge of the Old Testament, was the Stronghold ('Turn to the Stronghold ye prisoners of hope', a phrase that also provided the apt title, *Prisoners of Hope*, for Calvert's moving classic on the Burma war). Wingate planned for a Stronghold in brigade strength to be set up behind the enemy lines, but remote from main roads and open country, so that it could be defended against any attacks except by armour and heavy artillery. The Stronghold would be a heavily defended base, from which Columns could radiate and disrupt enemy activity and supplies across a wide area. Reverting to the original plan for the first Chindit expedition, the Chindit brigades would now be flown in to the area of Indaw, while, once again, it was intended that 4th Corps from Imphal, Stilwell from Fort Hertz, and Chiang Kai-Shek from the east, would all advance. Once again they were not ready, but the Chindits' future was secured by Mutaguchi, the Japanese commander, who chose the same day to launch his three-division attack on Imphal and Kohima.

The launch of the Second Chindit campaign, named Operation Thursday, on 5 March 1944 could not have been more dramatic. Some 83 Dakotas and 80 gliders were lined up ready. Three dropping zones had been chosen – code-named Broadway, Piccadilly and Chowringhee – with a Chindit brigade to fly in to each. This was guerrilla war on a grand scale. Then, within minutes of take-off, a photographic recce showed that Piccadilly had been blocked by tree trunks. Anguished discussion centred on whether security had been breached, and whether the whole force might be wiped out as they landed. Calvert agreed to go to Broadway with the whole of 77 Brigade and Wingate and Slim made the final decision to proceed. It was discovered later that the tree trunks laid out to dry were the normal practice for local Burmese farmers.

Calvert flew in to Broadway at the head of 77 Brigade and set up the first Stronghold. Wingate defined this as a defended airstrip and base for light planes; an asylum for Chindit wounded; a magazine of stores; an administration centre; and the orbit around which the Chindit Columns would circulate. The rapid build up of defensive fortifications with barbed wire, mines, pre-set fields of fire for Vickers, LMGs and 3-inch mortars, went so smoothly that Calvert felt confident enough to leave Broadway and lead a strong fighting patrol to Mawlu, some miles west of Broadway. From Mawlu he could block the vital road and rail link going north to the great Japanese base at Myitkyina (pronounced Michenar). When his patrol reached Mawlu there was a fierce action with the Japanese in which Calvert led a bayonet charge, and a young officer won the VC. The Chindits sustained casualties but drove out the Japanese. Calvert established this bloc – less permanent than a Stronghold – and it prevented any more traffic up to Myitkyina. It became known as White City from the number of parachutes festooning the trees.

At Broadway Calvert brilliantly proved the success of the Stronghold concept, which was successfully defended against wave after wave of Japanese attackers, and from which marauding Chindit Columns ranged over a wide area. The pilots of light planes said they knew they were approaching Broadway because of the stench of all the Japanese bodies stuck on the barbed wire. With his Royal Engineers training Calvert gave inspired leadership at both Broadway and White City, making them models for both offensive and defensive action, backed up by air strikes from US Mustangs. By holding Broadway and White City, the Chindits blocked supplies to the Japanese 18 and 56 Divisions fighting against Stilwell and Chiang Kai-shek's Chinese, and also to the three divisions – 15, 31 and 33 – which Mutaguchi launched towards Imphal and Kohima. When, later, Kirby wrote that the Chindit attack had no effect on the Japanese campaign, Sir Robert Thompson said that the attack was as if a German airborne division had landed on Salisbury Plain on D-Day.

By this time, Wingate's ever-active mind had been looking forward to the situation when the enemy forces would be retreating across south-east Asia towards Japan. He proposed that Chindit brigades should be dropped well behind the retreating Japanese forces in order to destroy them completely. This far sighted and forward looking plan for action by the Chindit brigades was later used by his many establishment critics to say that he was insanely ambitious.

On 24 March 1944, less than three weeks since the launch of Operation Thursday, the Chindits at Broadway and White City were immensely heartened by a visit from Wingate, who commended their splendid achievement. He left White City and soon afterwards his plane crashed and all were killed. Wingate's powerful personality and formidable mind place him among the great guerrilla leaders. Bernard Fergusson (later Lord Ballantrae), who commanded 16 Column, wrote in *Beyond the Chindwin*, 'Wingate was a military genius of a grandeur and stature not seen more than once or twice in a century'. At the same time, Wingate was abrasive and catankerous and seemed almost to enjoy making enemies. Certainly in the military establishment there was a phalanx of critics who have continued to denounce and deride Wingate ever since his death (see *Wingate and the Chindits*, pp.203–49).

Many Chindits were horrified when the weak and ineffective Lentaigne who, coming from 70 Division, had never accepted Wingate's ideas or his general philosophy, was appointed to succeed him. Shortly after Lentaigne's appointment, Slim decided to hand over the Chindit units to Stilwell's control. Calvert, who admired Slim as one of the great commanders, argued that he had a blind spot about the role of the Chindits. Certainly this decision, which Wingate would have been strong enough to reject, was the death warrant of many Chindits. Stilwell, notoriously and irresponsibly critical of 'cowardly Limeys', ordered 77 Brigade under Calvert to capture Mogaung. This illustrates a complete lack of understanding of the role of the Chindits, a specialist guerrilla force with no armour or artillery, and trained for guerrilla-type operations. Instead, Stilwell ordered them to attack Mogaung, a heavily fortified Japanese garrison. Calvert, 'the bravest of the brave', led his faithful 77 Brigade and, despite horrendous casualties, captured Mogaung. After Mogaung the whole brigade were flown out to hospitals in India because of their pitiable physical condition. This was a tragic end to one of the really original concepts of guerrilla war, which was peculiarly suited to the terrain of the Burmese jungle and the tactical situation of air superiority and effective radio communication. The Chindit concept was superseded largely by the development of the helicopter, although, as Giap was to show in Vietnam, helicopters cannot defeat effective guerrilla forces on the ground (see *Military Mavericks*, pp.221–4). It fell to Mountbatten to deliver the final blow and disband the Chindits. He said, dishonestly, 'We are all Chindit minded now.'

Calvert was invalided home at the end of 1944. Although recommended by his three battalion commanders for the VC, he received no award for his superb leadership from Broadway and White City to Mogaung – commanding a brigade for five months behind enemy lines. This was testimony enough to the power of the anti-Chindit prejudice. To his surprise, when back in England and restored to health, he was appointed to command the SAS in the final months of the war. This appointment was not popular with the SAS, who had built up a powerful team in Europe and rather resented Calvert as an outsider. The SAS remained active during the advance into Germany, and then a headquarters unit under

Calvert was flown into Norway to take over a large German naval base and 40,000 Russian POWs. This was a relatively uneventful time except for an excessively boisterous dinner night when Blair Mayne, in one of his violent outbursts, threw Calvert – no lightweight – over his shoulder, resulting in two black eyes.

After 1945, like many outstanding wartime leaders, Calvert returned almost reluctantly to the humdrum pursuits of peace. After Staff College, where he proved to be rather bolshie, and postings to Trieste and Pakistan, he had a staff job in Hong Kong at the time of the Korean War. This was also when the communist emergency in Malaya burst out. On Field Marshal Slim's recommendation, General Harding, commander in chief in Singapore, sent for Calvert since, as Slim said, 'He knows all about jungle warfare'. In the face of a rapidly deteriorating security position, Harding gave Calvert six months to get into Malaya and assess the situation.

He found a depressing scenario. During the Japanese occupation the main opposition had been the Chinese communists, and after 1945 this had become the Malayan Communist Party. The British administration was inept, with serious divisions between the civilian organisation, the police and the army, and between those who escaped in 1941 and those whom the Japanese imprisoned. By 1950 the communists set out to challenge British control by destroying the tin and rubber industries – the main source of Malaya's wealth. They enjoyed substantial advantages. In 1945 they had taken over many Japanese weapons, and also many British weapons after Operation 'Zipper' – named, as one cynic said, because everything was not buttoned up. The Chinese guerrillas had a powerful country-wide support group, the Min Yuen, but they had alienated the Malay people and they rejected the ideology of Mao Zedong when he came to power in China in 1949. When the attacks on the rubber plantations and the tin mines began, the rubber planters and tin miners refused to be daunted and prepared to fight back.

Calvert, who disliked his Hong Kong staff job, was delighted to be given an opportunity for action in Malaya. This was a serious and fundamental change for him. If ever there was a case of poacher turned gamekeeper, this was it. He now used his encyclopaedic knowledge of guerrilla war to fight against Chinese insurgents. He soon became a leader and expert in counter-insurgency, a field that opened up world-wide in the ensuing years. He spent six months visiting most parts of Malaya, getting to know the people, and going into the jungle with military patrols. He was appalled by what he found. On the military side there was lethargy, idleness, indifference and unacceptable attitudes. He reported that the CO of a Scots Guards battalion had said to him that 'it was not the job of the Guards to chase bare-arsed niggers'.

Calvert reported to Harding before the end of the six months. Based on his Chindit experience, he proposed a Long Range Penetration system with highly trained patrols going into the jungle to destroy terrorist bases. He backed this up with proposals to win the hearts and minds of the Malay and Chinese people, and the establishment of defended villages for the Chinese squatters who lived on the edge of jungle settlements and had often been terrorised by the communist groups. These plans of Calvert were the basis of what later became known as the Briggs Plan.

Calvert then seized another opportunity. He had witnessed the dismal spectacle in October 1945 of the disbandment of the SAS, and when, in August 1950, he was summoned to Whitehall to discuss his Malayan plans, he was able to obtain agreement to the establishment of the Malayan Scouts (SAS Regiment). What could have been a great opportunity swiftly became a near disaster.

Calvert was an absolutely inspiring leader in terms of practical skills in jungle fighting, but from the start both the new regiment and the training camp lacked the necessary military and professional backup. Most surprisingly, considering his immense prowess during the Chindit campaigns, his unit rapidly became notorious for drunken ill-discipline (see *Mad Mike*, Chapter 9, 'Malaya').

Many distinguished officers, notably Colonel John Woodhouse, have testified to Calvert's inspirational leadership but also confirm the riotous lack of discipline. The notoriety spread rapidly, and in June 1951, after less than a year, Calvert (who did have amoebic dysentery) was suddenly flown home to Millbank Hospital. From the sorry spectacle left by Calvert, many sound leaders restored high standards of discipline and helped to create the superb force which the SAS has remained.

After 1951, Calvert's career – after being unjustly convicted by court martial for a crime he did not commit – became a series of tragic disasters, but he did enjoy a brief period in the 1970s, when he became a respected commentator on issues of guerrilla war and counter-insurgency.

He had intended to produce a monumental work, *The Pattern of Guerrilla War*, but it was never completed. He did, however, write a short pamphlet which contained some interesting thoughts about guerrilla war. He argued that guerrilla war was always a war of the weak against the strong, and he compared the guerrilla leader to a surgeon who needed knowledge of the body politic and where its weakest points were. The guerrilla leader needed to understand the economy and where it was vulnerable, to weigh up psychological issues, and to consider the moral fibre of the people with their likely attitudes to a guerrilla uprising.

He gave careful thought to the qualities needed in a successful guerrilla leader. He needed to be well-educated, strong and healthy, aggressive and ruthless, and with a tortuous mind, enabling him to work his way into the enemy psyche. He needed the personality to win the hearts and minds of the people and the guile to achieve his ends. He saw Mao Zedong and Tito as the greatest modern guerrilla leaders, as they had a complete philosophy of war and were not merely technicians of war.

In looking at modern society he saw it as a grave disadvantage that so many men were tied down by their wish for a safe job, a home, and the need to pay their mortgage and work for their pension. Calvert tended to see an antagonism with the female sex and criticised wives who shackled their husbands to a safe routine life instead of 'the glorious uncertainty of guerrilla life'. He reckoned that these factors had weakened the French resistance and he had found it among possible underground leaders in Kent and Sussex in the spring of 1940. His personal situation may have coloured his view on these issues, since he never owned his own home, and he never had a wife or a mortgage.

He believed that, to gain support, a guerrilla group needed to have contact with teachers, university lecturers and youth leaders who could recruit young people to the guerrilla cause. These could be youths with a doubtful background 'who can be taken, brainwashed, kept physically and mentally exhausted, and drilled into a close-knit loyal and efficient fighting unit'. Likely recruits might come from men who felt rejected by society, including those rejected by elite military formations, who were anxious to prove their manhood. He touched on the issue of war leaders who were gay. This included Calvert himself and Blair Mayne, and raised the interesting question whether a gay man tries harder than others to prove his manliness in the harsh reality of military combat. In the course of his research, Calvert visited Angola and Vietnam and he included in his thesis the words of a young Vietcong guerrilla: 'It is far more interesting and exciting blowing up bridges than standing guard on them 24 hours a day' ('The Characteristics of Guerrilla Leaders', Calvert Papers, Imperial War Museum).

Calvert concluded – bearing in mind he was writing as an expert in counter-insurgency – that society needed to harness the energy and drive of the small minority of outstanding young men who might be potential rebel leaders. On the practical issues of guerrilla war, Calvert, writing from his great experience, was excellent, but his wider theories – seen perhaps from his lonely, increasingly right-wing and misanthropic view – seem fanciful and impractical. Unfortunately, he never established himself either as a commentator or as an historian, and he died almost penniless in a Star and Garter home.

The sad demise of Calvert was in contrast to some others whose early experiences in the Commandos, the Chindits and the SAS laid the foundation for successful careers. David Stirling put his energy and ability into several different fields, such as the Capricorn Africa Society and many security related and usually right-wing organisations across the Middle East – notably Saudi Arabia and the Yemen. Blair Mayne returned to his native Ulster and continued with his violent outbursts, after which he always paid for the damage. He was so respected by the people of Newtownards that they erected a statue to him. Sir Robert Thompson, the most successful of all the ex-Chindits, had been an RAF liaison officer with both Chindit operations. He subsequently had a most distinguished career as an expert in counter-insurgency and he became an adviser to presidents Ford and Nixon (see his autobiography, *Make for the Hills*).

The half century after 1945 became the age of insurgency, linked often to the problems of Israel and the Middle East, to Africa and its many post-colonial movements, to Indonesia and Borneo, and to Latin America. British and American military forces increasingly concentrated on counter-insurgency activity, and many soldiers trained in this field began to realise that their skills had a commercial value. Some joined the mercenary units, which flourished at the same time, often supporting dubious right-wing dictators such as those who dominated the Congo and sub-Saharan Africa. Others, like Andy McNab, published their reminiscences and added to the plethora of books on these fascinating topics.

CHE GUEVARA AND GUERRILLA WAR

Che Guevara, murdered in Bolivia in 1967, became, almost overnight, an idol and martyr for radical students around the world. After his death his writings and speeches made world-wide impact. His fame and authority as a guerrilla leader influenced many of the post-1968 revolutionary and urban guerrilla movements such as the Baader-Meinhof group – youngsters from well-to-do backgrounds like his own – ETA, the Red Army Faction and the Sandinistas. Despite his weaknesses, eagerly divulged by his critics, he still stands as a hero and an exemplar of what can be achieved by idealism and determination. Feared by the American establishment as a dangerous communist, he was too independent to submit to the discipline of a political party. He was driven instead by a passion to bring justice to the landless peasant, to downtrodden miners and 'the wretched of the earth'. His real threat to capitalist domination lay in his conviction, based on his Cuban experience, that a very small group of determined men can start a revolution and act as a catalyst for a mass movement of the people. Across South America, he witnessed the suffering, the sickness and the starvation inflicted on peasants, rural plantation workers, industrial workers and miners by the uncaring arrogance of the industrial muscle wielded by the USA. He devoted his life to changing this.

His reputation has, since 1967, risen or fallen depending on the films, TV series and countless books based on his romantic and colourful life, but his position as a guerrilla leader and as a serious thinker about guerrilla war has remained more constant. His thesis on guerrilla war is often linked in significance with that of Mao Zedong, yet, ironically, in his last disastrous campaign in Bolivia, which led to his death, he ignored almost all the criteria that he had laid down in his seminal work on guerrilla war.

Born in 1928 into a well-to-do, and even aristocratic, Argentinian family, he was brought up in an atmosphere of constant intellectual discussion, with a strong left-wing or Marxist slant, and with strong criticism of US imperialism. Che – a nickname he actually acquired later – was a sickly child, subject to frequent asthma attacks. For his health the family, at great cost, moved away from Buenos Aires to Alta Gracia, a town in the hills. He was a highly intelligent boy and, despite his frailty, he had fierce determination and gained a reputation as a daring leader of a street gang, but also as a boy who would undertake the meanest tasks without grumbling. He was often stricken for days with serious asthma attacks, and then he would read widely from his father's impressive library. At a time of industrial unrest, the Guevara family nearly always sided with the strikers – on one occasion, during a power workers' strike, Che's gang took their catapults and broke all the street lights in the town to show their support. During this time the family actively supported refugees and victims of Franco's fascist forces in Spain.

Asthma attacks frequently interrupted his education but, with his outstanding intelligence, he found it easy to catch up. Whilst at school he always appeared mature for his years, but undisciplined and moody. Partly because of his constant health problems he enrolled at the University of Buenos Aires to read medicine in 1947. His mother, a leading intellectual, introduced him to many leading Marxists and created an atmosphere of intellectual stimulation. Asthma attacks continued to dog him, but he passed his medical exams with ease. Even before he completed his degree, he set off with a close friend, Alberto Granado – a young doctor specialising in leprosy – to travel through the different countries of South America. This could have been a happy-go-lucky trip for two bright young men but for Che it was to have a deep and lasting impact. Wherever they went, they witnessed injustice, crippling poverty, corrupt, uncaring officialdom, and the mining companies grinding down their workers. Although they had great fun and shared in bizarre and hilarious scrapes, the experience convinced Che that all the countries they visited urgently needed reform. When he viewed the power of American companies and reactionary, corrupt governments, he began to think that the only way of overthrowing them was by military revolt.

The pair had vague hopes of going to Easter Island but abandoned the idea and travelled northwards through Chile. There, they were again horrified by the suffering and the human catastrophe endured by the miners working in the open cast copper mines. From Chile they crossed clandestinely into Peru, constantly amazed by the poverty and suffering, but awed by the kindness and hospitality of those who had almost nothing. As they travelled through the mountains they passed the remarkable ruins of Machu Picchu, the last refuge of the Incas from the Spaniards.

The pair had to resort to various tricks and subterfuges to get transport or even food, but they eventually reached Lima. Here they met a distinguished leprosy specialist, and they went to help at a leper colony, doing admirable work, often with the most seriously afflicted patients. They left the colony on a raft constructed for them by the lepers and, after a brief visit to Colombia, Che returned to his family in Buenos Aires and quickly passed his final medical examinations.

After a brief stay at home, Che went off to Bolivia, a country named after his hero Simon Bolivar. Here he was again appalled at the suffering caused by the draconian policies of the American companies. He then met an old friend who spoke to him of the volatile political conditions in Guatemala, and so Che went to Guatemala in December 1953. Here he saw at first hand the crude power of US imperialism used to overthrow the genuine reforming administration of Arbenz. An army, backed and armed by the CIA, overthrew Arbenz, but in doing so they created a fanatic, now convinced that armed struggle was the only answer to US imperialism. Che was prompted to return to serious study of Marxism and to investigate again the strategy and tactics of the Spanish Civil War, and the role of guerrillas in that war. Thus a radical young doctor with a hatred of injustice and suffering became an active revolutionary in Guatemala.

In Guatemala he met some Cuban exiles who were members of the 26 July Organisation, which commemorated Fidel Castro's first attack on Batista's Cuba, and he also met Hilda Acosta, whom he married shortly afterwards. After various adventures with the local police they both reached Mexico, and here, in July 1955, Che met Fidel Castro. They immediately established a sound rapport and found that they had similar ideas about revolution and the US-backed puppet governments of the region. Influenced by Castro's powerful charisma, Che joined the organisation as a doctor. Castro and Che had lengthy and fierce debates, which helped to clarify Che's views. He determined from then onwards to join any revolutionary organisation which was prepared to fight the real enemies: US imperialism, American companies which exploited the poor, the CIA and the repressive regimes it kept in power.

Che's experiences in South America had been sound training for his next expedition. His deep anger at the suffering, poverty and the 'degradation of under-nourishment' still drove him forward. His experience of walking vast distances, short of food and water and money, and cheerfully keeping going when others gave up, would soon mark him out as a leader among Castro's guerrillas.

The Cuba to which Castro and Che were to set sail in November 1956 had a bloody and turbulent history. In the mid-nineteenth century, Cuban rebels fought for ten years against the control of Spain, and slavery was

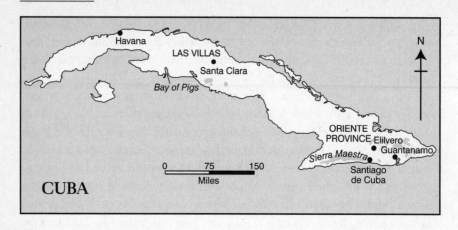

only abolished in 1886. Ten years later, the USA intervened on the side of the rebels and against Spanish control, and ruled with a military government until 1902 when a republic was established. Independence did little to curb US agricultural, industrial and economic domination. During the 1920s, and the prohibition era, Cuba became a safe haven for drink rackets, gambling, prostitution and organised crime, with the Mafia in the lead. Nothing really changed until after World War II and then, in 1952, Batista, a former president, seized power with the help of the army. This prompted an uprising led by Fidel Casto who was jailed for fifteen years. In 1955, Batista granted an amnesty to political prisoners and Castro was released from prison and fled to Mexico. The exiled members of his 26 July Organisation were protesting particularly against the widespread corruption of the Batista regime, and the domination of the country by US industrial power and crime syndicates.

In a remarkable parallel to Garibaldi's expedition with 'The Thousand' in 1860, Castro, Che and eighty ill-equipped and poorly trained men set out in a rusty old boat, the *Granma*. Even before they left, they were arrested by the Mexican police and only released after heavy fines were imposed – effectively depleting their funds for buying arms. Over six days, they suffered from constant and acute sea-sickness, they had to jettison their supplies in a storm and, finally, they landed in remote part of the Sierra Maestra on the eastern tip of Cuba. A coastguard had seen them and alerted the Cuban military forces of Batista. The leadership at the start of this campaign – ultimately one of the most successful guerrilla operations in the modern world – was almost ludicrously inept and incompetent. In the first action at Alegria de Pio on 5 December 1956, they made a series of near fatal blunders. They were betrayed by a guide whose loyalty they had not checked, they did not react to aircraft from the Cuban airforce and whilst resting with their boots off, their weapons laid aside, and no sentries posted, they were attacked by Batista's ground forces and virtually wiped out.

Another significant and symbolic incident took place during these early encounters – made much of by most biographers. Che's few remaining men were fleeing from Batista's troops when he had to choose between his box of medicines and a box of ammunition. He chose the ammunition. Any prospect of success appeared impossible, since they were reduced to about a dozen survivors, few guns, hardly any ammunition, no food or other supplies, and no apparent loyalty from locals who had betrayed them. Castro and Che's two small groups had split up, and before joining up again, Che and his group found a supportive peasant who gave them hospitality. Che temporarily left his weapons and vital supplies with the peasant, only to find that the welcoming neighbours had spread the news, and all the weapons were captured by the enemy. Castro severely reproached him: 'To abandon your weapons was criminal and stupid.'

Early in 1957, they attacked a small barracks and captured twelve rifles, but Che still made grave errors. For several months they made little progress, suffering from harsh conditions and low morale. Then, eventually, one or two volunteers from the local community joined them. Gradually they built up their support in the surrounding villages. Then the news spread that they were courteous to the local people, that they paid for their supplies, and were hoping to establish a fairer and more just society. All of this contrasted with the brutal attitudes of the Cuban Army, which people feared and loathed.

As the influence of the rebels grew, Che emerged as a positive leader. He trained his men to a higher standard of efficiency, and he let it be known that he demanded total loyalty and would be absolutely ruthless in dealing with traitors or informers. He remained a fierce disciplinarian and it was believed that he had shot a man for sleeping while on sentry duty. He punished or publicly humiliated men who fell short of his exacting standards. He stated publicly that war was harsh and even a suspicion of treason could not be tolerated. At the same time, from an old duplicating machine, he managed to produce a simple news-sheet which successfully spread their message.

Having witnessed rural poverty and suffering across South America, now, in the guerrilla situation, he was more than ever convinced that the downtrodden areas of the Americas were the ideal soil for revolution, and that agrarian reform must be the first demand of the guerrilla. By the beginning of 1957, the tiny rebel force had at least survived, and some outside factors began to favour them. On 17 January 1957, Castro commanded an attack on a small garrison at El Ilvero and, without loss, captured food, weapons and ammunition. Then their cause appeared to be threatened when a traitor, who had infiltrated their force, reached Castro but failed to kill him. He was executed. Next, some intrepid US journalists visited Castro's HQ and, in generally favourable reports, began to build up his reputation. Che said this was more important than a military victory. In February 1957 the well-known *New York Times* reporter Herbert Matthews, bluffed into thinking that Castro had large forces under his control, wrote articles that changed the whole image of Castro and presented him as a democratic leader opposed to communism. Matthews's articles caused a sensation, and soon afterwards a CBS film crew visited Castro's HQ.

While the rebels slowly built up their strength and extended the small area under their control, another anti-Batista group kept up a campaign of sabotage in Havana. In March 1957 they narrowly failed in an attempt to kill Batista but their leader, who could have been a serious rival to Castro, was captured and executed.

Other rebel groups now came to consult Castro, although Che remained highly suspicious of them. One of these, an anti-communist leader, was shortly afterwards caught and executed – another possible rival to Castro removed. He had other important backers in the wider community, and the rebels were heartened when the captured survivors of the *Granma* were acquitted in court. During the summer of 1957, highly confusing and conflicting factors and interests came into play. The US attempted to put pressure on Batista to restore democracy, and favourable publicity began to influence American public opinion. Even the CIA, hedging its bets, sent $50,000 to Castro's organisation. At about the same time, ironically, the communists backed the rebel movement.

By the autumn of 1957, the rebels effectively controlled a wide area in and around the Sierra Maestra and they had established a viable, if basic, civil administration. Journalists visited the hospital, the metal and leather workshops, the butcher and baker, the sugar factory and the office producing the newspaper. The rebels gradually established trade with the local peasants and a few traders, all of whom were paid in cash. At the beginning of 1958 they established Rebel Radio, which obtained great publicity for the rebel cause and demoralised the government. Castro and Che now appeared in a more favourable light in the American media, which tended to fall for many exaggerated claims. Castro received great help from Celia Sanchez, who had organised an arms shipment in the early days. She now became his lover, and also took over all the administration of the rebels' affairs.

During 1958, Batista was still under pressure from the USA to restore democracy; the powerful Roman Catholic church called for a government of national unity; and Eisenhower stopped military supplies to the Batista regime. The rebel cause did receive a setback, when a poorly organised general strike in Havana was easily repressed by Batista, but even this played into Castro's hands when the rebel leaders, who could have been rivals, were eliminated.

As the rebel organisation and achievements gained more favourable publicity, Batista was forced to take military action against them. Foolishly, he sent a large number of untried recruits and reservists in a campaign lasting ten weeks, which attempted to pursue the rebels into an isolated corner. The government forces made no significant headway against the rebels, who held all the high ground and knew the terrain intimately. Batista's men did capture one small town, but then had to make a humiliating withdrawal, and then the commander himself was ambushed. After all the clashes, the rebels released their prisoners after taking away their weapons and ammunition and this gave their reputation another boost.

For the rebels, having made very slow progress, suddenly things improved. Batista had put down a student plot in Havana with sickening brutality and the Cuban Army had carried out another campaign to strike terror into the people of the Sierra Maestra. Both of these backfired. Next, fifty volunteers, some of them armed, joined the rebels, who were now beginning to be recognized as a viable force. Equally significant, a small cargo ship safely delivered machine guns, rifles and ammunition to Castro's headquarters.

Shortly afterwards, Castro and Che led an attack in daylight on a small garrison town. They overwhelmed the garrison but suffered casualties. Although this victory was on a small scale, in some ways it was one of their most important. As a result of it, the Batista government withdrew its forces from small isolated garrisons which were vulnerable to rebel attack. In practice this handed over large areas to the rebels, and enabled them to establish their new and just regime. News of this spread more rapidly and had a wider impact even than the military achievements. Che, driven by his passion to establish a just and fair society for the oppressed rural poor, played a prominent part in the social reorganisation, which the new situation made possible. Under his direction, the rebels set up new administrative councils, hospitals, law courts and food supplies. This received an enthusiastic response. As the rebel strength increased, Castro reorganised the force and Che became commander of one of the three Columns which were set up. Both in size and function they were remarkably similar to the Column – which had been the key operating unit of Wingate's Chindits.

Through his modest newsletter, Che made valuable contact with journalists, who played a key role in publicising the cause. After careful vetting and with tight security, one or two were admitted to his base. One described a hospital with two doctors caring for twenty wounded men; a small metal workshop producing and repairing weapons; a tailor's shop producing uniforms, a cobbler producing and repairing boots and a bakery. To the visiting journalists, Castro appeared as the talker and dreamer, while Che, a fearsome debater on the great political issues they faced, at the same time was the man on the ground, who ensured that the policies were carried out.

During 1958, the rebels were strong enough to consider their next move. Castro entrusted the command of a major new strategy to Che, who was the most successful Column commander. The operation proposed that two Columns should drive westwards from the Sierra Maestra, through the mountains and into the central area of Las Villas. Che commanded about 300 men against regular forces of 10,000. He was undaunted by this because he thought that any regular soldier was the lackey of the dictator Batista and would always give in or run away rather than lose his life. This attitude also accounts for the constant reports of Che's bravery under fire, and his almost foolhardy and quixotic approach to danger.

Under his energetic command, the Columns moved rapidly westwards and established themselves in Las Villas. Then, to everyone's amazement, they captured the strategic town and fortress of Santa Clara. Before attacking Santa Clara, Che carried out a daring guerrilla strike by ambushing an armoured train and capturing a vast quantity of guns, two tanks and 'a fabulous quantity of ammunition.' This success and the effective work of suicide squads on the approaches to Santa Clara proved Che's outstanding qualities as a guerrilla commander – a far cry from the green and inexperienced man who had stumbled ashore only a few months before. The capture of Santa Clara and the province of Las Villas gave the rebels control over more than half of Cuba. Batista in Havana could not ignore a situation that clearly threatened his whole regime.

In the spring of 1958 there had been a call for a general strike in Havana to support the rebels. This failed completely and to some extent compromised the military plans. At the same time it confirmed Che in his belief, refuting the more orthodox Marxist view that revolution must come from a rising of the urban proletariat. Che now believed more confidently than ever that, at least in the Americas, for a revolt to succeed, bases must first be set up in the countryside, and from those bases the towns would be forced to surrender.

The most remarkable aspect of the Cuban campaign was the speed with which Che learnt his lessons and matured as a military commander. Having captured Santa Clara he had to hold his small force together and prepare for the inevitable counter-attack. This came in December 1958, when Batista launched a substantial assault with regular army units and a large number of recruits. Santa Clara contained a formidable fortress or citadel, and Che successfully defended this with his skeleton force. The troops of Batista were defeated.

The Eisenhower administration, under pressure from the United Fruit Company, actively intervened again in the political sphere, hoping to be able to get rid of Batista, and form an acceptable government before Castro took control by force of arms. The whole situation remained chaotic. Batista was using American planes against the rebels, when Raul, Castro's brother and one of the best Column commanders, kidnapped fifty Americans, only releasing them when the aerial attacks were called off.

After the defeat and repulse of Batista's forces at Santa Clara, all the rebel Columns moved rapidly towards Havana. Batista had no answer to this advance, while, increasingly, the Columns entered towns and villages to an enthusiastic welcome. On 1 January 1959, Batista and most of his cronies fled from Cuba, and there was a brief interregnum which was brought down by an effective general strike called by Castro. Che, at the head of the leading Column, entered Havana and immediately took control of the main army barracks. On 8 January 1959, Castro entered Havana as a conquering hero. The new Council of Ministers immediately announced that Che was a full citizen of Cuba. From that time onwards, he became a significant policy maker with Castro, and he held strongly to the view that the down-trodden of the Americas should look to Cuba for inspiration and help. If anything, he increased his hatred for the evil effects of US economic and political power.

Che always enjoyed a dazzling intelligence and power of observation, and after two years of guerrilla fighting he wrote with authority and conviction. His writings on *Guerrilla Warfare*, published in 1960, stressed the importance of the philosophical commitment to a juster society, going along with the development of military skills. The great lesson he deduced from his guerrilla experience was that a few determined men using guerrilla tactics could beat a modern army, even if it was armed with atomic weapons and tanks. The wisdom of that lesson will be debated later, but his views made a strong impact across the world. He considered the Cuban campaign to be a model for armed revolution across Latin America, and that guerrilla aims should always be to right the wrongs of society and build a new and just social order.

In formulating his theory he acknowledged his debt to Mao Zedong, and reiterated that guerrilla bands must have rural bases and a sanctuary from enemy attack. He claimed that the Cuban revolution proved the possibility of guerrilla war freeing a people from oppression: given a suitable terrain and serious injustice in society, a core of fifty men is enough to spark a revolution in a Latin American country.

The immediate impact of Che's views is seen in the worried reaction of Pentagon spokesmen, who expressed their strong fear of communist advance, and who identified the communist danger in North Vietnam, Cuba, Latin America and Africa. They stressed that communist guerrilla activity was a new form of war, and that it was easy for communist guerrillas to set up a guerrilla operation at little cost and bring whole areas under communist control. One rattled commentator suggested that it was just possible that the communists might not win if the west decided to unite economically, and, meanwhile, he looked apprehensively at the petty dictatorships and injustice in Mexico, Chile, Argentina and Bolivia.

The initial apprehension of the US military establishment was carried a step further in the *Small Wars Manual* – significantly not actually mentioning 'guerrilla war' in the title. It stated 'The US to protect its citizens world-wide can use its Marines, usually operating from US ships, to take action in a foreign country ... a marine landing is not an act of war', but it can include 'disarming of natives'. The US was swift to develop 'Special Forces' and a 'Strategic Corps'. The Rangers trained these forces in new techniques and new tactics, including the hunter-killer team aimed at eliminating guerrilla groups.

Che enunciated *General Principles of Guerrilla Fighting* and claimed that Cuba proved many things for the Americas: that popular forces can win a war against an army; that a revolutionary situation can be created; that in Latin America the rural areas are the best places for revolution; the people must be convinced that social wrongs cannot be solved peacefully; the guerrilla band is the armed nucleus of the masses; and it must fight for social reform in order to gain the total support of the masses.

Che often quoted Mao Zedong and Ho Chi Minh and, indirectly, Sun Tzu: 'Never fight if you cannot win; practise deception, treachery, surprise; attack the enemy's weak points; always exploit surprise; use hit and run tactics again and again; give the enemy no rest; continue the guerrilla struggle until it becomes a guerrilla army.' He believed that guerrilla war was the miracle by which a determined group could become the vanguard of a mass movement attempting to establish a new and just society.

In outlining strategy, Che – unintentionally quoting Mao – maintained that the enemy is always the best source of supply for weapons and ammunition, and the greatest danger is running out of ammunition in the middle of a fight. Arguing from his very slight experience of urban uprisings, he stressed the need to sound out the situation in the cities, to find out which figures in society would provide leadership, and to decide if a general strike would be supported. When this was ascertained, detailed plans must be made to sabotage water supplies, electricity, railways and roads.

Che considered tactics with forceful clarity, his freshness and sharpness stemming from his guerrilla campaign. His constant message was to conserve ammunition: 'never leave a dead comrade without taking his weapons and ammunition'; always use a few well aimed shots; equally important, keep all weapons in good condition, especially rifles, bazookas and machine guns, and in secure bases start to manufacture gunpowder. He was always concerned about the welfare of the people, and while he encouraged sabotage as a significant weapon, he warned his men against knocking out a whole industry, which would put people out of work.

While ideally the guerrilla operated in hilly and wooded areas, when he had to operate in unfavourable terrain, like flat and open country, he should quickly adapt to the less favourable conditions. He should be able to march twenty-five miles in a night, and, in darkness, discipline and control became even more essential. An attack in darkness should rely on concentration of fire, not marksmanship. He argued that the ideal guerrilla band numbered about ten, since that size of group was easier to feed and supply, to control in an attack, and to disperse when necessary.

Che's advice on tactics was often interspersed with the wider issues of social justice. He saw a guerrilla campaign as a crusade for people's freedom and justice, but it should be launched only after peaceful means had been exhausted. In the Americas, a revolt to destroy an unjust social order should start in the rural areas, and, recognising the peasant's yearning to own the land he works, should have agrarian reform as his banner. Emphasising self-control and moral conduct, Che believed that the guerrilla should appear as the elder brother of the peasant farmer, and then should, when victory comes, take the land from the rich and give it to the peasant.

After dealing with tactics and social aims, Che gave clear advice on actual combat. To be prepared for combat the guerrilla needs physical, mental and moral strength, preferably backed up by local knowledge. He must be prepared to work and fight at night, but, above all, to surprise, destroy, kill and sow panic among the enemy. He needs an iron constitution with strength to survive illness and wounds, and 'to live like a harassed animal – part of the very soil ... In Cuba it was literally a stinking life ... living on tubers, grain, and occasional pieces of meat.' Che was most specific that enemy wounded should be helped, and men should not be taken prisoner – instead disarmed, scolded and sent on their way. At the same time every effort must be made to save and rescue your own wounded. The guerrilla should carry the lightest possible pack, but always ensure that his rifle is clean, dry and slightly oiled – a nostalgic memory for most ex-soldiers. Apart from his weapon, his hammock and a blanket were indispensable, and sound shoes or boots the next most important thing. For most guerrillas, combat came as a relief from drudgery, despite the danger.

Hoping that his precepts would help guerrillas around the world, Che carefully outlined the organisation of the guerrilla group. The squad should be between eight and twelve men, with four squads in a platoon, and four platoons in a Column – about 160 men. The distribution of food, clothes, sweets and tobacco must be carefully controlled, as that is the most likely cause of resentment. He laid down necessary drills prior to an attack: reconnaissance, plan of ambush, digging of defensive positions, and, if there was time, to have overhead protection against mortar fire. Having often been outnumbered by Batista's forces, he advised that if a squad was surrounded, they should go to ground, dig in and await darkness, the guerrilla's natural ally. He believed that taking part in a campaign created bonds of brotherhood, and also good friendly rivalry between Columns.

Having made serious blunders during the first few weeks of combat in Cuba, Che strongly emphasised the need for security, and never to trust local farmers. The first actions of a guerrilla group were likely to be ambushes in order to obtain weapons and ammunition, so the group should always include some unarmed men, whose role was to carry off the loot.

In summing up his advice on organisation, Che paid generous tribute to the achievements of women, and also stressed the significance of education, indoctrination and propaganda, because so many peasants and potential supporters had extremely fuzzy concepts of liberty and freedom. It was important that the enemy of the guerrillas should appear as the hated criminal. Continuing his advice on propaganda, he stated, 'A small truth well presented is better than a glittering lie'. Throughout his lengthy thesis, Che Guevara always paid tribute to the charisma and leadership of Castro. He wrote, 'Fidel Castro had the best attributes of a fighter and statesman. His vision made possible our landing, our fight, our triumph'.

After the remarkable victory over the forces of Batista, Che soon emerged as the philosopher and mentor of the new revolutionary state. He sustained his hatred of American imperialism, and he backed ruthless policies against Batista's more brutal henchmen – ordering many executions and setting up work camps. Castro, initially, brought in some older men with administrative experience, but these were soon pushed out by the campaigners. As early as November 1959, Che drove through the law to nationalise the land, and Eisenhower dubbed him a dangerous communist. Having taken over the larger plantations – including over 800 million dollars of US assets, Che encouraged farmers to diversify and to learn new skills in order to lessen Cuba's dependence on its single-crop sugar economy. His main aim in establishing the state control of agriculture was to plough back huge profits for the benefit of rural areas, but he was to find – just as Nkrumah did in Ghana at about the same time – that there were few profits in that type of agricultural scheme.

In the wider field, Che saw Cuba as the embodiment of the underdeveloped countries struggling for their freedom against capitalist, and especially American, economic imperialism. He was often carried away by his own rhetoric, and his aims and hopes were often far removed from the realities of life. He was an outstanding orator, but his starry-eyed idealism did not always convince the workers. While he was remarkably indifferent to money – even for his family – his plan to create a society without money was just fanciful. When he was put in charge of the Cuban Bank, he discovered that all their gold reserves were held in Fort Knox. He swiftly withdrew them, just before the Eisenhower administration froze all Cuban assets. His passionate opposition to capitalism, and the buying and selling of man's labour, lay behind his utopian schemes for creating a happy, socialist society.

While he was deeply involved in setting up the new government administration, as early as 1959 he was sent by Castro as a roving ambassador to visit socialist states around the world. During this time he became a respected world figure, making passionate speeches to distinguished conferences in Asia, Africa and South America. He demanded help for the oppressed under-developed nations ground down by capitalist economic imperialism. He scoffed at the idea that there had been peace since 1945, and quoted Korea, Vietnam, the Congo, Bolivia, Colombia and others. He saw South America as the ideal territory and was heartened by the success of the Vietnamese guerrillas under Giap. In December 1964 he addressed the UN General Assembly and publicly denounced the action of the Belgian forces in the Congo, and the murder of Patrice Lumumba in 1961 on the orders of President Eisenhower and the CIA. In February 1965 he addressed an Afro-Asian Conference in Algiers, calling for all out war against imperialism. He had meetings with many socialist and non-aligned leaders like Nkrumah of Ghana, Sekou Toure, Nyerere of Tanganyika and Ben Bella. Early in 1965 he met President Nasser and divulged to him his idea of supporting the guerrilla movement in the Congo. Nasser bluntly warned him 'not to be another Tarzan, a white man among black men, leading them and protecting them'. Che ignored this warning and embarked on what was to prove a total disaster.

In 1960, the Belgian government, in a fit of panic and having made no preparations, irresponsibly granted independence to the Congo. In the ensuing election, Patrice Lumumba gained a massive majority and became prime minister. Then, with the support of powerful mining interests, the Belgian government, and various right-wing mercenary forces, the mineral-rich area of Katanga broke away. Facing this crisis, Lumumba appealed to the Soviet Union for aircraft to move his troops against Katanga. Then, before the end of 1960, and under intense US pressure, the United Nations recognised Katanga under Mobutu. Soon afterwards,

212

Patrice Lumumba was murdered. In Katanga, Tshombe emerged as leader and had the support of the US, the Belgians, the military force of the South African apartheid regime, a large number of white mercenaries – notably 'Mad Mike' Hoare – as well as a group of Cuban exiles working with the CIA and the mercenaries.

Even before he left for Africa, Che had become a pawn or shuttlecock between international factions. Castro was busy signing up detailed agreements with Moscow, while Che had denounced them. Che had gained the reputation of a passionate but impractical idealist, and many, like Ben Bella, found him dogmatic and stubborn. Just before he left Cuba, Che was accused of being a Trotskyite and pro-Chinese, and the elaborate secrecy surrounding his project was designed to absolve Cuba of blame in case of failure.

In April 1965, in conditions of total secrecy – including serious operations to change his now well-known appearance – Che, having visited Beijing, Moscow, Cairo and Dar es Salaam, arrived on the shores of Lake Tanganyika with a force of about 400 Cubans. He saw Africa as the most promising area of the world for a revolutionary upsurge against capitalist imperialist domination. He had made contact with many African leaders including Amilcar Cabral and Agostino Neto – who were to lead successful revolts against the Portuguese in Guinea Bissau and Angola – and he was buoyed up by his confidence in his great thesis that a handful of determined men, as they had proved in the Sierra Maestra, could overthrow an unjust regime. In spite of these contacts, Che arrived on Lake Tanganyika to find a disillusioned, ill-disciplined and demoralised force of poorly led Africans. Because of the total secrecy surrounding his journey, no leaders were there to meet him, and the one significant one, Kabila, was away in Cairo. In addition, Che was soon to find, as Nasser had warned him, that generally the Africans resented an outsider coming in and telling them how to do things.

Having arrived at his base on the Tanzanian side of Lake Tanganyika, Che very soon realised the gravity of the situation. Immediately there were discussions on whether guerrilla training should take place in the Congo, in Cuba, or in the existing camps in China and Russia. Most of the African leaders strongly opposed training in the Congo, since from the safety of exile they enjoyed a lavish life style far removed from the realities of the war. There was a serious language problem, since none of the Cubans could communicate with the Africans, and this was exacerbated by the secrecy surrounding Che's identity. The Africans wondered who was this foreigner who seemed to give the orders, and they were scandalised when they found out. Che also became embroiled in the problem of thousands of Tutsis, refugees from Rwanda after the massacre carried out by the Hutu the previous year.

Che swiftly worked out a plan for guerrilla operations to support the Congolese rebel forces, but he was made to submit it in writing and waited weeks for a reply. While he waited, he worked as a doctor. He was appalled at the high level of venereal disease among the African troops, and disgusted that they were spending money, raised for the revolution, in the lakeside brothels. When Chinese or Russian supplies arrived, there was immediate chaos and looting, and his suggestion of putting armed Cuban guards on the supplies was rejected. Che wrote: 'They are a parasite army, which didn't work, didn't train, didn't fight and demanded supplies and food by force'. He visited African units and found drunkenness, dissipation, a complete lack of discipline and no disposition to fight. When the first small actions took place, most of the Africans fled at the first shot. Che concluded that the Congolese revolution was irreparably doomed. An incident in June 1965 highlighted the grave military situation. From his villa HQ in Dar es Salaam – 700 miles away – Kabila, the overall African commander of the Congolese forces, ordered the Cubans to take part in an action on a position on the west shore of Lake Tanganyika held by Tshombe's forces and white mercenaries under 'Mad Mike' Hoare. Che was horrified at this absurd situation and did not take part himself. In fact Che was prevented from going to the front because this would show up the African leaders like Kabila who were not prepared to take part in action. Later, Che ignored this ban and went to the front on the north-west shore of Lake Tanganyika. He found a general shambles with irresponsible officers, no discipline, no leadership and no willingness to fight.

In the second half of 1965 the situation rapidly deteriorated. Che was totally frustrated and he had increasing outbursts of violent temper, which alienated his own Cuban troops, and made it difficult for anyone to tell him the truth of the situation. He suffered from frequent asthma attacks, compounded by malaria and dysentery. Castro continued to send supporting troops for Che, but they could achieve little against the increasingly effective troops of Tshombe and Mike Hoare's mercenaries, who advanced along the western shore of Lake Tanganyika. Then politics again obtruded. At a conference in Ghana, the leaders of the Organisation of African Unity were outraged at Tshombe's use of white mercenaries, with the result that Mobutu, the Katanga president, sacked Tshombe. At the same time, Julius Nyerere, president of Tanzania, saw the hopelessness of the situation: he withdrew his support for the Congolese forces and Che's 'heroic and absurd attempt to lead an African revolution'.

Castro, when he learned of the disastrous situation, sent practical help to assist in the withdrawal of the Cuban group across the lake to sanctuary in Tanzania. For political reasons in Cuba, Castro had made public Che's secret letter – written when he left for the Congo – in which he resigned all his offices, handed over all his possessions and renounced his Cuban citizenship. This publicity finally destroyed any confidence the Cuban troops still had in Che's leadership.

In the final débâcle, when, surprisingly, the Belgians, the CIA, and the South African mercenaries allowed Che to escape, he still wished to fight on with a band of about twenty seasoned veterans. In spite of his experiences and the catastrophe of his African venture, he clearly still believed in the erroneous conclusion of his guerrilla thesis. While most of the Cubans left on Russian aircraft to travel via Moscow to Havana, Che stayed for some time in Dar es Salaam to write his description of what he called 'the history of failure'. In *The African Dream* he vividly and movingly describes the suffering and disaster of his African expedition. He wrote, 'I felt entirely alone, in a way that I had never experienced before.'

After the African débâcle, Che spent some considerable time holed up in Prague, while all sorts of fanciful plans were made and unmade. Castro – although discouraged by Russia – was still prepared to give secret support to the idea of a rising in Latin America. Che – in spite of his recent experience – still believed that a small band of determined men, with sound leadership, could topple an unpopular regime, and there were plenty of those in Latin America. Plans were considered for Che to go to Argentina, to Venezuela and to Peru. Such confusion led to deep anger and then to charges of betrayal.

At last it was decided that Che's next operation would take place in Bolivia. Although a poverty-stricken land-locked country, a glance at the map overleaf will show that if a revolt succeeded in Bolivia, it could become a revolutionary base threatening all the surrounding countries – Argentina, Chile, Peru, Paraguay and Brazil. In the greatest secrecy, a training camp was set up in Cuba, and a number of Bolivians were trained. These men, as well as Monje, the main communist leader in Bolivia, were ready to help, because they were led to believe that the action in Bolivia was merely a prelude to a campaign in Argentina. When they realised that

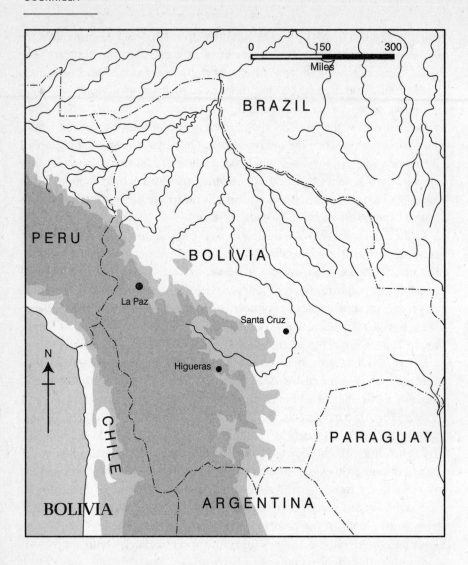

Che intended to lead an uprising in Bolivia they were outraged. Monje said that when the people of Bolivia found out that the guerrilla movement was led by a foreigner, they would turn their backs on it. Monje has been charged with treachery towards Che's expedition, but as soon as he discovered his deception by the Cubans, he openly opposed them. He went so far as to move their initial base camp into an area totally unsuitable for guerrilla war. He did not believe in an armed struggle in Bolivia at that time.

In Bolivia, the military dictator Barrientos profited from the close links and strong support of America for his regime. In the country there were few democratic rights, the army controlled every part of society, miners worked in appalling conditions and peasants lived in abject poverty. In spite of this, there was no impoverished population waiting to be liberated, and Che foolishly deceived himself that he could succeed in such a situation. Ignoring these major adverse factors, Che, in the greatest secrecy, left Havana in October 1966 and travelled via Moscow, Prague, Madrid and Brazil. He arrived in Bolivia in November 1966, and found that nothing had been done at his proposed base camp. He quickly organised two camps and started serious training, but from the start there was resentment at the system of discipline and at his autocratic attitude. Lax security, where the population did not give overall support, caused immediate and serious problems.

A young French journalist, Regis Debray, found Che's expedition and later made an interesting comment about Che's policy. He said that the Sierra Maestra was peculiarly favourable to guerrilla activity, whereas in Bolivia the jungle was singularly hostile. Guerrillas, loaded down with heavy packs, their clothes and shoes quickly ruined, had to use machetes to cut their way through the jungle and were quickly exhausted.

In February 1967 Che led the first expedition, partly as a reconnaissance. They traversed grim jungle-covered mountains, crossed dangerous rapids where some men were drowned, they had no accurate maps, they found hardly any settlements, and, in the severe conditions of this hostile terrain, morale and discipline broke down. They returned to their base in an atmosphere of defeat and chaos, having achieved nothing. More dangerous and more significant, their security had been fatally compromised and the Bolivian forces were now taking action.

In March 1967, in the face of growing military opposition, Che, using classic guerrilla tactics, ambushed an army patrol, killed several men, took prisoners and captured weapons and ammunition. Although it was a minor tactical success, this ambush virtually sealed the fate of the whole expedition, since the Bolivian military force – incompetent though they were – had spotter planes and helicopters and were able, almost at their leisure, to strangle the guerrilla units. A series of minor clashes during April and May 1967 drove Che's forces deeper into a hostile and remote jungle area, and further lowered their morale because no peasants joined them. Under this constant pressure, Che lost his personal touch with the guerrillas and was seen as moody, unpredictable and autocratic. All his problems were exacerbated by an almost complete breakdown in his communication system. As early as May, Walt Rostow, the distinguished

American National Security Adviser, commented that the guerrillas only survived because of the poor quality of Bolivian troops. Soon afterwards, US Rangers went to Bolivia to train their forward troops.

The hopelessness of Che's situation was highlighted by his failure to establish any effective contacts in the towns, and he gained no benefit when masses of striking miners fought with government forces. From June onwards he became seriously ill and was often too weak to walk. The hostile terrain, the adverse climate, the shortage of medicines and food and the failure to gain any effective local support presaged almost certain defeat. When patrols were sent to recover dumps of supplies left in caves it was found that traitors had disclosed their whereabouts to the authorities.

Although Che was wandering ineffectively through the Bolivian jungle with a small band of guerrillas, his situation was discussed at a very high level. The USSR, not wanting to provoke the USA at that time, was furious when it was discovered that Cuba was supporting the guerrilla activity. In July 1968. Kosygin, the USSR prime minister, addressed the UN General Assembly and met President Johnson. They discussed Che's action, and both the USA and USSR – for different reasons – put strong pressure on Cuba to back off. Kosygin visited Cuba and received an extremely hostile reception, but he gave a blunt alternative: if Cuba did not withdraw support from Che, the USSR would cease to support Cuba.

By August 1967 Che confessed in his diary that he was a 'human wreck'. His small group made for a secret camp, where medicines and food had been secreted. The Army, informed by a traitor, had destroyed it. Che considered this was the hardest blow he ever received. Then he heard that Tania, a resolute fighter who had been with him in Africa, had been killed in an ambush. In September, the few remaining guerrillas set out on a desperate march to the small remote town of La Higueras, where he hoped there would be medical supplies and food. The march defied all sense and broke every guerrilla rule. The exhausted and decrepit group moved slowly along a main road in broad daylight, knowing that there was a price of 4,000 dollars on the head of Che. They did not even go into the jungle at night. Then their advance guard was attacked and destroyed, and Che with a group of about seventeen survivors managed to hide in a jungle ravine, though the whole area was full of pursuing government troops. On 7 October, as large numbers of troops moved in there was a fierce fire-fight and the remaining survivors were killed or captured.

Che's capture posed very serious problems for the Bolivian authorities. Bolivia did not have the death penalty and they did not have a secure prison, so, to hold him as a prisoner appeared to be fraught with danger of rescue attempts or the kidnapping of hostages. It was swiftly decided that he must be killed: in the school at La Higueras soldiers drew lots and Lieutenant Teran carried out the execution. The body was immediately taken away by helicopter. The government's denials that he had been executed swiftly crumbled and were proved false by the post-mortem.

After his experience in the Cuba campaign, Che believed passionately in the possibility of a determined revolutionary group overthrowing an unpopular regime – this was his most important message and also his greatest mistake. He had focused his hatred on the American economic imperialism he had witnessed in his travels around South America in the 1950s. Thus, when his execution quickly created a martyr, a hero and an icon, his message appealed to many disaffected and often well-to-do young people around the world. While his famous image dominated student rooms, his message encouraged many urban guerrilla groups like the Angry Brigade, the Red Army Faction, the Baader-Meinhof Group and many more.

Timing played an important part in the creation of his legend. His deliberate execution on 8 October 1967 – encouraged, it was believed, by the CIA and the American administration – came just before the social, cultural and educational upheavals of 1968. His growing legend seemed to link world-wide protest movements: anti-Vietnam protests in Washington; anti-colonial risings in Algeria and elsewhere in Africa; support for Ho Chi Minh with chants of 'Ho, Ho, Ho Chi Minh'; the Sandinistas in Nicaragua; and the Basque separatists.

Thus his death achieved far more than his life, but while most biographies eagerly assess the legend, few examine his role as a theorist and practitioner of guerrilla war. His exposition on guerrilla war, written with brilliant and acute observation after the Sierra Maestre campaign, was a masterful thesis on every aspect of guerrilla war and was intended to encourage world-wide revolt against American capitalist economic exploitation. While his exposition was outstanding, most commentators failed to see that – fatally and tragically – he deduced and passed on a totally false conclusion. After the victory in Havana in January 1959, he constructed a powerful polemic in favour of guerrilla war, but he failed to realise that the conditions for the success of Fidel Castro's campaign had been unusually favourable. He therefore preached his doctrine and believed that across Asia, Africa and Latin America this would become a bible for would-be revolutionaries. This was a disastrous and ultimately fatal blunder. Che was buoyed up by the Cuban success and his own conceited self-confidence, but, as he was to find in the Congo and in Bolivia, people rarely rise up to follow a foreigner, however charismatic. How unfortunate that he did not heed Nasser's warning not to try to be a Tarzan! Thus his Congo expedition had almost no hope of success, and in Bolivia, the in-fighting between Russia and China, between Maoists, Trotskyites and local communist parties, destroyed any hope of winning a guerrilla campaign.

The legend of Che, with numerous books, films, TV programmes, and millions of posters and T-shirts, will doubtless flourish for years. His controversial role and character invite frequent re-assessment. Thirty years after his execution a new book claimed, unconvincingly, that Castro had deliberately sent Che to his death. Many more articles and biographies have posed the question: 'Who betrayed Che?' The answer is that he was betrayed by his own rhetoric and the false lesson he learnt from his outstanding thesis on guerrilla war.

AL-QAEDA: BIN LADEN AND THE ISLAMIC STRUGGLE

The most distinguished guerrilla leaders of the modern world, who proved themselves in battle and then went on to found a new regime, followed military precepts which had been enunciated in 350 BC by Sun Tzu and worked out in practice by successful commanders thereafter. The essential factors were to establish a secure base, which could be hidden or easily defended; strike like a hawk and then disappear; imbue followers with strong loyalty to the cause – social or racial justice, patriotism or religion – for which they are prepared to sacrifice their lives; the leader must gain the respect of his fighters by taking part in battles and the military campaign, and then establish discipline in order to control both the strategy and tactics. Tactical success varied little over the centuries, from Judah Maccabee onwards. The precepts were clear: attack the vulnerable points of the enemy, withdraw and regroup; always study the terrain and the weather; always avoid a pitched battle; always gather intelligence; confuse the enemy about your intentions; never be predictable. Obedience to these rules, from the time of Sun Tzu to the twentieth century, has brought success to guerrilla operations. It was hoped that the end of the Cold War and the twenty-first century would usher in an era of peace. Yet the world today is threatened more widely than ever before, by a force which has learnt all the lessons of guerrilla war, which has a world-wide organisation – Al-Qaeda – led by a sinister and charismatic leader, Osama Bin Laden.

Bin Laden, suddenly placed on the world stage after the attack on the World Trade Center in New York on 11 September 2001, had in fact been building up his forces for decades before that. Brought up in Saudi Arabia in the port city of Jeddah on the Red Sea, as a young man he led a life of pampered luxury in a large family of immense wealth. His father, Muhammad Bin Laden, had come to Saudi Arabia from the Yemen, and although he was illiterate he was an able businessman and built up his wealth through his contacts with the Saudi royal family, thereby winning contracts to build or restore the most holy Islamic shrines in Mecca and elsewhere.

Muhammad had many wives and over fifty children, including twenty sons. There were tensions in the family. Bin Laden's mother Hamida – a Syrian not a Saudi – was ostracised by some of the family, who even referred to her as the concubine. Bin Laden remained devoted to his mother, and harboured deep feelings of resentment about her treatment. He shared in the luxurious lifestyle of the family, and after graduating in Engineering, Business Administration and Islamic Studies from the university in Jeddah, he joined the family construction firm. He entered the gilded set of wealthy Saudi young men with the customary Cadillac. He enjoyed travelling with the family to Europe and to Britain. His visits included London and Oxford, and there was a brother at Millfield, the English public school. There is some evidence that he also enjoyed visiting Beirut, where he established a reputation for taking part in the night-life, with women and drink, and was known for his arrogance, based on his great wealth and his formidable height – six feet five inches.

This appears an unlikely background for an outstanding guerrilla commander or a fanatical religious zealot – yet Bin Laden became both of these. The key influence in Bin Laden's change was Abdullah Azzam, an Islamic teacher. Azzam, with a background in the Egyptian Muslim Brotherhood encouraged an aggressive Islamic fundamentalism. He emphasised the historic struggle of Islam against the infidel, and stressed the injustice of the Christian and Jewish powers from the time of the crusades to the Palestine refugee camps. Under the tutelage of Azzam, Bin Laden came to admire as a role model the great Islamic warrior Saladin. A Kurd, Saladin was educated in Syria and became a passionate Sunni Muslim. In the 1170s he established an empire stretching from Morocco to Baghdad and he determined to drive the crusaders from Lebanon and Jerusalem. He crushed the Assassins, and in 1187 inflicted a major defeat on the crusaders. Saladin, in contrast to the hideous cruelty of the crusaders, was renowned for chivalry and mercy. Saladin died in 1193, having patched up an uneasy truce with King Richard the Lionheart, and he is revered as the greatest Islamic warrior.

While Azzam remained the most powerful influence on Bin Laden, through his teaching and his powerful organising ability in the worldwide network of Islamic fundamentalism, outside events were shortly to make a dramatic impact on the impressionable young Bin Laden. In 1968, his father Muhammad died in an air crash, and although he had been remote from Bin Laden, his presence had exerted a restraining influence. After his father's death, he came more and more under the religious influence of Azzam and he was also involved, through the Bin Laden construction conglomerate, in the building of mosques. This appeared to fuel his religious zeal.

In 1975, the assassination of King Faisal, the son of Ibn Saud, gave some indication of the deep divisions playing on Saudi society and the fearsome aspirations of the fundamentalists. Soon after this, President Sadat of Egypt, who had succeeded Nasser in 1970, made his dramatic move to bring to an end the dispute with Israel. Having announced his intentions to the Egyptian parliament, Sadat went to Israel and addressed the Knesset. This brave gesture, encouraged by President Jimmy Carter, was thwarted by the intransigence of the Israeli prime minister, Begin. Sadat, trying to rise above the fury and the hatred, virtually signed his own death warrant, and exemplified that bloody feature of Middle East politics – a peacemaker is more likely to be killed by an extremist on his own side than by the enemy. The Israeli president Rabin paid this penalty in 1995 when an Israeli extremist assassinated him. All these events made a deep impact on Bin Laden as he struggled more deeply with the problems of his faith and the threatening world situation.

Middle East tension increased substantially during the 1970s and came to a climax in 1979, the start of a new Muslim century. In Iran, the exiled Shiite leader, Khomeni, returned home when the Shah was overthrown in January 1979 and established a strict Islamic regime. The Shiite revolt boded ill for Islamic unity and further divisions developed as a result of the peace treaty with Israel. Bin Laden was more directly and emotionally involved by the next dramatic event when, in 1979, fundamentalists stormed the Grand Mosque in Mecca in protest at the corruption and domination of the Saudi royal family. Bin Laden suffered further mental anguish when the mosque was recovered by French paratroops. This succession of psychological blows took place when Bin Laden was already deeply committed to the Islamic struggle. Then, in December 1979, when the Soviet Union invaded Afghanistan, Bin Laden was totally outraged. Thousands of young Muslims responded to the call for Jihad, as left-wingers had done in the 1930s in the Spanish Civil War. Bin Laden joined them.

The Soviet invasion ushered in more than twenty years of conflict in which all the great issues of guerrilla war were illustrated. Had the Soviet leaders known their history, they might have hesitated before campaigning in this bleak and threatening land. Afghanistan had been overrun by Persian, Mogul and Sikh conquerors, as well as Alexander the Great, Genghis Khan, Tamerlane and, more recently, the British and the Russians. The Afghans always fell back on their traditional guerrilla warfare, with the resilience to drive out the invader, and then revert to their murderous tribal rivalries.

In the 1830s, the British, fearing the intrigues and advance of Russia, sent a large expedition, which captured Kandahar and Ghazni, and established a

223

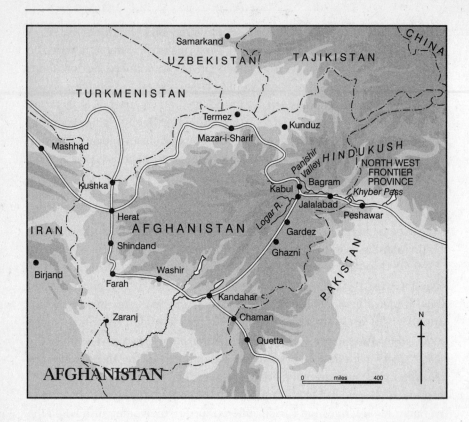

puppet ruler in Kabul. With crass insensitivity, with their drunkenness and womanising, they outraged the local Muslim people. Then, in the winter of 1842, the egregious General Elphinstone, who handed over his guns to the Ghilzai warlord Akbar Khan in return for a promise of safe passage, led the whole British community – about 17,000 altogether – into total disaster. On the desolate road from Kabul to Jalalabad, every man, woman and child was slaughtered, save only Doctor Bryden, a Scottish surgeon who, sorely wounded, escaped to tell the tale. The Afghan guerrillas had won another great victory. British and Russian intrigues – misnamed the 'Great Game' – continued until 1919. Meanwhile a fragile independence for Afghanistan was established, and this lasted until the 1970s.

During the 1970s, the Soviet Union, conscious of turbulence on its southern border, had deliberately extended its influence in Afghanistan. In 1978, a group of Soviet-trained army officers carried out a coup, and established the Democratic Republic of Afghanistan (subsequently DRA). President Taraki, a client of Russia, attempted to impose a Marxist programme of reform, including land distribution and collectivisation –

that most disastrous of all Marx's ideas. Such a policy was anathema to most Afghans. In 1978, the Imams called for Jihad against the atheist communist regime. The Mujahidin quickly came forward to lead the opposition. Frequently, the DRA regular army officers led their units to join the rebels. At Herat in 1979, a whole division of the DRA army went over to the Mujahidin.

The DRA regime controlled most of the cities, while the opposition controlled the villages and countryside. By the end of 1979, because of the chaos and virtual civil war, Brezhnev decided to intervene, intending to support the DRA, establish order quickly and withdraw. Little did he realise that this was to be Russia's Vietnam. In the first phase of the invasion, which started on Christmas Eve 1979, the DRA army, which the Soviets hoped would do most of the fighting, was consistently beaten. Then, when the Soviet forces were drawn in, they found that they were ill-prepared and ill-equipped for the type of guerrilla war which they now faced. What was intended as a brief incursion, based on their experiences in Hungary and Czechoslovakia, lasted for nine years, killed 1,300,000 people and created 5,000,000 refugees, nearly one third of the Afghan population.

Just as Angola was torn apart by the proxy warfare of the great powers, so Afghanistan rapidly became an arena for a savage guerrilla war, with the Mujahidin gaining support in money, weapons and supplies from a galaxy of countries each of which had their own reasons for opposing the Soviets. These included the US, the United Kingdom, France, Saudi Arabia, China and Egypt. Most of the aid was channelled through Pakistan, which, like Iran, was apprehensive at major Russian moves so close to its borders. This arrangement gave Pakistan increasing power, and it tended to support the more extreme religious groups. The Soviets, with their highly mechanised forces, were soon to find that the terrain in Afghanistan – mountains, deserts and forests, with tenuous and inadequate roads – suited its guerrilla opponents. Roads, which passed through narrow defiles, were ideal for Mujahidin ambushes, and the caves in the mountains were ideal for their secure bases.

By 1979 Bin Laden had achieved little, but he had gained useful experience in the family construction business. In 1979 he went to Peshawar in Pakistan, the nearest large town to Jalalabad and Kabul. From Peshawar he travelled frequently into Afghanistan with his mentor Abdullah Azzam, who now cultivated even more extreme attitudes towards Jihad. Although Bin Laden did fight with the Mujahidin, his main role at this time was to raise funds and to gain practical support for the struggle against the

Soviets. He provided large supplies of machinery and bulldozers – often from his own firm – to build roads, bridges and defensive bunkers for the Mujahidin fighters. Ironically, he co-operated with the CIA and with agencies of the Saudi government. At this time he worked closely with Ayman Zawahiri, an outstandingly able man who was to play a big part in the development of Al-Qaeda. By the mid 1980s, Bin Laden and Zawahiri, together with Azzam, had set up training camps and so-called guest houses, which were used extensively by volunteers coming from all over the world to fight in the Jihad. Bin Laden used his wealth – estimated at that time as 250,000,000 dollars – to raise even more funds, especially from Saudi Arabia. During this phase of building up the Al-Qaeda network, Azzam developed and clarified his fanatical views, not only about driving the infidel Russians from Afghanistan but continuing the Jihad until all Muslim lands were re-conquered and brought under Islamic control. His influence on Bin Laden was powerful and obvious. An interesting question has been raised about the different influences on Bin Laden. In 1951 the American author Isaac Azimov wrote the science-fiction novel *The Foundation*, which, later, was translated into Arabic as *Al-Qaeda*. In the novel the main character in the clash of empires is killed, but leaves video-taped messages for his followers, and to confuse his enemies. The remarkable similarity to the story of Bin Laden raises the ironic point that he might have read *The Foundation* and then based Al-Qaeda on the original concept of an American Jew.

After 11 September 2001, Bin Laden was demonised by western governments and the world media, but in the early days of the struggle against the Soviets he was very much under the influence of the two more powerful personalities Azzam and Zawahiri. Bin Laden travelled into Afghanistan and controlled much of the construction work carried out to support the Mujahidin. He did take part in some of their operations, and shared their hardship, but his more significant work was to build up his recruiting system, to mastermind the publicity – notably by videos, which were widely circulated – and to extend the Al-Qaeda system.

While this work continued, the Mujahidin were fighting a classic guerrilla war against the Soviet invaders. The ambush has always been a key tactic of guerrilla fighters, and the Mujahidin, drawing on generations – indeed centuries – of experience, used it with devastating effect. Some military historians argue that guerrilla war reverses the military precept of the concentration of force, but the ambush shows an absolute and exact concentration of force at a single point. The Mujahidin used their extensive knowledge of the terrain, and initially planned their ambushes to obtain weapons and supplies. The Soviets remained largely a road-bound force and had to use the roads to supply their overstretched units.

Some of the most effective ambushes took place on the main road, Highway 157, leading south from Kabul to Gardez. A particularly successful one was carried out in the summer of 1980, where this road wound through a narrow gorge close to the Logar river. The Mujahidin had gained detailed intelligence that a convoy of over one hundred vehicles would move south at a particular time. They set up the ambush with a group of about fifty fighters armed with rifles, some machine guns and, what was to become the favourite weapon of the guerrillas, the Rocket Propelled Grenade or RPG – a Soviet-made anti-tank weapon. As the end of the convoy reached the killing zone, the Mujahidin struck. They attacked first at the back of the convoy and met little resistance. They destroyed over 100 vehicles and rapidly removed the food, weapons and ammunition the convoy had been carrying.

The Mujahidin were careful not to become predictable but, over the years, they carried out several more ambushes in that area because the terrain was ideal. The attack groups varied in number from ten to fifty men, and, as more captured weapons became available, they were able to use mortars and heavy machine guns along with RPGs, and AK47s. After suffering a number of humiliating reverses, the Soviets did eventually change their tactics. They started to carry out a helicopter sweep ahead of a convoy, though the Mujahidin later claimed that they used this as the call to stand-to. To lessen the impact of an attack, convoys were spread out, and helicopter gunships were put on stand-by when a major convoy was moving. Gradually the Soviets increased the firepower of the convoy escorts, and trained them to take cover when attacked, and wait for the helicopter gunships. The Mujahidin soon realised this, so they then made swift attacks and sped off with their booty before the gunships arrived. They also discovered that an RPG could bring down a helicopter.

One of the best-known ambushes of the early days of the war took place in October 1980 just north of the Bagram airbase, where the road crossed the Panjshir valley bridge. The Mujahidin had obtained detailed information that a large convoy would leave the base travelling north and would return towards evening. A group of 200 Mujahidin armed with RPGs, mortars and heavy machine guns set up the ambush. In the late afternoon, as the convoy returned, the attackers allowed the front half to cross the bridge, and then attacked the whole length simultaneously. Most of the Soviet troops, realising they were close to the airbase, abandoned their vehicles and rushed to the river to get home. There was virtually no command or control against the attack, and as darkness fell, the Mujahidin were able, almost at their leisure, to take away large supplies of food and weapons. In this war of ambush and surprise attacks, the Mujahidin were much quicker than their enemy to learn important tactical lessons. For example, they tried to attack just before dusk so that the value of the helicopter counter-attack would be reduced. The Mujahidin were particularly strong in the south of the country, which the Soviets never fully controlled, and there were many ambushes on the roads radiating from Kandahar.

The Russians exacted brutal reprisals and often destroyed villages which had supported the Mujahidin. They also scattered anti-personnel mines indiscriminately. Despite this savagery, in the middle of a battle the Mujahidin were often supplied with bread and milk by the local women. Increasingly, the Mujahidin also used mines – some captured and some of their own making – to attack Soviet tanks and other vehicles. They learnt to identify likely landing places for helicopters, and they carried out many successful attacks just as a helicopter landed. In spite of their successes, by the mid-1980s the Soviets appeared to be winning the war, and that was when the US began to provide Stinger missiles to the Mujahidin – this proved a decisive weapon.

The Afghans remained dedicated to Islam, to Jihad, and to the struggle against the Soviets, but there were still many dangerous clashes between the rival Mujahidin groups. While the western media is aware of the many wars between Roman Catholics and Protestants, it is generally less aware of the bloody struggles between Shiite and Sunni Muslims. These stretch from the Shia rebellion against the Sunni, in AD 814, to the Sunni–Shia clash between Iran and Iraq in the 1980s. What an appalling role religion has played in the history of world conflicts!

Soon after the Soviet invasion, Brezhnev had a stroke, and he was followed by a number of ineffective successors until Gorbachev came to power in 1985. He tried to achieve a quick victory by the use of massive firepower, but like many before him, he failed. Then, after the bloody battle of Jalalabad, he sought a way out of the impasse, and accepted a deal brokered by the United Nations. In February 1989 the Soviet forces withdrew. Thus a hardy and dedicated band of Mujahidin fighters, by holding to all the sound precepts of guerrilla war had driven out one of the world's super-powers of the 1980s. Sun Tzu would have been proud of them.

When the Soviets left in 1989, Bin Laden, who had not been a major military figure, saw new opportunities. He used his wealth and power to embark on a vast building programme of training camps and military bases, mostly in the caves in remote mountain areas. At the same time, his powerful mentor Azzam was assassinated by a car bomb in Peshawar, and Bin Laden's elder brother was killed. This removed two restraining influences.

Having built up his training camps, Bin Laden now developed a training programme for the recruits who flocked to his cause. Al-Qaeda was formally established and the foundations laid for a worldwide organisation to achieve Bin Laden's primary aim of driving the American forces out of the Holy Lands of Arabia. His views on the elimination of Americans, Jews and Christians became more extreme.

He established over twenty camps in Afghanistan, most of them close to the border with Pakistan, and it is estimated that more than 50,000 volunteers have been trained there. Recruits from all over the world, including the most prosperous countries of the west, arrived in Pakistan and were sent at once over the border to their camp. First, they had to swear an oath of loyalty to Bin Laden and to Al-Qaeda. Then training started on weapon-handling – particularly on AK47s, Kalashnikovs and Rocket Propelled Grenades. After mastering the weapons, recruits passed on to training in bombing and explosives, and to the identification of urban targets. Later in the course, the volunteers learned the techniques of assassination, and how to use chemicals, such as cyanide, to kill people on a large scale in cities – for example in the ventilation systems of major buildings. Technical training was accompanied by fearsome indoctrination with Bin Laden's extreme version of Islamic fundamentalism and anti-western propaganda. After completing the course, volunteers usually returned to their own country to set up their own training cadres.

While Bin Laden looked to the wider struggle against the infidel west, there was not universal support for his views or his organisation in Afghanistan. His most formidable opponent was Ahmed Shah Massoud, nicknamed the Lion of Panjshir, who was the most successful of all the guerrilla leaders. In north-west Afghanistan and the Panjshir valley, he survived seven Soviet offensives. As a commander, he rose above the traditional Afghan attack just to secure booty. He studied guerrilla leaders like Mao Zedong and Che Guevara, and created a well-trained guerrilla force. After the Soviet withdrawal, Massoud, with his Northern Alliance troops, captured Kabul in 1992 and toppled the rump communist government. He continued to fight the fundamentalist forces of the Taliban. Speaking of his campaign against the

Soviet forces he said 'Afghanistan needs two things – the Koran and Stinger missiles'. He also wanted his country cleared of Afghan-Arabs.

In 1990 Bin Laden was able to return to Saudi Arabia as a popular hero, as one of the Mujahidin warriors who had driven the Soviets out of Afghanistan. He was idolised by the young. They saw him as the multi-millionaire who had given up everything to take part in the Jihad and to share in the danger and suffering of the front-line fighters against the Russians. His training camps then welcomed thousands of Saudi youths. At first he was favourably received by the Saudi royal family, but quite soon his openly expressed and fanatical views on Jihad against Americans, Jews and Christians began to alienate the Saudi authorities.

On 2 August 1990, Saddam Hussein invaded Kuwait, and this proved to be another turning point for Bin Laden. He offered the Saudi government his support and the use of the battle-hardened Mujahidin – who had just driven the Russians out of Afghanistan – to remove Saddam Hussein and his Iraqi troops. He reasoned that if the Mujahidin could conquer a super-power, surely, with the active support of the Saudi government, the removal of Saddam Hussein should not be too difficult. He was therefore totally outraged and humiliated when his offer was rejected and the Saudi royal family and government instead then invited the Americans and the western alliance to conduct the Gulf War. Bin Laden constantly re-iterated that once the Americans moved in – to desecrate the sacred soil of Arabia – they would never leave. They were primarily interested, not in democracy, as they claimed, but in oil.

As he developed and expressed more and more extreme views, Bin Laden was soon put under virtual house arrest in Jeddah – no great hardship where the Bin Laden family had palaces to spare. This period of frustration was terminated when, in 1991, he was ejected from Saudi Arabia and went to the Sudan, where he was made welcome. Increasingly, he saw himself at war with Saudi Arabia, with America and with most of his own family who had humiliated both him and his mother. In the Sudan he continued to set up training camps, and, by a big increase in the Al-Qaeda network, to recruit thousands of volunteers.

In the Sudan, he used his wealth as well as his expertise in the construction industry to invest and build up businesses to support the religious struggle. He also developed his plans and strategy for what he saw as the guerrilla war, which would eventually remove America and infidel western forces from Arabia. The flow of eager young Muslims to his training camps proved the power of his appeal. When volunteers flocked from all over the

Middle East; from France, Algeria and Morocco; from London and the Muslim communities of northern England; from the American continent; and from the Islamic centres of South East Asia and the Philippines, Bin Laden began to see the possibility of achieving his wider aims.

He hoped that with the support of Al-Qaeda he would be able to take control of Afghanistan as the first step towards his ultimate goal. If this happened, he reckoned that he would be able to increase the production of heroin. Afghanistan already produced over half the world's supply, and he calculated that this could finance his strategy while causing untold damage to the rich western nations where it was sold. He reckoned next that in Pakistan, which generally supported the Taliban, the government was vulnerable. There, Islamic extremists were backed up by intense anti-American feeling because of America's continuing support for Israel. He calculated that if an extreme Islamic group took over the fragile Pakistan government, it could provide him with a power base, which included nuclear weapons and the rockets to deliver them. This would also give him the chance to gain further Muslim support by the ability, almost at will, to create crises with India over the running sore of Kashmir.

His ultimate global strategy would include the removal of the Saudi royal family, and the creation of a fundamentalist Islamic state – a view more widely supported by the Saudi people than many western commentators seem to realise – and this would give him control over a quarter of the world's oil supply. This would neatly confirm his contention that America was motivated not by support for democracy but by oil.

Thus Bin Laden's dreams and ambitions – and the ultimate nightmare for the West – would give him control of much of the world's oil supply, a further massive income from the trade in heroin, the world-wide activity of Al-Qaeda, and the backup of the nuclear power of Pakistan.

While Bin Laden nurtured these hopes, and built a powerful base in the Sudan, the vicious civil war in Afghanistan, which followed the Russian withdrawal, caused more carnage and destruction as the Taliban slowly seized control. From Khartoum, Bin Laden observed this progress, and started his own campaign. In 1993, he was further offended when – albeit on a humanitarian mission – American troops entered Somalia, another devout Muslim country. Al-Qaeda struck, and in a successful ambush killed 18 American soldiers. Bin Laden denied any involvement, but, as he was to do so often, commended the action of the Islamic warriors.

In the same year, 1993, came the first attack on the World Trade Center in New York, when six people were killed and hundreds injured. The attack had been masterminded by Ramzi Yousef, an experienced Al-Qaeda operator, who had been trained and financed from Bin Laden's camps. Again, Bin Laden denied any knowledge but commended the action.

By the mid-1990s his extreme views and widening influence had been traced by the intelligence services of the US and of Saudi Arabia. Under pressure from both of these, the Sudan government succumbed and once again Bin Laden was banished. In 1996 he left the Sudan for Afghanistan, where he was welcomed by the Taliban. His exile was seen as a success for the west, but it gave Bin Laden a safe and secure base with fanatically loyal supporters, who could not be suborned even by offers of substantial rewards. It was the one place in the world where the CIA could not reach him.

From the security of Afghanistan, and protected by the Taliban, Bin Laden was able to step up the actions of Al-Qaeda. In June 1996, they bombed the US military complex in Dhahran in eastern Saudi Arabia, and killed 19 servicemen. Soon afterwards Bin Laden called for more action against all Americans and Jews worldwide, and he signed the fatwa calling for Jihad.

In 1998 he was interviewed by an American journalist, and he came across as a calm, soft-spoken, giant of a man, but one who presented a chilling image. He clearly enunciated his policy which was, through world-wide guerrilla attacks, to remove American and Allied forces from Arabia, to put an end to American support and arms supplies to Israel, and to end the bombing of Iraq and the killing of innocent Muslim women and children. When questioned about the danger of Al-Qaeda's attacks killing innocent civilians, he quoted Hiroshima as a typical western attack on an Asian nation, and added that in Jihad, if people die, it is the will of Allah. Bin Laden's absolute conviction and chilling self-confidence certainly attracted vast numbers of young people but his views alienated many other Muslim people around the world. Several Muslim countries, notably Egypt and Saudi Arabia, did their best to eliminate him.

1998 brought the armed struggle to a new peak. On 7 August, Al-Qaeda, in operations that had taken years to plan, bombed the American embassies in Nairobi, Kenya, and in Dar es Salaam, Tanzania. In the Kenya attack 200 were killed and thousands injured, and slightly fewer in Dar es Salaam. On 20 August, President Clinton interrupted his summer break at Martha's Vineyard to announce that, in retaliation for the attacks on the East African embassies, cruise missiles had been launched against Al-Qaeda targets in Afghanistan. US intelligence was either inaccurate or out of date because, although some Al-Qaeda members were killed, Bin Laden was elsewhere. The cruise missile attack on Afghanistan was followed by another on a factory in the Sudan. Again, incorrect intelligence meant that this was a fiasco and ultimately counter-productive – creating widespread anger across many Muslim communities. Soon afterwards, in November 1998, Bin Laden was formally indicted in the US and a $5,000,000 reward offered for his capture.

By the year 2000, Bin Laden felt confident enough to taunt Clinton and America, saying that the war had hardly started. This taunt was soon followed by another American blunder. Their intelligence should have known that the Yemen, whence Bin Laden's family had originated, was a significant Al-Qaeda base. Once again, bad intelligence and lax security made it possible for a relatively simple attack by a little local boat in Aden harbour to kill 17 US sailors and cause millions of dollars' worth of damage to the modern and sophisticated USS *Cole*.

Whilst Bin Laden pursued his wider ambitions, in Afghanistan he enjoyed the loyal admiration and protection of the Taliban. This youthful Islamic fundamentalist movement was formed in 1994 by Mullah Omar from the predominantly Pashtun Mujahidin who had fought effectively against the Soviets. Centred on Kandahar and the south of the country, the Taliban, in a murderous civil war, slowly extended their power. In September 1996 they were strong enough, after months of bombardment, to capture Kabul. Then they drove out the rump government of Tajiks, Uzbeks and Hazaras, whose main support lay in the north of the country, where the formidable leader Massoud held sway.

The Taliban, now harbouring their famous guest, gained some initial support in Afghanistan from those people who hoped above all for an end to decades of fighting, and for an end to corruption and the depredations of the warlords. As soon as they grasped power, the Taliban imposed a fiercely repressive regime. The quaintly named Ministry for Ordering What is Right and Forbidding What is Wrong, which was far more repressive than the better known religious police of Saudi Arabia, set out to control the behaviour of the whole country. Music, films, videos, television, and alcohol were all banned. They even banned kite flying – a pastime so beloved by young Afghans. The greatest impact of this savagely puritanical policy fell most harshly on women. All women were forced to wear the *burka*, which covered them from head to foot and included gauze covering to the face. Women were forbidden to work outside their home, and girls' schools were closed. Thousands of men had been killed in the decades of fighting, and now, the widows, who were often the sole breadwinner for fatherless families, were denied the chance to work. The hospitals, all over the country, trying to cope with tens of thousands of war casualties, and staffed largely by women, were suddenly bereft of most of their staff. These harsh regulations were backed up by draconian punishments: the death sentence of stoning for adultery, amputation of the hand for theft, and beatings for failure to observe the daily prayer times. Despite these savage and unpopular measures, such was the hold of the Taliban, and so deep the Islamic convictions of the people, that no one succumbed to the temptation of $5,000,000 to betray Bin Laden.

The brutal and chaotic rule of the Taliban, which safely harboured Bin Laden, stretched into the new millennium. A dramatic start to this was planned, with a bomb attack on Los Angeles airport – thwarted only by the alert vigilance of a customs officer on the Canadian–US border. The real significance of that incident is that, although it failed, it was not a serious setback to the operations then planned by Al-Qaeda. Secondly, it appeared not to alert the West to the huge potential threat from Islamic extremists, from the Taliban and from Al-Qaeda, which, as Peter Bergen writes in *Holy War Inc.*, 'is a Hydra-headed monster'.

Thus the attack on the World Trade Center on 11 September 2001 came as an almost total surprise to the majority of American people and of the world population. The atrocity was almost immediately condemned by most world leaders and by the majority of Muslim countries. Al-Qaeda and Bin Laden appeared and remained in the world's headlines, which, over the following months, gave graphic details of the American campaign of bombing and rocket attacks on Afghanistan. As American bombers pulverised the Taliban strongholds, few believed that anyone could possibly have survived such an attack. This false assumption – which has cost thousands of infantry lives from the battle of the Somme onwards – enabled Al-Qaeda and the Taliban to regroup and adapt to a new situation. From one perspective there was a new situation, but from the perspective of Afghanistan and its neighbours in Central Asia, 11 September changed very little.

The media demonisation of Bin Laden and Al-Qaeda over-simplified many crucial issues and overlooked the complex situation in those countries lying to the north of Afghanistan. Maps began to appear, with those large arrows – so beloved of war reporters and generals in high command – but they rarely focused on Turkmenistan, Uzbekistan, Tajikistan or Kyrgyzstan, which stretch from Iran and the Caspian Sea in the west, to the bleak borders of China in the east. Yet this remote area and its hostile terrain was about to regain its historical significance.

It was once the Washington and London of the ancient world, where Alexander the Great wooed and married the voluptuous local beauty Roxana, where the Silk Route brought prosperity and stability, where Tamerlane, from his capital in Samarkand, built an empire stretching into Russia, China and India. The development of the sea route from Europe to the Far East may have pushed Central Asia into the background, but now it is emerging again from its backwardness and poverty as the great powers begin to comprehend the significance and relevance of Al-Qaeda and the wider issues of Islamic fundamentalism.

The deep religious feelings of the people of Central Asia were driven underground when, particularly after the Russian Revolution, the Soviet regime deliberately extended its influence and provoked a smouldering guerrilla war with the Islamic patriots. Stalin, regardless of ethnic details, divided the whole territory into Soviet republics, and, as the colonial powers did with their colonies, developed the area to provide raw materials for Soviet industry and the home market. For decades after 1917, the countries of Central Asia suffered from the worst effects of the Soviet policy of collectivisation and Stalin's brutal and uncaring removal of different ethnic groups to satisfy his economic aims. He backed up this destructive regime by a calculated campaign to crush all Islamic movements. Thousands of mosques were closed or destroyed, Islam was proscribed, and tens of thousands of refugees fled to China, Iran or Pakistan.

Soviet repression, both of Central Asia and of Islam, continued into the 1970s, and then, after the invasion of Afghanistan in 1979, the Soviets drafted thousands of local men into their military forces. Many of these had hidden sympathy with the Mujahidin and, later, were to use their military training and experience to support the guerrilla activities against the Russian-backed successor regimes, and to support the new leaders of Islamic militancy.

The success of the guerrilla struggle of the Taliban and Al-Qaeda in forcing the Russians to leave Afghanistan was a factor in the break-up of the Soviet Union in 1991, and the establishment of the Commonwealth of Independent States. Throughout Central Asia, the Russian-backed leaders dreaded the Soviet withdrawal, but most of the people welcomed it. Thousands of new mosques were built, but the upsurge in Islamic activity was accompanied by widespread economic disaster, because the economies of all the countries had been geared to the Soviet system, and had relied on Soviet support, which was suddenly withdrawn. Suffering, poverty and starvation spread across the whole area, and as the generally incompetent rulers of Uzbekistan, Tajikistan, Turkmenistan, Kyrgyzstan and, further north, Khazakstan, failed to overcome their social and economic problems, more and more young men turned to the Islamic militants. Khazakstan suffered more than the others, because its territory had been used for Soviet nuclear experiments, and many of its people lived in a radioactive wasteland. These disasters were exacerbated by the widespread breakdown of the infrastructure, which had largely been run by the Russians, who, after 1991, rapidly left.

Across Central Asia, as the tragedy and suffering continued, and as more power accrued to the guerrilla groups of Islamic militants, a new factor emerged. World leaders began to realise that this poverty-stricken territory contained oil and gas resources equal to those of the Middle East. Just as some countries were destroyed by the proxy wars of the Cold War rivals, now Central Asia may miss a great opportunity because outside powers follow a different agenda. Will Russia, China, the US, Iran or Pakistan co-operate to develop the oil potential and the untold riches it could bring? Each of these countries has its own interest and plan, and the well being of the sad people of Central Asia is not their highest priority. Despite these adverse factors, it is just possible that the Taliban and Al-Qaeda may have, inadvertently, contributed towards a solution of the problem. Could it be that the alliance of the US, the European powers, Russia and China, forged to fight terrorism, could be carried over into co-operation in the peaceful development of this potentially rich and prosperous land? Yet, the biggest obstacle to a happy outcome from the present impasse is the rising strength of young Islamic militants – the very people that a solution would benefit most. After all, thousands of miles of oil pipelines through wild and rugged territory are the easiest targets for guerrilla attacks.

The desperately poor country of Tajikistan illustrates most of the problems besetting the area. After independence from the Soviet Union in 1991, the various Islamic guerrilla groups mounted endless attacks on the government in a civil war, which lasted five years. The Tajik people have spread into all the neighbouring countries – including Russia – and during the civil war many Tajik fighters went to Afghanistan and were linked to Massoud and the Northern Alliance. Russia and Uzbekistan, which had an old-style communist ruler, Karimov, supported the weak Tajik government against the Islamic militants. The young Tajik fighters founded the Islamic Renaissance Party, and sought help across Central Asia and from Pakistan and Saudi Arabia. The bitter civil war, which caused horrendous casualties and suffering, was finally concluded by a UN brokered compromise, which produced a coalition government – something almost unheard-of in Central Asia at the time.

The Islamic movements – themselves deeply divided over both their aims and beliefs – flourished on the poverty and suffering of the people, but seemed to have few ideas on how to solve the economic problems. When the Tajik civil war ended, the outside world did little to help a country with 60% unemployment and with tens of thousands of the young and able fleeing to Russia or China or anywhere to escape the grinding poverty. It appears that only in 2001 did the West realise the significance of Tajikistan and the Islamic movements.

One such group, though initially with peaceful aims, plans to re-establish the medieval Caliphate, which was founded by Abu Bakr who succeeded Muhammad, and lasted with varying success until the 1920s. Called Hisb ut Tahrir, it aims to bring all Muslim lands under one highly centralised regime based on Sharia law. It looks back to the earliest days of Islamic expansion after the death of Muhammad, and plans an expansive Jihad only after the widest Islamic society has been established. While its present aims renounce violence, it does illustrate the wild ferment of ideas that are sweeping over Islamic lands, and it is considered highly dangerous by the fragile but dictatorial regimes of Central Asia.

A different type of movement, and more immediately menacing, arose in Uzbekistan, as a protest against the repressive rule of Karimov, the pro-Russian puppet ruler after 1991. The Islamic Movement of Uzbekistan (subsequently IMU) gained powerful support from many young men who had received military training from the Russians. It is led by a charismatic young man – a former sergeant in the Russian airborne forces – known as Namangani, who has set up the best organised and classic guerrilla force in the whole area. He has established his bases in the remote mountainous region of west Tajikistan, and also over the border at Mazar e Sharif and Konduz in Afghanistan. He lies low and carries out training during the winter months, and then, relying on partly trained secret helpers – sleepers – carries out attacks almost at will on government forces and installations in Uzbekistan and Kyrgyzstan. Namangani enforces strict discipline and, indeed, his rules about his supporters being polite, not molesting women, and paying for all supplies, might have come from Giap himself. He was even strong enough to call for Jihad against Karimov, the beleaguered ruler of Uzbekistan. Although since September 11 the word Jihad has had terrifying resonance, a call for Jihad has not always been effective. During the campaign of Lawrence of Arabia against the Turks in 1917, the Germans encouraged the Turks to call for Jihad, and even put it about that the Kaiser had become a Muslim.

The IMU achieved remarkable results from the guerrilla tactics of a cadre of a few hundred determined men. In the poverty-stricken territories of Kyrgyzstan, where the only flourishing activity was the drugs trade and the sale of girls for prostitution, the payment for goods and services made the IMU popular. Namangani finances his operations from the wider drugs trade, and he has been closely linked with Al-Qaeda and Bin Laden. Millions of dollars have flowed in to support the IMU, and its leaders have been able to purchase sophisticated weapons and even helicopters – usually seen as an anti-guerrilla weapon. Namangani has sufficient resources to provide weapons for his sleepers, and has been able to launch operations across Uzbekistan and even close to Tashkent and Samarkand. He gained much support when his forces captured some Japanese geologists. This and the kidnapping of some climbers, including some Americans, together with his skilful handling of the publicity, brought him widespread prestige.

The World Trade Center attack on 11 September 2001 brought the IMU dramatic new challenges. There was immediate American pressure on Uzbekistan to provide air bases for bombing raids on the Taliban, and after tortuous discussions this was agreed. This had the advantage for the IMU that they could step up their call for Jihad against the infidels, but it had more serious disadvantages. Suddenly, American and World Bank money was pouring into Uzbekistan, Tajikistan and Kyrgyzstan, and their governments quickly strengthened their campaign against the IMU because of its close links with Al-Qaeda and Bin Laden. The new situation also created a dilemma for Russia, but because of the need to be associated with the world-wide war on terrorism it had reluctantly agreed to the American move. For the US it was a most significant development, giving it for the first time military bases in Central Asia, and in a former part of the Soviet empire. Some have asked – as Bin Laden did of the US presence in Saudi Arabia – will they ever leave?

The 11 September attack directly involved all the world powers in the affairs of Central Asia. While America gained valuable bases, Russia faced serious difficulties. It was deeply unpopular across most of the area, because of the anti-Islamic policies of the Soviets, and because of the damage to the economy and infrastructure after its withdrawal in 1991. To this was added the effect of the two Chechen wars, 1994–6, and 1999–2000. During these wars, Russia pursued an aggressive anti-Islamic policy and condemned all Islamic movements. This dangerous background encouraged Russia to co-operate with the US in the anti-terrorist campaign to destroy the Taliban, Al-Qaeda and the IMU.

The anti-terrorist alliance also brought in China with its own agenda. The vast, bleak desert area of Xinjiang, lying to the north of the Himalayas abuts on to Tajikistan, Kyrgyzistan and Khazakstan. In spite of its remoteness, over the last decades there have been frequent border disputes and guerrilla raids from Islamic forces against Chinese installations in Xinjiang. Now, although strongly opposed to terrorism, China has followed a wiser and more constructive policy than either the US or Russia. It has created an alliance with its neighbours, which seeks co-operation over economic and military issues, border disputes, and the ever-present problem of guerrilla attacks and terrorism.

With the US, Russia and China now involved in the Central Asian imbroglio, Pakistan, so long the base and training area for the Taliban, Al-Qaeda and other guerrilla groups, is still a key factor in the situation. Under President Zia ul Haq, and particularly since General Musharraf's coup in 1999, it supported the Taliban and, foolishly, alienated its neighbours in Central Asia by failing to curb the guerrilla training camps and Islamic schools – madrassahs. Pakistan's support for the guerrillas ties in with the on-going clash with India over Kashmir, and for years Pakistan has sent its Kashmiri fighters to train with the Taliban.

After the break up of the Soviet Union, Pakistan thought to extend its influence in central Asia by supporting Islamic militants, in the hope that they would overthrow the old Soviet-dominated governments. Some Pakistanis had advocated a wiser course, suggesting that the country should develop economic links, and encourage the trade in oil to be routed towards Karachi, the closest port to Central Asia. This proposal was pushed aside by the militants. The Pakistani government faces a major problem in the criminal under-cover operations of drug traffickers, arms salesmen, smugglers and a variety of Islamic extremist groups, which are too powerful for it to curb, and are eager to prolong the conflict. Bush's blunt ultimatum after 11 September forced Musharraf into a dramatic volte face – to stop supporting the Taliban. Naturally, this caused violent outbursts from Islamic groups and all supporters of the Taliban and Jihad. The world media focused on these protests, but the majority of Pakistanis accepted the situation. In the new changed world scenario, having co-operated with the US, Pakistan clearly hopes to recover its influence, to improve its relations with Central Asia, and to restore hope of trade and oil projects.

While the Pakistani government clearly regrets its past support for guerrilla activities, and is still precariously vulnerable, circumstances have proved generally more favourable to its western neighbour Iran. Despite the damage it suffered during its eight-year war with Iraq (1980–8), when, of course the US and the West tended to back Saddam Hussein, Iran is well placed in the post-2001 situation. It has always opposed the guerrilla attacks of the Islamic extremists – even when the US was supporting the Taliban in the 1980s. Now Iran, in spite of the Shia–Sunni division, is popular with the governments of Central Asia because it stood up to the Taliban and IMU. It is also a significant player in the new Great Game because, with its oil wealth, it was able to purchase millions of dollars' worth of arms and even nuclear and rocket technology from Russia during the 1980s.

Saudi Arabia, the final piece in the jigsaw, has been considered as a supporter of Islamic extremists, and many of its young people have enrolled with Al-Qaeda and Bin Laden. In the new situation after 11 September, the Saudi royal family may regret its indecisive and less than coherent policies, when many guerrilla fighters trained in the camps of Afghanistan have returned home, and are sympathetic to the critics of the current Saudi regime.

Central Asia, because of its forbidding terrain and the warlike traditions of its people, has always been the home of guerrilla war. Now, as the great powers eye its potential wealth in oil and gas – with estimates into billions and trillions of dollars – there remains a slight hope that sound sense and co-operation may achieve a peaceful development of the oil riches, bring some prosperity to the long-suffering people and defeat the warmongers.

The basic issues of guerrilla war, from Sun Tzu onwards are clear: find a secure base which the power of the enemy cannot destroy; avoid pitched battles; attack when the enemy is unprepared; give followers effective training; encourage the enemy's arrogance; keep him under strain; give followers a cause which will establish conviction, loyalty and discipline; never allow one setback to damage the cause; attack swiftly like a hawk; always confuse and deceive the enemy; use spies and agents to obtain information on how to damage the enemy. The ultimate test of guerrilla success is whether it removes an alien or unjust power from the homeland.

Bin Laden, Al-Qaeda and the other guerrilla groups appear to have met the majority of these criteria. He has a secure base and followers with total conviction; he is able to strike like a hawk. He avoids pitched battles and manages to keep the enemy under strain. He has established effective training camps secure from enemy attack. Bin Laden and Al-Qaeda argue that they are waging war, Holy War, by using guerrilla methods.

This sacred mission has been linked to the issue of justice for the Muslim peoples of Palestine, and the continuing American support for Israel. The almost unbelievable gaffe of President Bush in calling for a crusade against terror (surely he should have known of the bestial image the Crusaders still have throughout the Middle East), illustrates the chasm of misunderstanding between Al-Qaeda and the West. There is no doubt that unless the Palestinian issue is settled with justice and fairness, the Jihad will continue, with an ever-increasing number of young men – and now young women – prepared to sacrifice their lives to the cause.

Since 11 September, western governments and the media have often been astonished when an Al-Qaeda plot is discovered. On 24 June 2002, in a tone of hurt surprise, *The Times* published the headline 'Tunisia attack marks Al-Qaeda comeback'. What is more truly surprising is that Al-Qaeda – whether or not Bin Laden was killed in the American attack on Afghanistan – with their network of highly trained and dedicated followers, have not carried out further attacks. Significantly, only weeks after the attack on the World Trade Centre, Bin Laden stated: 'America will not live in peace before peace reigns in Palestine, and before the army of infidels leaves the land of Muhammad' – a clear statement of guerrilla aims.

EPILOGUE:
2004 – THE GUERRILLA SCENE

Four years into the twenty-first century, does the world appear to be a happy, peaceful place, buoyed up by massive wealth created by modern scientific technology, with the surplus wealth of the most advanced countries devoted to alleviating the poverty and suffering of the poorest? Hardly. The person who, when the Cold War finished, invented the phrase 'The Peace Dividend' must be wondering what happened to that idea. Instead of enjoying peace and serenity, the world of 2004 is deeply beset by fear, hatred and insecurity.

This book has put forward the argument that Sun Tzu laid down the major precepts for guerrilla war, and that little has changed since then. Mao Zedong quoted him in detail, as did Che Guevara, but one major factor has been added since the time of Sun Tzu – religion. From the time of Muhammad there has been religious conflict: between Shia and Sunni from the early years of Islam to the Iran–Iraq War, when the USA and the west eagerly supported their ally Saddam Hussein; between Islam and the Christian west, highlighted by the Crusades and their unspeakable atrocities, which made such an impact that naughty Arab children are still curbed by the threat of the Crusaders; during the swift advance of Islam across north Africa, southern Europe and western Europe, past Constantinople and up to the very walls of Vienna. While Christianity was threatened by Islam, from the time of Martin Luther, Christianity itself engaged in religious wars between Protestant and Roman Catholic. These wars devastated central Europe in the seventeenth century, and Christianity has continued its bloody internecine struggle to this day in the intransigent ghettos of Belfast and across Northern Ireland.

Perhaps the most dangerous element in the religious basis of all these historic conflicts and in the present world-wide terrorist threat is an idea, espoused by all the major religions, which has caused more damage, suffering, human misery and anguish than any other single idea: the belief in life after death. This notion enabled the medieval Christian church to terrify its followers with threats of everlasting hell and damnation. In contrast, Islam promised heaven to those men who died for their faith while fighting in Jihad. What a tragedy for the world that not one of the great spiritual leaders – Abraham, Moses, Jesus, Muhammad or the Buddha – was brave enough to say that he did not believe in life after death. Is this the biggest confidence trick in human history? Imagine if the religious factor was removed from the major conflicts in the world – how many would be left?

At the beginning of 2004, the main concern in the world appeared to be the accuracy of the intelligence reports that influenced the decisions of US President Bush and UK Prime Minister Blair to go to war with Iraq because Saddam Hussein was thought to possess weapons of mass destruction – chemical, biological and nuclear. The western intelligence system plays a major role in the fight against international terrorism and costs an estimated 30 billion dollars annually.

Terrorist strikes continued despite the vigilance of police and intelligence services. In March 1995, Japan witnessed the ominous disaster of a lethal poison released on the underground by a religious fanatic. In 2003, hundreds of young westerners, mostly Australian, were killed or injured in a pleasure resort in Bali, Indonesia, the most populous of the Muslim countries. In the USA in 1995, Timothy McVeigh, a psychopathic drop-out, killed 168 people in Oklahoma City, and in response the police rounded up Arab-looking people. This knee-jerk reaction was due to the fact that the first attack on the World Trade Center, two years earlier, had been carried out by Islamic militants. In February 2004, a suicide bomber, thought to be a Chechen patriot or terrorist, struck on the Moscow underground, and in March the Madrid bombings once again highlighted the comparative ease with which terrorists can strike.

Each terrorist attack produces pained surprise in much of the western media. This is remarkable, since it is well known that Bin Laden spent years in Afghanistan and on the borders of Pakistan training thousands of young volunteers from around the world – from the USA, from the UK, from Germany, France, Malaysia and many more countries in the Middle East and North Africa. After training and taking an oath of allegiance, most of his followers went home to lie low and to be available when called upon.

Bin Laden – whether in this world or the next! – must be viewing the situation in early 2004 with satisfaction. He can witness the growing tensions in Saudia Arabia, whence came so many of his volunteers, and where frustrated and unemployed young people readily support any criticism of the wealthy ruling families. Bin Laden consistently keeps to his basic demand that the infidels should be removed from the sacred lands of Arabia. After the attacks on '9/11', while the wealthy, westernised sheiks at the head of Saudi Arabian companies expressed formal regret, most of the workforce was exultant. In its propaganda, Al-Qaeda quoted the attitudes of American neo-conservatives, with their fanatical support for Israel, and found it easy to claim there was a link between Christianity and Zionist Judaism. In the months before the 2003 Iraq War, Al-Qaeda openly advised Bush not to let the Zionists lead him by the nose into war. Now, across the world, major scrutiny focuses on Bush's motives for going to war, fuelled by the statement of one of his former senior ministers that, from the first day he became president, Bush intended to attack Iraq. In the welter of fierce and conflicting opinions about the problems of the Middle East, whether balanced or extreme, all return to the basic issue that the Middle East will never be at peace unless and until the USA stops backing Israel and there is justice for the Palestinians.

In the tense atmosphere as the post-Iraq war crisis dragged on into 2004, with the US government understandably stressing the real danger of weapons of mass destruction, a dramatic new development took place. It may strengthen the hands of the hawks in Washington, and it has certainly changed the whole terrorist scenario.

Dr Abdul Qadeer Khan, the great hero of Pakistan, who nurses a fanatical hatred of the west, produced nuclear weapons for his country and strengthened its hand immeasurably in the continuing struggle with India over Kashmir. In February 2004, he confessed to Pakistani President Musharraf that, since the 1980s, he had sold nuclear secrets to Iran, Libya and North Korea in return for vast rewards. He had passed on techniques for enriching uranium, together with technical details for nuclear development. His team, backed by millions of dollars, had operated across Malaysia, the Middle East, Germany, the Netherlands, China, Japan, and some parts of Africa. He came under suspicion, and due to American pressure, was dismissed from his post after '9/11', but his downfall came from information procured by the UN weapons inspectors in Iran, and from Libya, demonstrating its more open policy. But his televised confession can only be a charade. As early as 1975, when Pakistan was incensed and alarmed at India's testing of an atomic bomb, Khan was sent to the Netherlands to steal blueprints. In 1993 he was involved in swapping nuclear techniques with North Korea. Khan's activities cannot have been unknown to the Pakistani government, and the fact that they were kept secret from the west for so long is another massive failure for western intelligence.

Dr Khan's revelations created another crisis for Musharraf. He had already survived two assassination attempts carried out by Muslim extremists because of his co-operation with America and was in such a weak position politically that he had no alternative but to pardon the national hero. Musharraf's vulnerable position highlights a western nightmare of a 'worst case scenario' and brings the focus back again to Bin Laden and Al-Qaeda.

Bin Laden outlined his strategic plan years ago. Now, with a slight change in the volatile political situation in Pakistan, it could come dramatically closer to realisation. If Musharraf is overthrown, the top military commanders in the country, who are mostly sympathetic to Bin Laden, could easily take over, and they would have control over the first array of nuclear weapons held by a Muslim country.

In neighbouring Afghanistan, the Taliban reduced the production of opium poppies; if he took control there, Bin Laden intended to raise it substantially so that he would be able to control 90% of the world's supply of heroin. This would have provided him with massive revenue and do untold damage in Europe and America where most of the heroin is sold.

Bin Laden's third step looks to Saudi Arabia, where most of his fifty siblings and their families still enjoy a fabulously wealthy life style. The rising tide of opposition to the regime of the Saudi royal family brings the possibility of dramatic change much closer. If change does come, thousands of Bin Laden's trained volunteers would be ready and waiting to play an effective role in another volatile political situation. If an uprising takes place, how loyal would Saudi military forces be to the remote and wealthy ruling families?

While terrorists in Afghanistan have been temporarily cowed, the situation there is fragile and uncertain. If extremists overthrew Musharraf over the border in Pakistan, followers of Bin Laden and Al-Qaeda might easily restore their control over much of the country.

It is not entirely fanciful to envisage a situation where a Pakistani regime with nuclear weapons, controlled by hard-line rulers linked to Al-Qaeda, was backed up by the substantial profits of the heroin trade. Such a regime would be in a powerful position to stir up revolt by the numerous Al-Qaeda supporters in Saudi Arabia and, from its geographical proximity, could easily threaten the oil trade from the Persian Gulf through the Straits of Hormuz.

A constant factor in this alarming scenario is the continuing support of the USA for Israel, and the continuing injustices perpetrated against the people of Palestine. Such feelings of injustice are not confined to extremists or terrorists, but are held by increasing numbers of concerned people throughout the Middle East and around the world. Their fears and anxiety are renewed every time Israeli helicopter gunships shoot people in the Gaza Strip, or Israeli tanks open fire in the Square of the Nativity in Bethlehem.

Bin Laden's guerrilla plans seem far from finished, backed up as they are by his demand that it is a religious duty of his followers to acquire weapons of mass destruction.

SELECT BIBLIOGRAPHY

General Interest
Asprey, Robert B. *War in the Shadows*, New York, Doubleday, 1975
Ellis, J. *A Short History of Guerrilla War*, London, Deutsch, 1975
McTernan, Oliver. *Violence in God's Name*, Darton, Longman, Todd, 2003

Guerrilla War Origins
Oman, C. W. C. *The Art of War in the Middle Ages*, Oxford, 1885
Pearlman, M. *The Maccabees*, London, 1973

The Age of Napoleon
Alexander, D. W. *Rod of Iron*, Wilmington, USA, 1985
Chandler, David. *Dictionary of the Napoleonic Wars*, Arms and Armour Press, 1979
—*Napoleon's Marshals*, Macmillan, 1987
Douglas, J. *Tale of the Peninsula and Waterloo*, Leo Cooper, 1997
Haythornthwaite, P. *Napoleonic Source Book*, Arms and Armour Press, 1990
Urban, M. *The Man who Broke Napoleon's Codes*, Faber, 2000
Wheeler, W. *Letters of Private Wheeler*, Windrush Press, 1997

Garibaldi in South America, Prelude to Italy
Ridley, Jasper. *Garibaldi*, Constable, 1974
Viotti, Andrea. *Garibaldi – The Revolutionary and his Men*, Blandford, 1979

The Boer Commandos: Guerrilla War in Africa
De Wet, Christian. *Three Years War*, Constable, 1902
Nasson, Bill. *The South African War*, Arnold, 1999
Pakenham, T. *The Boer War*, Abacus, 1992
Reitz, D. *Commando*, Faber, 1929

Michael Collins: Guerrilla War in Ireland
Barry, Tom. *Guerrilla Days in Ireland*, Dublin, Irish Press, 1948
Coogan, Tim Pat. *Michael Collins*, Arrow Books, 1991
Kee, Robert. *Ireland a History*, Weidenfeld and Nicolson, 1980
Oxford Companion to Irish History, Oxford, 2002

Lawrence and Guerrilla War

James, L. *The Golden Warrior*, Abacus, 1995
Lawrence, T. E. *The Seven Pillars of Wisdom*, Cape, 1935

Mao the Guerrilla Leader

Mao Zedong. *On Guerrilla War*, Cassell, 1962
—*Basic Tactics*, Pall Mall, 1967
Short, Philip. *Mao A Life*, Hodder and Stoughton, 1999
Spence, Jonathan D. *Mao Zedong*, Weidenfeld and Nicolson, 1999

Tito: From Guerrilla to World Statesman

Djilas, Milovan. *Tito*, Weidenfeld and Nicolson, 1981
Maclean, Fitzroy. *Disputed Barricade*, Cape, 1957
Zilliacus, Konni. *Tito of Yugoslavia*, Michael Joseph, 1952

Guerrilla Fighters: World War II

Hoe, Alan. *David Stirling*, Warner, 1994
Messenger, Charles. *The Commandos*, Kimber, 1985
Rooney, David. *Wingate and the Chindits*, Arms and Armour Press, 1994
—*Mad Mike*, Leo Cooper, 1997
Weale, Adrian. *Secret Warfare*, Hodder and Stoughton, 1997

Che Guevara and Guerrilla War

Castaneda, Jorge. *Campanero*, Bloomsbury, 1997
Guevara, Ernesto. *Guerrilla Warfare*, University of Nebraska Press, 1980
—*The African Dream*, Harvill, 2000
Sinclair, Andrew. *Che Guevara*, Fontana, 1979

Al-Qaeda, Bin Laden and the Islamic Struggle

Bergen, Peter. *Holy War Inc*, Weidenfeld and Nicolson, 2001
Jalali, Ali Ahmad and Grau Lester. *Afghan Guerrilla War*, Compendium, 2001
Rashid, Ahmed. *Jihad*, Yale University Press, 2002
Robinson, Adam. *Bin Laden*, Mainstream Edinburgh, 2001

INDEX